The Dawn of Software Engineering

From Turing to Dijkstra

Edgar G. DAYLIGHT

Edited by Kurt De Grave.

Cover portraits, top: Alan M. Turing. King's College Library, Cambridge. AMT/K/7/9 and AMT/K/7/14.
Bottom: Edsger W. Dijkstra, 1963 and est. 1956. Archive of E. G. Daylight, courtesy of the Dijkstra family.

LONELY SCHOLAR™
SCIENTIFIC BOOKS

© 2012 Karel Van Oudheusden
Cover design © 2012 Kurt De Grave

Published by Lonely Scholar bvba
Sint-Lambertusstraat 3
3001 Heverlee
Belgium
editor@lonelyscholar.com
http://www.lonelyscholar.com

D/2012/12.695/1
ISBN 9789491386022
NUR 980, 989

For Alida & Helena

"No thorough understanding of anything can be had without a knowledge of its origins, its roots."

— Theodore Vail, Founding AT&T President

Contents

1. Introduction

It is not uncommon to find accounts that portray computing's history as a beautiful road from logic to practice. A major example is about the purported road from Alan Turing's now-famous 1936 paper 'On Computable Numbers' [291] to the first universal computers.

Many people today are led to believe that Turing is the father of the computer, the father of our digital society, as also the following praise for Martin Davis's bestseller *The Universal Computer: The Road from Leibniz to Turing*[1] suggests:

> At last, a book about the origin of the computer that goes to the heart of the story: the human struggle for logic and truth. Erudite, gripping, and humane, Martin Davis shows the extraordinary individuals *through whom the groundwork of the computer came into being*, and the culmination in Alan Turing, *whose universal machine now dominates the world economy.*
> [50, first page, my italics] [53, back cover, my italics]

These words are from no one less than Andrew Hodges, the biographer of Turing.

The central thesis in Davis's book is that logic and especially Turing's work have played a central role in the advent of the first universal computers[2]. He tries to defend this claim by writing mostly about logicians and mathematicians — including Frege, Cantor, Hilbert, Gödel, Turing, and Von Neumann — and intentionally leaving the work of the many engineers out of the picture[3].

Davis does not elaborate on the early work of the many engineers and numerical analysts like Konrad Zuse and Howard Aiken. As a result, his claim about Turing's priority with regard to the first universal computers is unwarranted. Both Zuse and Aiken had already built "universal" computers by 1941 and 1944, respectively. They did not use the adjective "universal" to describe their machines because they did *not* depend on developments in logic, nor on Turing's 1936 notion of universal machine in particular, to further their early research[4].

To put it gently, Davis overstates Turing's role in the history of the computer[5].

A second example of a road from logic to practice is one that starts with Church's λ-calculus and ends with existing programming languages. In particular, Boris Trakhtenbrot views McCarthy's LISP programming language as a realization of Church's λ-calculus [290, p.559]. He claims that McCarthy started out with pure LISP and "gave [it] up" by adding imperative features (such as assignments, gotos, and side effects) in the interest of computational efficiency [290, p.564]. McCarthy has countered such claims repeatedly, stressing that he started with imperative programming and only gradually worked toward a functional style of programming [187]. Similar counterclaims have been made by Herbert Stoyan who has researched the history of LISP. In Stoyan's words:

> There are people who believe that there once was a clean "pure" language design in the functional direction which was comprised by [programmers in Artificial Intelligence] in search of efficiency. This view does not take into account, that around the end of the fifties, nobody, including McCarthy himself, seriously based his programming on the concept of mathematical function. It is quite certain that McCarthy for a long time associated programming with the design of stepwise executed "algorithms". [284, p.299]

Besides Trakhtenbrot, also Davis has documented the history of programming languages, as the following two statements from his bestseller illustrate:

> [Frege's Begriffsschrift] was the ancestor of all computer programming languages in common use today. [50, p.53][53, p.45]

> [S]omeone knowledgeable about modern programming languages today looking at Gödel's paper on undecidability written that year [1930] will see a sequence of 45 numbered formulas that looks very much like a computer program. The resemblance is no accident. [53, p.102]

By describing Frege and Gödel as pivotal actors in the history of computing[6], as opposed to solely logic, Davis presents a very biased view of how the developments took place. The first statement seems to suggest that Frege's work was a prerequisite to modern day computer programming. The statement is very similar to the commonly held belief that the Babylonian mathematicians were really writing algorithms. As explained by the historian Mike Mahoney, that's precisely what the Babylonians were *not* doing [180]. Just like the framework of Babylonian mathematics had no place for a metamathematical notion such as algorithm, Frege's work had no place for the notion of a computer programming language. Frege was working on problems related to the foundations of mathematics, not programming.

The second statement about Gödel holds, at best, for mathematical logicians who are experienced in programming, like Martin Davis himself. It certainly does not hold for the vast majority of computer programmers in both academia and industry. Glancing at, reading, or even trying to understand Gödel's 1931 paper [105] will not make the computer programmer think of a computer program.

Unsurprisingly, then, also Turing's 1936 paper itself has been represented anachronistically in the historical literature. Davis explains Turing's automatic machines by resorting to current-day terminology and practice, using words like *hardware*, *software*, and *program*. He furthermore states that

> [Turing's] universal machine in particular is the first example of an interpretative program. [50, p.165][53, p.147]

With hindsight, such a statement is (or could be) technically correct and harmless. But, again, it is deceptive to use such a statement when documenting logic's and Turing's role in the history of science and technology. In 1936, Turing did *not* view his universal machine as an interpretative program. He, too, was solving a problem related to the foundations of mathematics, not programming.

It is irrelevant whether Davis thinks that Turing viewed his 1936 paper with such modern applications in mind or not. (I am confident that Davis does not make this mistake himself.) But by presenting an anachronistic narrative Davis leads many of his readers to believe that Turing did foresee it all. For historically accurate accounts of Turing's 1936 paper, I refer to Charles Petzold's *The Annotated Turing* [240] and to Chapter 4 in Mark Priestley's *A Science of Operations* [245].

Even in later decades when interpreters were actually being built, leading computer programmers like McCarthy did *not* initially view Turing's universal machine as an interpretative program in any practical sense. Hence, Davis's anachronistic statement does not even hold 20 to 25 years later! Although McCarthy had by 1960 already written a paper [185] in which he had connected the universal Turing machine to his LISP programming system, he did not see the practical implication of LISP's universal function *eval*. It was his student Steve Russell who insisted on implementing it. After having done so, an interpreter for LISP "surprisingly" and "suddenly appeared" [187, p.191][284].

A final example of inaccurate folklore concerns the historical roles of Church and Turing, written in the July 2011 issue of the *Communications of the ACM* in the section 'Solving the Unsolvable' by the editor in chief, Moshe Y. Vardi. In his words:

> In 1936–1937, Alonzo Church, an American logician, and Alan Turing, a British logician, proved independently that the Decision Problem for first-order logic is *unsolvable*; there is no algorithm that checks the validity of logical formulas. The Church-Turing Theorem can be viewed as the birth of theoretical computer science. To prove the theorem, Church and Turing introduced computational models, recursive functions, and Turing machines, respectively, and proved that the *Halting Problem*—checking whether a given recursive function or Turing machine yields an output on a given input—is unsolvable.

The previous passage is inaccurate in several respects. First, it is perhaps more appropriate to say that Alan Turing was a mathematician, not a logician. Second, Vardi's description gives the impression that both Church and Turing deserve equal credit for proving the unsolvability of the Decision Problem. But we should not lose sight of the fact that Church's proof was already published and in Turing's hands *before* Turing submitted his own paper for publication. This is not simultaneous by any academic standard, however generous one may wish to be[7]. Third, it was also due to the work of Gödel and others, like Herbrand, that the definition of a recursive (i.e. computable) function was introduced, not solely due to Church. Moreover, it was not Turing who introduced what we today call a "Turing machine". Turing introduced his automatic machines which do not contain an input nor an output as is the case with the later devised "Turing machines". Turing's automatic machines compute a real number with ever increasing accuracy, never ceasing execution. The implication is that, strictly speaking, Turing did not prove the unsolvability of the Halting Problem. Church, on the other hand, *did* prove the unsolvability of what was later called the "Halting Problem". He did this in terms of his notion of "effective calculability" which is based on normalization[8]. In later years, Post, Church, Kleene, and Davis recast the concept of Turing's automatic machine into that of a "Turing machine". During the 1950s it was Davis, not Turing, who introduced the words "Halting Problem" which he defined in terms of the recast notion of a "Turing machine"[9].

In Chapter 2 I will elaborate on some of the claims made in the previous paragraph. For now, it suffices to note how easy it is to forget or be ignorant of the actual developments that did take place in the past. Here we have the editor in chief of a reputable magazine being inaccurate in several respects in just one paragraph!

"So what?" you may ask. "Isn't Vardi's account accurate enough for his readership?" After all, Turing did prove a theorem that comes very close to what we would today call the unsolvability of the Halting Problem. So why be so picky about Vardi's words?

The quick and cliché answer is that Vardi is glorifying the work of some at the expense of the work of others. Conceptualizing the "Turing machine" took several years and was also due to the work of Post, Church, Kleene, and a logician who also became a computer programmer: Martin Davis. It was not just Turing. Vardi's passage is only one of many; it is not hard to find several similar passages, written or spoken by leading researchers in computing. Such accounts strengthen my skepticism about the centenary celebration of Alan M. Turing in the year 2012.

The historical answer is that actors like Turing were, during the mid-1930s, trying to solve a problem in mathematical logic. They were not, as we now tend to believe, thinking about halting computer *programs*. They did not, in 1936, anticipate that their work would be of extreme value in the future field of computing. By seeking heroes like Turing, we are often, albeit unintentionally, disrespecting their true accomplishments! The pending and outstanding problem of the day was the Decision Problem. It had to do with the foundations of mathematics, not with the foundations of computer programming.

Furthermore, Vardi's passage presented above is, due to its inaccuracies, of value to the history of science itself. The passage suggests that Vardi did not thoroughly study Church's and Turing's papers even though Church and Turing are considered by him to be among the fathers of what is commonly called theoretical computer science. As mentioned, Vardi is by no means exceptional in this case: many, if not most, researchers in computing have not read Church's and Turing's papers[10]. In retrospect, this is no surprise, given that their papers address a fundamental 1936 problem in mathematical logic. These papers are extremely hard to grasp for the modern-day computing professional.

The observations just made raise the question whether other major players in computing ever read or became knowledgeable of the work of Church and Turing. In particular, did ACM[11] Turing Award winners like Edsger W. Dijkstra and Tony Hoare grasp Turing's work while they were advancing the state of the art in programming? This is one of the questions I will address.

1.1   From Turing to Dijkstra

The focus of this book lies on Turing's influence on programming and his influence on Edsger W. Dijkstra's thinking in particular. It comes at the expense of discussing the work of others like Post and Church[12].

Turing's involvement with computer building was popularized in the 1970s and later. Most notable are the accounts by Brian Randell [249], Andrew Hodges [136], and Martin Davis [49][50][51]. A central question is whether John von Neumann was influenced by Turing's 1936 paper when he helped build the EDVAC machine, even though he never cited Turing's work. This question remains unsettled up till this day. As remarked by Charles Petzold [240, p.164], one standard history [36] barely mentions Turing, while the other, written by a logician [51], makes Turing a key player[13].

The influence of Turing's 1936 paper on computer programming, on the other hand, has barely been documented. This is a rather peculiar observation when one notes that the first Turing Award was given in 1966 to a *programmer* (Alan J. Perlis), as were several subsequent Turing awards. In 1966, the potentially significant connection between Turing and Von Neumann concerning the EDVAC was not public knowledge: the popular accounts of Randell (1973), Hodges (1983), Davis (1988, 2000), and others had yet to be published!

Therefore, instead of only documenting Turing's alleged role in the advent of the first universal computers, it is no less fundamental to examine why Turing's 1936 paper was, and is, of great importance for the field of computer programming. Serving this purpose, Chapter 2 shows that (i) many first-generation programmers did not read Turing's 1936 paper, let alone understand it, and (ii) those computer practitioners who *did* become acquainted with Turing's 1936 work during the 1950s–1960s received it in at least one of the following three ways:

1. The Turing machine was viewed as a model for a digital stored-program computer[14]. Furthermore, some researchers tried to actually build Turing machines during the 1950s, i.e. *after* the first all-purpose[15] computing machines were already available.

2. Turing's notion of universal machine helped lay the foundations of *automatic programming*, i.e. the activity of seeking automatic

techniques and programming styles to overcome the tediousness of instructing computers.

3. The unsolvability of the Halting Problem as, for example, presented in Davis's 1958 book *Computability and Unsolvability* [47], helped researchers lay bare certain limitations in automatic programming. The 1972 Turing Award winner, Edsger W. Dijkstra, was definitely one of the first to do so.

The first item alludes to the 1950s when switching theorists, hardware engineers, and some mathematical logicians tried to close the gap between Turing's theoretical 1936 paper and already existing stored-program computing machines. Notable actors are the switching theorist Edward F. Moore and the logician Hao Wang. The second item will mainly be illustrated by discussing the work of two strong and early proponents of machine-independent programming languages: Saul Gorn and John W. Carr, III. These men grasped Turing's 1936 notion of universal machine in the context of programming languages and also explicitly referred to the work of the logicians Gödel and Kleene. The third item will be illustrated by discussing Dijkstra's indirect reception of Turing's work. It will turn out that Dijkstra was one of the first programmers to apply the unsolvability of the Halting Problem in the context of programming. He used it as preparatory work for his now-famous 1968 letter 'Go To Statement Considered Harmful' [69]. Likewise, he applied it in his 1978 correspondence with the American Department of Defense (DoD) on a technical programming example in order to convey the need to separate language design from language implementation [76]. Dijkstra's work, in short, shows that undecidability has practical implications in software engineering today.

In Chapter 3 I investigate how the mathematical aesthetics of the Amsterdamers, Dijkstra and Aad van Wijngaarden, led to the advent of the recursive procedure in imperative programming in 1960. Even though Dijkstra and Van Wijngaarden hardly needed the recursive procedure themselves in their programming, they persuaded Peter Naur to include it in the definition of the programming language ALGOL60. In the immediately following years, ALGOL60's recursive procedure was used in unanticipated and innovative ways, for example in recursive descent compilation and QuickSort. Moreover, in sharp contrast to the hard-core engineering practices of several leading British and West-German researchers, it was Dijkstra's quest for mathematical generality which led to practical breakthroughs in compiler writing, breakthroughs which are related to modern developments such as the now widely used virtual

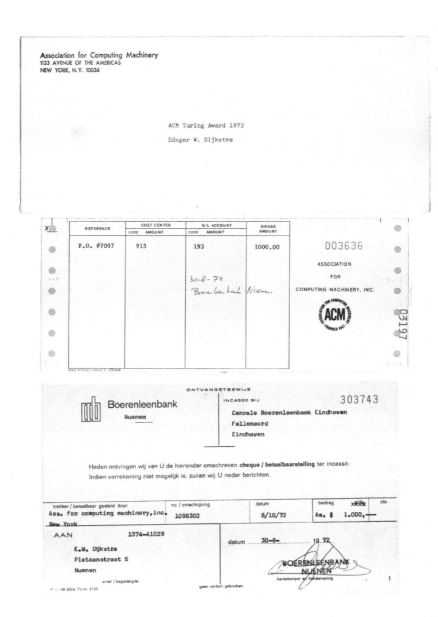

Figure 1.1: The receipt of Dijkstra's Turing award from my personal collection; see *www.dijkstrascry.com*.

machine. History thus shows that mathematical elegance can lead to useful and practical results in software engineering.

The focus on Dijkstra in Chapter 3 comes at the expense of others and most notably the German computer builder Konrad Zuse, the Swiss mathematician Heinz Rutishauser, and the American computer architect Robert Barton. In the second half of the 1930s, Zuse was already successfully constructing computing machines. After the second world war, Zuse designed his programming notation Plankalkül on paper. This notation influenced Rutishauser's work in the 1950s which helped lead the way via the ALGOL58 language to the later ALGOL60, a machine-independent and universal programming language intended primarily for numerical computations. ALGOL60, in turn, influenced the design of the Burroughs B-5000 computer in the USA; Barton was its chief architect.[16]

Zuse had been building computing machines in Germany between the mid-1930s and mid-1940s. One of them, the Z4, survived the Allied bombings [162, p.7]. While the war was ending, Zuse took his Z4 and moved westwards, away from potential Soviet occupation. Later, the Z4 would end up in Zurich where it would be used by the Swiss mathematician Rutishauser. After first working on numerical problems, Rutishauser started to seek specific techniques to overcome his tedious programming efforts. While doing so, he introduced algebraic expressions and a technique to translate them into machine code.[17]

The ALGOL60 programming language, officially defined in May 1960, had at least two features which distinguished it from programming tradition. One feature was its block structure: an ALGOL60 program is essentially a series of nested blocks. Like a set of Russian dolls, each block is enclosed inside another [294, p.29–30]. This textual form of recursion is complemented by another key feature of ALGOL60: the recursive procedure. Executing an ALGOL60 procedure has the potential of calling itself directly or indirectly and, thus, exhibiting a dynamic form of recursion.

Both forms of recursion in ALGOL60 resulted in a radical break with established practices of programming. In Valdez's words:

> In FORTRAN there is a clear continuity with machine language and assembly language, while ALGOL, which was much influenced by the ideas of Zuse and Rutishauser, requires a radical rethinking of programming.[18]

IBM's FORTRAN was, just like ALGOL60, intended for numerical computations. But, in terms of programming features, both languages were very different indeed.

A FORTRAN program (during the second half of the 1950s) consisted of a sequence of subroutines, each of which was allocated to a specific and fixed part in storage before the program was executed. During execution, the program would jump from one part in storage to another, executing the instructions of the corresponding subroutine. The close correspondence between the textual FORTRAN program and the storage layout required to execute the program implied that it was relatively easy to build a FORTRAN compiler.

An experienced FORTRAN programmer knew in advance exactly how much fixed storage his program would require during execution. An experienced ALGOL60 programmer, by contrast, had no such control over his ALGOL60 programs. The storage requirements of an ALGOL60 program would typically change during the execution of the program; that is, there was no fixed correspondence between the textual ALGOL60 program and the storage layout required to execute the program. The storage allocation was dynamic and, as a result, it was more difficult to build a compiler[19] for ALGOL60 than for FORTRAN. Moreover, managing the dynamic allocation of storage by means of a runtime system required considerable overhead by itself, a bit similar to the operating systems developed in later years.

The outstanding problem of the late 1950s and 1960s in programming was to close the large gap between the ALGOL60 language and the machine, i.e. between the dynamic and the static[20]. Several leading British and West-German researchers tried to accomplish this by restricting the ALGOL60 language in terms of dynamic language constructs; for instance, by eschewing the recursive procedure. These actors were, essentially, approaching the FORTRAN style of programming, as elaborated on in Chapter 3. In later years, others like Barton designed new machine architectures (i.e. *stack* architectures) which could handle dynamic storage requirements and which also contained *virtual memory* systems. Barton and his colleagues closed the gap from the machine side by making the machine more dynamic[21].

Barton's B-5000 machine did not sell well, as Dent recollected in later years:

> [T]rying to sell a machine where neither the operator nor the user nor the programmer knew where the program was in memory was very difficult. [82, p.49]

Academics like Dijkstra, however, did become strong proponents of Burroughs machines. In 1973, Dijkstra even joined Burroughs as a research consultant while conducting his work from his home in Nuenen, the Netherlands [3, p.92].

In 1960, Dijkstra took the ALGOL60 language in full generality and implemented it surprisingly quickly together with his close colleague Jaap Zonneveld. He did not close the gap between ALGOL60's dynamic storage requirements and the machine by restricting ALGOL60. As we shall see, he succeeded in *bridging* the gap by unifying seemingly disparate language and compiler concepts. His rallying cry for generalization was heard in 1962, as the following words of Maurice Wilkes illustrate:

> [Dijkstra] has indicated, and with good reason, that compiler writing may well become trivial, and is becoming trivial, and he has illustrated this very brilliantly in his compiler. [...] Dijkstra has reduced the writing of [an] Algol compiler to a triviality, in terms of his notations [...] [231, p.198–199]

Moreover, Dijkstra viewed the gap between language and machine to be a temporary problem because he anticipated the advent of new machine architectures, like the Burroughs B-5000, in the near future (cf. Chapter 3).

Dijkstra's later case against the goto statement, in turn, is best viewed as a way of closing another gap, namely the conceptual gap between the static ALGOL60 program text and its dynamic process on an *abstract* stack-based machine. Indeed, during the 1960s, Dijkstra like many others approached the semantics of an ALGOL-like language from an operational perspective. Discarding goto constructs from an ALGOL60 program would increase its lucidity when reasoning in terms of how the abstract machine operates when the program at hand is executed[22].

Dijkstra was only one of several researchers to make a case against the goto during the 1960s, so why did his 1968 letter 'Go To Statement Considered Harmful' [69] create the most waves? I argue that this was indirectly due to Turing's 1936 paper and, in particular, due to Böhm's and Jacopini's 1966 paper entitled 'Flow diagrams, Turing machines, and languages with only two formation rules' [23].

In their 1966 paper, Böhm and Jacopini essentially gave the go-ahead signal to those who favored goto-less programming. By elaborately using Turing machines, Böhm and Jacopini proved a fundamental result in programming which, when recast from Dijkstra's perspective, states that goto-less programming does *not* come at the expense of computability. That is, an ALGOL-like language does not lose computational power when discarding the goto statement. Some experts in the programming community had indirectly been waiting for this theoretical go-ahead signal and it was Dijkstra who reaped the benefit (cf. Chapter 2).

Discussions with Four Turing Award Winners

Although the focus of this book lies on Turing and Dijkstra, it would be a methodological mistake to solely elaborate on their accomplishments. To achieve a richer, contextual understanding of their legacies, I have conducted discussions with four Turing Award winners: Tony Hoare, Niklaus Wirth, Barbara Liskov, and Peter Naur. Each discussion centers on his or her research contributions and, while doing so, sometimes also spontaneously addresses the question as to how Turing's and Dijkstra's work were received and how his or her research and practice were affected by it.

The fact that Wirth and especially Naur express their reservations of Dijkstra's later work is not a matter of right or wrong, it is a matter of explicating each other's research agenda and the extent to which they understood each other's agenda. In this respect, my aspirations come close to those of the late Mike Mahoney who has written about research agendas in computing following his primary dissertation adviser Thomas Kuhn [182].

In each discussion I have sympathized with the discussant, trying as much as possible to crawl under their skin. My first discussion was conducted in Cambridge (UK) in spring 2010 with Tony Hoare and is primarily about his reception of logic, including Turing's work. My second discussion was conducted in Zurich in fall 2010 with Niklaus Wirth. It is mainly about his engineering perspective toward the field of programming. A month later, I met Barbara Liskov in Boston to discuss her work on layered operating system design and her developing thoughts on data abstraction during the 1960s and 1970s. My fourth discussion was conducted in spring 2011 in Gentofte, Denmark, with Peter Naur. Some fragments from that very long discussion concerning ALGOL60 and Turing are presented here. I refer to my booklet *Pluralism in Software Engineering: Turing Award Winner Peter Naur Explains* [55] for the complete dialog and, in particular, Naur's critical comments about Dijkstra's research.

Only by conducting discussions with more first-generation programmers in the near future does it become possible to distill a general impression of the software engineering field at large, and of Turing's and Dijkstra's influence in particular. While Chapters 2 and 3 serve to be scrutinized, I recommend reading Chapters 4–7 in a more recreational manner. As will become apparent, some comments made by Hoare and Naur have served well in Chapter 2. Likewise, specific comments from Wirth and Liskov are very helpful to those who are interested in programming methodology and structured programming especially.

2. Turing's Influence on Programming

The year 2012 is one of celebration and remembrance: Alan M. Turing was born in 1912 and Edsger W. Dijkstra, the 1972 Turing Award winner, passed away 10 years ago. Turing and Dijkstra are considered by many to have been very influential actors in the history of computing. As a tribute to both men, I shall examine how the work of the former influenced that of the latter and, by doing so, lay bare some early principles of programming.

With his 1936 paper 'On Computable Numbers, with an Application to the Entscheidungsproblem' [291], Turing came second place, i.e. after Church, to solving the fundamental Entscheidungsproblem (Decision Problem) in mathematical logic. Grasping Turing's solution and its implications requires appreciation for the work of mathematical logicians, including Hilbert, Gödel, Church, and Kleene. Unsurprisingly, then, Turing's paper is rather difficult to understand for the modern-day computer professional (cf. [240]). A similar remark held for first-generation programmers in the 1950s, as the following words from 1953 illustrate:

> Türing Machine: In 1936 Dr. Turing wrote a paper on the design and the limitations of computing machines. For this reason they are sometimes known by his name. The umlaut is an unearned and undesirable addition, due, presumably, to an impression that anything so incomprehensible must be Teutonic. [89]

According to Dijkstra, Turing's seminal 1936 paper had, at least until 1950, not attracted much attention in the mathematical world at large [81]. Moreover, Hoare tried to comprehend Turing's paper during the early 1950s but with difficulty, as will follow from my discussion with him in Chapter 4. To understand Turing's work better, he later read Davis's 1958 book *Computability and Unsolvability* [47], but also without full comprehension. Likewise, Naur tells me that he became acquainted with

Turing's work early on, but only started studying it in detail during the early 1990s (cf. [218, 219]). Toward the end of his professorship, Naur asked several computer professionals in conferences whether they had ever heard of Turing's 1936 paper. The vast majority of answers were negative (see Chapter 7).

The previous observations raise the following questions. Did Dijkstra, himself, read Turing's 1936 paper and, if so, when? To what extent did he grasp Turing's work? Did it perhaps help him further his own research in the design and implementation of programming languages? Attempting to answer these questions will bring some early principles of programming languages to the fore.

Many other computer practitioners of the 1950s were either not aware of Turing's 1936 paper, or did not clearly see the connection between it and computing. The 1973 Turing Award recipient Charles W. Bachman, for instance, "did not really know who Alan Turing was" prior to 1973 [116, p.100]. And, the leading lady in compiler building, Grace Hopper, said the following in 1978:

> I think I can remember sometime along in the middle of 1952 that I finally made the alarming statement that I could make a computer do anything which I could completely define. I'm still of course involved in proving that because I'm not sure if anybody believes me yet. [139, p.9]

The last sentence shows that Hopper and, hence, also many of her colleagues, were not well acquainted with Turing's theory of computation. For, the crux of Turing's work is that there *are* well-defined problems that cannot be computed (i.e. are algorithmically unsolvable).

The previous paragraphs are not meant to belittle researchers in computing; they serve to illustrate that the implications of Turing's work only surfaced gradually, if at all, in certain quarters of computing. It is in this context that I will salute Dijkstra's ability to connect the undecidability results of Church and Turing, in the form of Davis's Halting Problem (or in a form equivalent to it), with the practical programming problems that he and his contemporaries faced.

2.1 Advances in Mathematical Logic

Before contextualizing Turing's 1936 paper, I present some technical definitions from mathematical logic. The reader can safely skim across them and start reading in detail from Section 2.1.2.

1) successor $\qquad \lambda x[x+1]$
2) constant functions $\qquad \lambda x_1 \ldots x_n[k]$
3) projections $\qquad \lambda x_1 \ldots x_n[x_i]$
4) composition

$$f(\overrightarrow{x}) \quad = \quad h(g_1(\overrightarrow{x}), \ldots, g_m(\overrightarrow{x}))$$

5) primitive recursion

$$f(0, \overrightarrow{y}) \quad = \quad h(\overrightarrow{y})$$
$$f(x+1, \overrightarrow{y}) \quad = \quad g(x, f(x, \overrightarrow{y}), \overrightarrow{y})$$

Table 2.1: Five schemas to define the class of primitive recursive functions. The functions g and h are previously defined functions and $\overrightarrow{x}$ denotes a sequence $x_1, \ldots, x_n$ of variables, a sequence which may be empty [282].

Mathematical logic took shape in the second half of the 19th century. Of prime interest was the study of functions and, in particular, functions defined by induction. In 1888 Dedekind provided a proof that an inductively defined function is unique [57]. This result influenced Peano in formulating his now-familiar axioms for the positive integers; he used definition by induction for his fifth axiom (cf. [120, p.83–97] and [237]), a definition which would be called *primitive recursion* by the 1930s [282].

The class of primitive recursive functions is defined by the five schemas in Table 2.1. Let the successor functions, the constant functions, and the projection functions be called initial functions. Then we call a function *primitive recursive* if and only if it can be obtained from some initial functions by finitely many applications of the composition and primitive recursion schemas.

Kurt Gödel used primitive recursive functions in his ground-breaking 1931 work entitled 'Uber formal mentscheidbare satze der Principia Mathematica und verwandter systeme. I'. In modern-day computing terminology, Gödel's proof along with a later contribution by Rosser amount to the following incompleteness result: for any consistent system of axioms[23] whose theorems can be generated by a computer program[24], there will always be true statements about the natural numbers that are unprovable within the system[25].

In order to write his 1931 paper, Gödel had studied the limitations of formal mathematical systems and systems of logic. A *formal mathematical system* is defined in terms of a formal language, axioms, and inference rules. By applying inference rules to the axioms, expressable in the formal language, one obtains theorems within the formal system. These theorems can, in turn, serve as a basis for further derivations within the formal system.

A *system of logic* is a formal system with a model and a means to interpret the formulae generated within the formal system into the model. For example, a theorem derived within the formal system can, after interpretation, express a truth about the natural numbers. Hopefully non trivial facts about natural numbers can be derived, thereby demonstrating the power of the formal system at hand.

Essential to Gödel's proof was his technique which we now call Gödel numbering or Gödel's device. He used it to associate a natural number with each symbol in his formal system, and, likewise, to associate a sequence of numbers with each formula. Extrapolating this idea further, Gödel used a sequence of a sequence of numbers to encode a derivation (i.e. a sequence of formulas). By doing so, Gödel, following a hint of Hilbert, was able to arithmetically interpret syntactical metamathematical statements[26] — details which we need not go into here.

Gödel numbering paved the way for the aforementioned incompleteness result which can be restated as follows: the properties of the set of natural numbers, mathematicians' most basic structure, lies beyond the reach of what first-order logic and the axiomatic method have to offer. Gödel numbering was also used in subsequent work by Church, Kleene, Turing and several others. Church used it to show that there is no decision procedure for arithmetic, nor for the predicate calculus (cf. [58]). Kleene used it to derive his Normal Form theorem (cf. [52, p.236]), described later. Turing used Gödel numbering to uniquely identify each of his machines with integers, a key element in the construction of his universal machine (cf. [291, Section 5] and [240, p.138]).

Though Gödel used primitive recursive functions in his 1931 paper, he knew very well that not all effectively calculable functions are primitive recursive functions. Already in 1928, Ackermann had defined a function by double recursion which was not primitive recursive[27]. Therefore, in 1934, by following up on an earlier suggestion by Herbrand, Gödel proposed a wider class of functions which he called the *general recursive functions*. This class strictly includes the primitive recursive functions and allows for partial functions.

2.1.1 Kleene's Normal Form Theorem

During the early 1930s, Gödel visited the USA a couple of times, including Princeton where Alonzo Church conceived the type-free λ-calculus in an attempt to lay bare the foundations for logic and mathematics [290, p.557]. In this context Church's PhD student Stephen C. Kleene confirmed in his dissertation (1934) that all primitive recursions and his least number operator μ can be effected in the λ-calculus. Kleene's objective was, in part, to prove that every general recursive function is λ-definable. According to his recollections:

> I couldn't help but reflect that I could [accomplish that objective] if I could get every general recursive function by a combination of primitive recursions (with explicit definitions) and least-number operations. [156, p.377]

Kleene succeeded in his objective by using Gödel numbering to prove his Normal Form theorem, namely that every general recursive function can be written in the normal form $\psi(\mu y\,[\rho(x_1,\ldots,x_n,y)=0])$ where

1. ψ and ρ are ordinary or "primitive" recursive functions,

2. for all x_1, ..., x_n there exists a y such that $\rho(x_1,\ldots,x_n,y)=0$, and

3. $\mu x\,[A(x)]$ denotes the least natural number x such that $A(x)$, or 0 if there is no such natural number[28].

In plain English, any general recursive function can be obtained by using only primitive recursive functions and just one least number operator μ. Or, in Kleene's own words:

> Thus the extension of general over primitive recursive functions consists only in that to substitutions and primitive recursions is added the operation of seeking indefinitely through the series of natural numbers for one satisfying a primitive recursive relation. [52, p.246]

Kleene proved his Normal Form theorem in his now-famous 1936 paper 'General recursive functions of natural numbers' [153] and, as an aside, he also showed how his Normal Form theorem leads rather directly to Gödel's incompleteness result.

In later years, Kleene refined his Normal Form theorem. In particular, in 1938, he omitted the second assumption (presented above as item 2.) and, hence, also considered general *partial* recursive functions. In this regard, Kleene's Normal Form theorem can be recast as follows:

> There is a primitive recursive predicate $T(e,x,y)$ and a primitive recursive function $U(y)$ such that for any general partial recursive function $\varphi(x)$, there is an index e (corresponding to the system E of equations defining φ) such that $\varphi(x) \approx U(\mu y\,T(e,x,y))$

where $\approx$ means that the two members are either both defined with same value or both undefined (cf. [156, 282]).

Since Kleene's proof of his Normal Form theorem was published, equivalence proofs for formalisms in computability theory became routine [48, p.11]. We will revisit Kleene's Normal Form theorem later in the modern context of computer programming.

2.1.2   Turing's machines and Turing machines

Gödel's 1931 incompleteness result left the door open for somebody to devise a decision procedure for arithmetic. That is, the possibility remained of there being a finitary method which, for an arbitrary formula φ, could tell whether φ or $\neg\varphi$ is a theorem or whether it is undecidable (cf. DeLong [58]). In 1928, Hilbert and Ackermann had described this decision problem (the Entscheidungsproblem) as the main problem of mathematical logic [123, p.77], a problem which would eventually be resolved in the negative due to the work of Church [40, 41].

Coming in second place to resolving the Entscheidungsproblem, Turing's 1936 paper 'On Computable Numbers' [291] was rather peculiar, compared with the work of Church and Gödel, in that he introduced an "automatic machine" as a model for a human computing a real number[29]. Each of Turing's machines, in essence, computes a real number r, just as a very disciplined and patient human can compute r on paper with a pencil and eraser [291, p.249–251]. Consider, for instance, the real number $1/3$, which is equal to $0.01010101\ldots$ in binary notation. The dots in the sequence signify the fact that the digits 0 and 1 alternate forever. Turing explained how to construct an automatic machine that computes the sequence $0.01010101\ldots.$ Likewise, to compute $1/4$, which in binary notation is equal to 0.01, Turing's corresponding automatic machine prints the digits 0 and 1, and then forever prints the digit 0 in accordance with the sequence $0.0100000\ldots.$ In short, Turing was only interested in machines that print digits forever and *not* in machines that print a finite number of digits [240, p.76].

Important in Turing's paper was his construction of the universal machine, a construction which relied on Gödel numbering but which I shall not delve into here. In the words of Hodges:

> Turing had the vital perception that operations and numerical data could be codified alike [... I]n a remarkable application of that perception, Turing showed that 'it is possible to invent a single machine which can be used to compute any computable

sequence'. This invention was his *universal machine.* [137, p.4, Hodges's italics]

By 1946 and perhaps a bit earlier, but definitely not during the 1930s, Turing had become well aware of the fact that his 1936 universal machine could, essentially, serve as a mathematical model of an all-purpose computer[30]. Turing, Von Neumann, and their close associates may well have been the only people to have seen this connection during the 1940s[31]. It was by presenting his 1950 paper 'Computing machinery and Intelligence' [293], in which he devoted a section to 'The Universality of Digital Computers', that Turing was able to change the common perception among some of his contemporaries[32].

The work of Church, Turing, and Post of the 1930s led logicians like Post [243], Kleene[33], and Davis [47] to reformulate Turing's automatic machines during the 1940s–1950s. The recast machines compute integer functions[34] instead of real numbers, similar to the way real computing machines work. In this modified setting, a machine is provided with a finite number of digits as input, representing an integer. The machine then either computes forever and, hence, does not halt. Or, the machine only prints a finite number of digits and halts. In Petzold's words:

> In the Kleene and Davis formulation, machines that don't halt are considered *bad* machines. Determining whether a Turing Machine will properly complete its calculation and halt was termed — by Davis — as the *halting problem.* [240, p.234, Petzold's italics]

In the previous quote and in the rest of this book, the words "Turing machine" describe the reformulated machines, *not* Turing's original automatic machines.

At this point it is interesting to delve a bit deeper into Martin Davis's own recollections. In a 2008 interview, he explained that after having given a course on mathematical logic in 1950–51, which included the work of Turing, he became one of the world's first programmers by programming the ORDVAC [146, p.565–566]. Doing so allowed him to connect Turing's theoretical work with physical computing machines:

> I began to see that Turing machines provided an abstract mathematical model of real-world computers. (It wasn't until many years later that I came to realize that Alan Turing himself had made that connection long before I did.) [34, p.60]

Davis's realization of the *connection* between Turing's work and real-world computing machines cannot be emphasized enough. It led him to write his 1958 book, *Computability & Unsolvability* (cf. Calude [34, p.60]). As Davis stated himself, the book was technically not novel, but placing Turing machines to the fore was [47, p.vii–viii]. In fact, one of the reviewers of his book derided the connection he was proposing with actual computing machines[35]. It was Davis's book which initiated the study of computability in the curriculum of computer science majors (cf. Petzold [240, p.328]).

In his book, Davis also formulated and proved a theorem stating the unsolvability of the Halting Problem[36]. In plain English and under some widely accepted assumptions, the unsolvability of the Halting Problem amounts today to stating that:

> [I]t is impossible to devise a uniform procedure, or computer program, which can look at any computer program and decide whether or not that program will ever terminate. [197, p.153]

This theoretical result has had practical implications in the design and implementation of programming languages, some of which are described in this chapter.

The theoretical work in mathematical logic was paralleled by the work of many engineers who built physical programmable computing machines. Between 1938 and 1941, Konrad Zuse built his Z3 machine in Germany [259, 316]. During and after World War II, engineers in the USA and England built several machines, which were primarily used by applied mathematicians to solve numerical problems. Among those involved were Howard Aiken, Presper Eckert, Herman Goldstine, John Mauchly, John von Neumann, Alan Turing, and Maurice Wilkes [49, 50].

The advent of the physical programmable computing machine had a great impact on the field of numerical analysis. Unlike the logicians and the electrical engineers, the numerical analysts, by their very profession, took programming seriously [179, p.3]. Several of them, such as Edsger W. Dijkstra (1930–2002), gradually became more involved in seeking automatic techniques and programming styles to overcome the tediousness in programming their machines. The corresponding activity, first called *automatic coding* and later *automatic programming*, would eventually include the design of high-level programming languages and their implementation by means of compilers and runtime systems.

2.2 Different Receptions of Turing's 1936 Paper

During the 1950s, an increasing number of computer practitioners began to view the Turing machine as a model for a digital stored-program computer, including Van der Poel [241], Burks [31], and Moore [200]. Concerning the latter, Edward F. Moore was a switching theorist who in 1952 wrote a paper entitled 'A Simplified Universal Turing Machine' [200]. In his paper, Moore started off by connecting Turing's 1936 work with his own field of expertise and then noted that Turing's machines were initially used by Turing to model humans, and that in later years they had become models for actual computers [200, p.50]. In his words:

> In fact, several present-day digital computers do actually use magnetic or perforated paper tapes as auxiliary memories, instead of merely as input-output media. Hence, a Turing machine *could also be* considered a mathematical model [...] of a digital computer. [200, p.50, my italics]

Moore also wrote that the universal Turing machine "can, loosely speaking, be interpreted as a completely general-purpose digital computer" [200, p.51].

Besides switching theorists and hardware engineers, also mathematical logicians tried to close the gap between Turing's 1936 theory and practical computing machinery. In 1954, Hao Wang presented 'A Variant to Turing's Theory of Computing Machines', which was published three years later [296]. To simplify Turing's theory and to make it more accessible to the machine designer, he defined a machine which is equivalent in power to a Turing machine but which cannot erase data from its tape. In his words: "erasing is dispensable, one symbol for marking is sufficient, and one kind of transfer is enough" [296, p.63]. Lecturing to computer designers, Wang talked about physically realizing his machines and, likewise, about the "physical realization of a universal Turing machine" [296, p.87–88]. Being concerned about *both* logicians and engineers, he made three analogies:

- "Just as logicians speak of theorems and metatheorems, there are programs and metaprograms.

- Just as logicians distinguish between using and mentioning a word, automatic coding must observe the distinction between using an instruction and talking about it.

- Just as logicians contrast primitive propositions with derived rules of inference, there is the distinction between basic commands and subroutines." [296, p.88]

Wang concluded by expressing his hope that logic and computing would bond deeper than had been the case up till 1954.

Also in post-war western Germany, researchers such as Hasenjaeger tried to build actual Turing machines, even though their own Konrad Zuse had already succeeded in building several computing machines independently of both Turing and Von Neumann[37]. According to Hasenjaeger's recollections, he and his colleagues, in an attempt to materialize a "Turing tape", were greatly aided by Wang's variant machine in which erasing is dispensable[38]. For, the practical implication of Wang's machines is that writing on the tape may be realized by punching holes in the tape. Although this particular technique of the West-Germans never worked quite well, it did pave the way for their register[39] version of the Turing machine [119, p.183].

Besides viewing the Turing machine as a model for a digital stored-program computer, there were also researchers who focused on Turing's key notion of universality in the context of programming. Two such researchers were Saul Gorn and John W. Carr, III. As we shall see, they advocated a universal machine-independent language in computing. By doing so, they contributed greatly to introducing the language metaphor and, hence, the word "language" — as in "programming language" — into computing during the 1950s.

To set the stage, it was spring 1954 and the venue of interest was a conference in Washington D.C. called *Automatic Programming for Digital Computers* [288]. Instead of having a programmer tediously write down machine code, the conference attendees wanted to be able to provide the programmer with a more mathematical notation in which he could express himself more easily. The research challenge was to design a computer program that could automatically translate the mathematical expressions of the programmer into the instructions of the machine. Various automatic-translation programs were presented and discussed at the conference.

Most presentations at the 1954 conference covered mathematical notations and automatic translation programs that only worked for a specific kind of machine. Two exceptions, however, were the presentations of Gorn [108] and Brown & Carr [28]. These three researchers discussed translation techniques that were applicable for any type of machine. To obtain such a general technique, they realized that the mathematical notation, intended for the programmer, had to be independent of any computing machine. Furthermore, Gorn, Brown, and Carr sought a *universal* machine-independent *language*, i.e. a language that was close to the universal language of mathematics and, hence, applicable to a large class of mathematical problems.

Brown and Carr distinguished in their paper between the "outside human language" (i.e. the "language of mathematics and formal logic") and the "less understandable interior instruction languages" [28, p.84]. They wanted to bridge the "gap" between such languages and, hence, contribute to the emerging discipline called automatic programming.

While many people at the aforementioned 1954 conference hardly used the word "language" in their lectures — Hopper, for instance, did not use it a single time — Gorn and Carr did so extensively. Furthermore, their inspiration to do so clearly came from mathematical logic. Carr, for instance, referred to metamathematics in his paper:

> Most machine users know intuitively "how to program", now must come the stage where this intuition is formalized and transferred into the heart of the machine itself. What are the steps by which a code is developed?

> Such investigations would appear to lead into the regions of *metamathematics*, where the problems deal with the generation of systems rather than the systems themselves. [28, p.89, my italics]

Likewise, Gorn referred to metamathematics and Gödel in particular [108, p.75].

Gorn and Carr's inspiration from mathematical logic becomes even more apparent when studying their 1957 work. At Purdue University, Carr gave a lecture in which he advocated an "outside-in view" (i.e. a problem-oriented view) toward computing, and where he viewed computers as "symbol manipulators". The machine user "must become much more problem oriented and much less equipment oriented" [38, p.21]. In this regard, Carr mentioned the work of Turing, Post, and Markov, and the "Universal Turing Machine" in particular. Gorn, in turn, did not only refer to Turing's 1936 paper, but also explicitly referred to Kleene's Metamathematics [155] and the equivalence between general recursive functions and Turing's machines. The central notion of interest was Turing's universal machine, as Gorn's words illustrate:

> On the one hand the sequence of imperative and interrogative sentences which constitutes a code of instructions causing a general purpose machine to produce a desired output may be looked upon as the recursive [i.e. computable] definition of that output[.]

> [O]n the other hand such a sequence of instructions may be looked upon as the set of specifications of a *special purpose machine* designed specifically to give the desired output, and which the *general purpose machine* copies and imitates. From this second point of view the general purpose machine is the equivalent of the "Universal Turing Machine" which could produce anything producible by any special machine by its ability to accept and react to the description of such a machine as input data. [109, p.255, my italics]

Gorn furthermore introduced the contradistinction between *syntax* and *semantics* in the emerging field of what many would later call computer science [109, p.260–261]. He promoted the language metaphor by making an analogy between verbs and nouns, on the one hand, and order types and variables on the other hand. That is, he projected linguistics (verbs and nouns) onto the practice of coding a machine (order types and variables) [109, p.259]. As a result, the phrase "programming language" eventually became standard jargon in computing. The metaphor of language has proved to be extremely successful; it is, after all still with us today[40].

Gorn and Carr were, of course, not the only researchers in automatic programming who had grasped Turing's 1936 notion of universality. In the spring of 1959, a working conference was held on automatic programming in Brighton, England, where Andrew Booth in his opening address credited the late Dr. A. M. Turing[41] as he who "first enunciated the fundamental theorem upon which all automatic programming is based" [106, p.x]. Continuing, Booth said:

> In its original form the theorem was so buried in a mass of mathematical logic that most readers would find it impossible to see the wood for the trees. Simply enunciated, however, it states that *any computing machine which has the minimum proper number of instructions can simulate any other computing machine, however large the instruction repertoire of the latter.* All forms of automatic programming are merely embodiments of this rather simple theorem and, although from time to time we may be in some doubt as to how FORTRAN, for example, differs from MATHMATIC or the Ferranti AUTOCODE from FLOW-MATIC, it will perhaps make things rather easier to bear in mind that they are simple consequences of Turing's theorem. [106, p.1, my italics]

Given that Turing's work was recognized to be of fundamental importance, Booth continued his speech by openly wondering why Turing's 1936 work had received so little recognition until recently; that is, only after the advent of the computer did Turing's work "assume importance". Booth's answer, in short, was that the first computing machines were used almost exclusively by their constructors and, hence, by people who were intimately aware of their internal construction. It took some years before the machines were used for scientific applications, devised by people who were and wanted to remain ignorant of the machine itself and, hence, had to rely on automatic programming techniques. At that same conference, Stanley Gill, too, elaborated on Turing's notion of universal machine and discussed a "hierarchy of programming languages" [106, p.186]. All of this happened before the 1960s.

The 1950s was also a decade in which the majority of logicians were separated from the computer practitioners — a notable exception was, as we have seen, Hao Wang. To illustrate the separation between both groups, it is worthwhile mentioning the 1961 conference that was held in Blaricum, the Netherlands, and organized by logicians. Among the attendees were Beth, Wang, McCarthy, Burks, and Chomsky. Their goal was to discuss the impact that the computer might have on mathematical logic. In more specific terms, their objectives were to (i) survey various non-numerical applications of computers (e.g. language translation, theorem proving) and (ii) address some aspects of the theory of formal systems. Selected works were published in a book [27] in 1963 with a preface stating:

> Symbol manipulation plays an important role both in the theory of formal systems and in computer programming and one would therefore expect some important relationships to exist between these domains. It may therefore seem surprising that specialists in the two fields have only recently become interested in one another's techniques. This situation is probably due to an original difference in motivation and to a phaseshift in time.

The book shows how logicians and other researchers interested in logic were discovering and sometimes rediscovering the fruitful interplay between mathematical logic and the programming of a real (i.e. finite) computing machine. For example, Beth rediscovered the finiteness of practical computing and discussed the implications this had on conducting proofs in mathematical logic [27, p.29–30].

In the seventh chapter of the book, 'Programming and the Theory of Automata', A.W. Burks explained the relationship between a Turing machine and Von Neumann's cellular automaton and then formalized the notion of automatic programming. One of Burks's main claims was the within-limits interchangeability of software and hardware [27, p.114].

Three Receptions of Turing's 1936 Paper

The discussion presented so far shows that, if Turing's 1936 paper was received at all, then it was received in the following two ways:

- The (universal) Turing machine was viewed as a model for a digital (all-purpose) stored-program computer. Furthermore, some researchers tried to actually build Turing machines during the 1950s, i.e. after the first all-purpose computing machines were already available.

- Turing's notion of universal machine helped lay the foundations of automatic programming.

As I will show later, Dijkstra followed a third route during the 1960s by projecting the unsolvability of the Halting Problem onto his own domain of expertise: imperative programming languages. Hence, as a third reception of the recast work of Turing, we have:

- The unsolvability of the Halting Problem helped some researchers lay bare certain limitations in automatic programming.

To the best of my knowledge, these three receptions of Turing's work have not been described in the literature before.

Dijkstra's Contemporaries

To contextualize Dijkstra's reception of the unsolvability of the Halting Problem, I first discuss the work of some of his contemporaries and reintroduce Kleene's Normal Form theorem in the modern context of computer programming.

In 1956 a conference was held at Dartmouth with a corresponding volume called *Automata Studies* [272], edited by Shannon and McCarthy. Among the contributors were Davis, Kleene, Minsky, Moore, Newell, Von Neumann, and Simon. Turing had also been invited to contribute (before his death in 1954) but had chosen not to do so due to his preoccupation with his work on morphogenesis [157, p.6–7].

Many participants at the Dartmouth conference had been influenced by cybernetics before and some, like Simon, were thus accustomed to viewing both humans and computers as adaptive information processors. According to the historian Kline, cybernetics divided into three different avenues: minimal self-organizing systems, simulation of human thought, and artificial intelligence [157, p.4].

The simulation of human thought was of prime interest to Newell and Simon. These two researchers had by 1957, together with Shaw, implemented a system for automatic theorem proving. Their system was called the Logic Theory Machine (LT) and served the purpose of trying to better understand how effective human problem solving works in reality, such as finding a proof of a mathematical theorem, playing chess, or discovering scientific laws from data [225, p.218–219]. IPL was the interpreted language used to implement LT, a system that was symbolic in nature and thus very different from the many numerical programs that were written during the 1950s [224, p.232].

Artificial intelligence, in turn, was of prime interest to Minsky and McCarthy. Both men shared Shannon's aspiration "to someday build a machine that really thinks, learns, communicates with humans and manipulates its environment in a fairly sophisticated way" [157, p.10]. It is in this context of symbolic processing that McCarthy showed interest in Turing machines and would later design and implement his LISP programming language.

When working at IBM in the summer of 1958, McCarthy first tried to use the imperative programming language FORTRAN to write a program that would differentiate algebraic expressions, such as the expression y^2. To calculate the derivative of y^2, McCarthy realized that he needed recursive conditional expressions. Since FORTRAN did not contain recursion, he tried to add it to the language, but without success. This, in turn, led him to develop his own programming language LISP, heavily influenced by IPL [274, p.27].

Although LISP was partly inspired by Church's λ-calculus and although it is, today, tempting to believe that McCarthy viewed LISP as a realization of the λ-calculus, McCarthy has emphasized repeatedly that he "didn't really understand the lambda calculus" and that it is a "myth" to believe that his intent was to realize it in a programming language [187, p.190]. This claim is backed up further by Herbert Stoyan's historical research [284, 285]. For example, Stoyan writes:

> [I]t is an important fact that McCarthy as mathematician was familiar with some formal mathematical languages but did not have a deep, intimate understanding of all their details. McCarthy has stressed this fact [...] His aim was to use the mathematical formalisms as languages and not as calculi. This is the root of the historical fact that he never took the λ-calculus conversion rules as a sound basis for LISP implementation. [284, p.299]

While McCarthy was clearly aware of Turing's 1936 work during the 1950s (see, for example, [183]), it is important to keep in mind that Turing's work can be understood at different levels. For example, McCarthy had already written a paper [185] in 1960 in which he had connected the universal Turing machine to his LISP programming system. But, he also stressed in later years that this paper was only intended for theoretical purposes. In particular, he did not see the practical implication of LISP's universal function *eval*. It was his student Steve Russell who was eager to implement it. And, after having done so, an interpreter for LISP "surprisingly" and "suddenly appeared" [187, p.191][284]. In Stoyan's words:

> When McCarthy was working on this function S. Russell saw it and suggested translating it by hand — as he had done so often — and adding it to the program system. McCarthy recalls: "... this EVAL was written and published in the paper and Steve Russell said, look, why don't I program this EVAL and you remember the interpreter, and I said to him, ho, ho, you're confusing theory with practice, this EVAL is intended for reading not for computing. But he went ahead and did it. That is, he compiled the EVAL in my paper into 704 machine code fixing bugs and then advertised this as a LISP interpreter which it certainly was, so at that point LISP had essentially the form that it has today, the S-expression form ...". [284, p.307]

Concerning pure LISP, McCarthy and his close colleagues did not yet realize that, using modern terminology, it was a Turing-complete programming language. According to McCarthy's recollections:

> I didn't understand that you really could do conditional expressions [and] recursion in some sense in the pure lambda calculus. [187, p.190]

In this regard, it is also interesting to present Christopher Strachey's contribution in a panel discussion, published in 1966, about imperative and declarative languages (DLs). In Strachey's words:

> I am not convinced that all problems are amenable to programming in DLs but I am not convinced that there are any which are not either; I preserve an open mind on this point. It is perfectly true that in the process of rewriting programs to avoid labels and jumps, you've gone half the way towards going into DLs. When you have also avoided assignment statements, you've gone the rest of the way. With many problems you can, in fact, go the whole way. LISP has no assignment statements and it is remarkable what you can do with pure LISP if you try. [167, p.165]

Strachey was starting to come to grips with the practical implications of universality and also undecidability. The latter is illustrated by presenting his short 1965 letter which he wrote to the editor of the Computer Journal under the title 'An impossible program' [286]. In that letter, Strachey started by describing what Davis would have called the unsolvability of the Halting Problem:

> A well-known piece of folk-lore among programmers holds that it is impossible to write a program which can examine any other program and tell, in every case, if it will terminate or get into a closed loop when it is run.[42]

Though Strachey had known Turing personally, it does not seem to be the case that Strachey had read Turing's 1936 paper or Davis's 1958 book.

> <continued> I have never actually seen a proof of this in print, and though Alan Turing once gave me a verbal proof (in a railway carriage on the way to a Conference at the NPL in 1953), I unfortunately and promptly forgot the details. This left me with an uneasy feeling that the proof must be long or complicated, but in fact it is so short and simple that it may be of interest to casual readers. The version below uses CPL[43], but not in any essential way. [286]

Strachey continued his letter by essentially proving the unsolvability of the Halting Problem. To do so, he introduced $T[R]$ as a Boolean function taking a routine (or program) R with no formal or free variables as its argument such that, for any R:

- $T[R] = True$ if R terminates if run, and

- $T[R] = False$ if R does not terminate if run.

He then asked the reader to consider the routine P which he defined in CPL as:

```
rec routine P
    ♮L:    if T[P] go to L
           Return ♮
```

Finally, he noted that, if $T[P] = True$, then the routine P will loop, and it will only terminate if $T[P] = False$. Therefore, in each case, $T[P]$ has exactly the wrong value and this in turn contradicts the existence of the computable function T. In short, Strachey had presumably reinvented Cantor's diagonal argument, the essential idea underlying the proof of the unsolvability of the Halting Problem[44].

In 1966, Böhm and Jacopini elaborately used Turing machines in order to prove a fundamental result in programming language theory, namely that "every Turing machine is reducible into, or in a determined sense is equivalent to, a program written in a language which admits as formation rules only composition and iteration" [23, p.366]. Iteration here refers to a modern *while-do* programming language construct in the sense that it can express potentially unbounded searches.

The implication of Böhm and Jacopini's result is that if the programming language under study admits the aforementioned formation rules, then language constructs like goto statements and recursive procedures are logically superfluous. This observation is related to the above remark that Strachey made when discussing imperative and declarative languages, an observation which will resurface when discussing Dijkstra's case against the goto statement.

All in all, the 1960s can be viewed as the decade in which some leading researchers in programming were starting to come to grips with *practical* implications of universality and undecidability. This point of view will be strengthened in Chapter 4 when discussing the 1972 paper 'Incomputability' [133] with one of its authors, Tony Hoare.

The Impact of Kleene's Normal Form Theorem on Programming

The work of Böhm and Jacopini clearly illustrates the reception of Turing's 1936 paper in the context of programming. This, in turn, raises the question of how far Böhm and Jacopini had penetrated through the mathematical logic literature. I am tempted to state that Böhm and Jacopini were not thoroughly familiar with Kleene's *Metamathematics* [155] or computability theory in general. The reason is that their fundamental result on programming almost immediately follows from Kleene's Normal Form theorem. In fact, modern books on computability theory, written by logicians, use Kleene's Normal Form theorem to derive a stronger form of Böhm and Jacopini's result (e.g. Fitting [93] and Smith [281]). These books are very educational in that they explain Kleene's work in terms of high-level programming languages. I shall now use part of Smith's account [281] to demonstrate this.

To explain how Kleene's earlier research leads to a stronger form of Böhm and Jacopini's theorem, it is instructive to distinguish between LOOP programs and WHILE programs. As noted by Smith, the former were introduced by Meyer and Ritchie in a 1967 paper as programs which only consist of assignment statements and bounded iteration (loop) statements [193]. A WHILE program can be obtained from a LOOP program by, optionally, adding one or more *while-do* constructs; i.e. unbounded searches.

A primitive recursive function can be specified by a chain of definitions by primitive recursion and composition. This chain leads back ultimately to initial functions, such as the successor function S, which are effectively computable by a simple algorithm. An example of a primitive recursive function is multiplication ($\times$) whose definition partly relies on S. Continuing in this manner, it is possible to build up longer chains of definitions for primitive recursive functions. A common example is the factorial (!), defined as follows:

$$0! \quad = \quad 1$$
$$(S\,y)! \quad = \quad y! \times S\,y$$

The second clause exemplifies both primitive recursion and composition: the factorial is defined in terms of itself and in terms of $\times$ and S. It is, furthermore, easy to see that the factorial, as defined above, can be computed by a program containing nested 'for' loops, a program which ultimately calls the primitive operation of incrementing the contents of a register by one. Each 'for' loop has predetermined and fixed bounds.

The factorial example can be generalized to the following provable statement. Any primitive recursive function is effectively computable by a series of (possibly nested) 'for' loops and, hence, expressible as a LOOP program. Furthermore, the converse also holds: every LOOP program defines a primitive recursive function. Further details are presented in Meyer and Ritchie's 1967 paper [193] and also in Smith [281].

Continuing with WHILE programs, it is immediately clear, today, that Kleene's least-number operator μ corresponds to a *while–do* construct (and that it cannot be implemented as a LOOP program). Hence, it follows from Kleene's Normal Form theorem $\varphi(x) \approx U(\,\mu y\,T(e,x,y)\,)$ that any general recursive function φ, on input x, can be computed by a corresponding WHILE program that contains at most one *while–do* construct. Given the equivalence between general recursive functions and Turing machines (cf. Kleene's *Metamathematics* [155]), we have thus, rather directly, obtained a stronger form of Böhm and Jacopini's theorem[45].

2.3 Dijkstra's Reception of Turing's 1936 Paper

Dijkstra, born on 11 May 1930 in Rotterdam, studied mathematics and theoretical physics at the University of Leiden, and subsequently conducted PhD research at the Mathematisch Centrum in Amsterdam. He defended his dissertation in 1959 under the title *Communication with an Automatic Computer* [59]. During the late 1950s and 1960s, he contributed to advancing the state of the art in programming. For instance, he helped define and implement the machine-independent programming language ALGOL60 [10], the topic of Chapter 3. During the 1960s, he and his colleagues at the Technische Hogeschool Eindhoven (THE) implemented the THE operating system which relieved the programmer from having to write system software [70, 190].

Already during the early 1950s, at the Mathematisch Centrum, Dijkstra had at least two opportunities to become acquainted with Turing's 1936 paper. First of all, Dijkstra and Van der Poel were both PhD students of Prof. Van Wijngaarden. Therefore, Dijkstra may very well have come across Van der Poel's 1952 machine design [241] which refers to Turing's universal machine, or they may simply have discussed Turing's work. Second, in March 1953, the mathematician Tamari gave a presentation, most likely in French, at the Mathematisch Centrum about Turing machines and Post's word problems [289]. Nothing related to this presentation is, however, mentioned in the 1953 scientific annual report of the Mathematisch Centrum [149], nor any sign of reception of those ideas.

We have to move to 1962 in order to find documented evidence of Dijkstra mentioning Turing. In that year, at the IFIP congress in Munich, Dijkstra gave an invited talk entitled 'Some Meditations on Advanced Programming' [64]. In this talk, Dijkstra showed that he was aware of some of the work of Turing and Von Neumann.

> However, as I told you, the sky above the programmers' world is brightening slowly. Before I go on to draw your attention to some discoveries that are responsible for this improvement, I should like to state as my opinion that it is relatively unimportant whether these are really new discoveries or whether they are rediscoveries of things perfectly well known to people like, say, Turing or von Neumann. [64, p.536]

Dijkstra was in 1962 also well aware of the message conveyed by Burks and others, discussed previously, namely that hardware and software are within limits interchangeable [64, p.536].

While it is not clear whether Dijkstra had, by 1962, become acquainted with Turing's 1936 theory of computation[46], he clearly had done so by 1964. For in April of that year, Dijkstra gave a Dutch presentation [68] in which he talked about the practical (i.e. finite) limitations of electronic computers. In the beginning of his talk, he briefly but explicitly mentioned Turing and his theory of computation, "Turing machines", and unsolvable problems[47].

2.3.1   A Case Against the Goto Statement

In 1962, after his IFIP address in Munich, Dijkstra became Professor of Mathematics in Eindhoven and started working on the THE operating system which he viewed as a "society of sequential processes, progressing with undefined speed ratios" [70]. Dijkstra and his colleagues were much concerned about the intellectual manageability of the progress of such a process. It is in this setting that Dijkstra conceived of the idea of writing his 1968 letter 'Go To Statement Considered Harmful' (cf. [294, p.207]). According to Dijkstra, even for one process, the goto statement is "just too primitive; it is too much an invitation to make a mess of one's program" [69].

Dijkstra started his 1968 letter by stressing that his concern about the goto statement was already a few years old:

> For a number of years I have been familiar with the observation that the quality of programmers is a decreasing function of the density of **go to** statements in the programs they produce. [69]

At the end of his letter, Dijkstra acknowledged that Zemanek had expressed doubts about the goto statement as early as 1959, and also mentioned Landin, Strachey, and Hoare as inspirators. Likewise, in 1974, Knuth mentioned several people who had, prior to Dijkstra, made a case against the goto statement [161]. Naur, for instance, had already done so in 1963 [204], and Van Wijngaarden had illustrated in 1964 how to get rid of gotos to labels by replacing them with calls to procedures generated from the corresponding labels [25, p.27][169]. Knuth also mentioned Schorre and Forsythe as pioneers in trying to avoid using goto statements in their programs [161, p.264]. Finally, Landin's explanation in 1966 concerning the programming language ALGOL60 serves well in describing the intellectual climate of the mid-1960s:

> There is a game sometimes played with ALGOL60 programs —
> rewriting them so as to avoid using labels and **go to** statements.
> It is part of a more embracing game— reducing the extent to
> which the program conveys its information by explicit sequencing.
> Roughly speaking this amounts to using fewer and larger
> statements. The game's significance lies in that it frequently
> produces a more "transparent" program —easier to understand,
> debug, modify and incorporate into a larger program. [167, p.163]

Landin's words suggest that, besides Dijkstra, many other ALGOL
researchers[48] had, prior to 1968, viewed the quality of a program as
inversely proportional to the number of the goto statements it contains.

Nevertheless, it was Dijkstra's letter which created the most waves [161,
p.265]. Besides attracting immediate attention (cf. [299, p.247]), Dijkstra's
letter polarized the computing community. On the one hand, many ALGOL
researchers, if not followed, at least eagerly studied Dijkstra's suggestion
to abolish the goto statement. On the other hand, many computer
practitioners and researchers who favored FORTRAN became upset and
even angry because of Dijkstra's letter. For, all of a sudden, they were
branded as "sinners" in using the goto statement in their otherwise-correct
programs [161, p.294][294, p.211]. A typical reaction went along the
following lines:

> I find the emotional tone of this attack [by Dijkstra] as disquieting
> as the "scientific" analysis. How many poor, innocent, novice
> programmers will feel guilty when their sinful use of go to is flailed
> in this letter? [257]

Dijkstra said he received "a torrent of abusive letters" after his letter
was published (cf. [161, p.265]). In subsequent years, articles titled "X
considered harmful" were published with in one case even "Dijkstra
considered harmful"[49]. The 1972 ACM National Conference devoted an
entire session to the topic [138, 168, 314] and the December 1973 issue of
Datamation contained several articles about structured programming and
elimination of gotos [11, 42, 84, 188, 194]. The controversy concerning
Dijkstra's letter would continue well into the 1980s and later, as stated
explicitly by Benander et al. [20, p.222].

Dijkstra's letter was not in accord with his original intentions,
however. Initially, Dijkstra had submitted a paper to the editor of
the Communications of the ACM, Niklaus Wirth, under the moderate
title 'A case against the goto statement'. It was the editor who, in the
interest of speeding up publication, single handedly decided to publish the
paper as a letter under the far more provocative title 'Go To Statement

Considered Harmful'[50]. Not surprisingly, many authors in later years referred to Dijkstra's letter while giving him the impression that they hadn't studied its contents [79, p.346].

According to Valdez, the controversy concerning Dijkstra's letter was not a "yes/no" conflict, but a "yes, but ..." argument which "operated at different levels, depending on how the letter was perceived" [294, p.212]. Valdez's point, in short, is that the main issue for Dijkstra was clear program development, not the banishment of goto per se. In the words of Dijkstra's close colleague, Niklaus Wirth, "the absence of jumps is not the initial aim, but the final outcome of [structured programming]" [304, p.257]. Closely related to Wirth's explanation, Dijkstra in later years also remarked that

> [I]f you wish to see algorithms not as pragmatic pieces of text that you feed into an IBM computer, but if you prefer to treat them as a mathematical object, [then] the GOTO statement is a complexity generator. [294, p.219]

Dijkstra conveyed to Knuth in January 1973 that he felt uncomfortable with the hype surrounding his letter[51]:

> Please don't fall into the trap of believing that I am terribly dogmatical [sic] about [the go to statement]. I have the uncomfortable feeling that others are making a religion out of it, as if the conceptual problems of programming could be solved by a single trick, by a simple form of coding discipline!

The "others" who were "making a religion out of it" were primarily FORTRAN advocates who were opposing the ALGOL school of thought[52]. I have already explained in Chapter 1 the difference in programming philosophy between proponents of FORTRAN and ALGOL-like languages. The proponents of FORTRAN organized their programs in terms of the machine. They were accustomed to thinking in terms of goto constructs. ALGOL researchers, by contrast, intentionally tried to organize their programs in a problem-oriented way. As we have seen, several of them tried to avoid using goto constructs.

Dijkstra's case against the goto statement was written with the purpose of closing the conceptual gap between the static program text (the syntax) and its dynamic process on an *abstract* stack-based machine (the semantics). Like many others, Dijkstra viewed the semantics of an ALGOL-like language from an operational perspective during the 1960s. Discarding goto constructs from the language would reduce the gap between its syntax and its semantics.

In his letter, Dijkstra described his abstract-machine semantics of an ALGOL-like language in terms of a coordinate system. He stated that every programming language clause "should satisfy the requirement that a programmer independent coordinate system can be maintained to describe the process in a helpful and manageable way". By first showing how this can be accomplished by various clauses, including the procedure mechanism and the repetition clause, Dijkstra then explained why goto clauses make it "terribly hard to find a meaningful set of coordinates in which to describe the process progress" [69].

The goto statement is, in general, a complexity generator, as Dijkstra put it later [294, p.219]. It would, however, be of much less concern if the Halting Problem were a decidable problem. It is here where we see Dijkstra connect his insight into the theory of computation with programming:

> As is well known[53] *there exists no algorithm to decide whether a given program ends or not.* In other words: each programmer who wants to produce a flawless program must at least convince himself by inspection that his program will indeed terminate. In a program, in which unrestricted use of the goto statement has been made this analysis may be very hard on account of the great variety of ways in which the program may fail to stop. After the abolishment of the goto statement there are only two ways in which a program may fail to stop: either by infinite recursion —i.e. through the procedure mechanism— or by the repetition clause. This simplifies the inspection greatly. [80, p.10, my italics]

The above excerpt was not part of Dijkstra's official letter but it shows that he *applied*, albeit indirectly, the unsolvability of the Halting Problem in order to infer a criterion of elegance in higher level programming.

Dijkstra, like so many others, was a computer programmer who had no training in mathematical logic. It is not self-evident that by 1968 he had acquired sufficient knowledge of the theory of computation in order to make his case against the goto statement. His appeal to the unsolvability of the Halting Problem was only one part of his theoretical insight. The other crucial part was his reference to Böhm and Jacopini's paper [23]. In his letter, he wrote:

> In [23] Guiseppe Jacopini *seems* to have proved the (logical) superfluousness of the **go to** statement. [my italics]

Böhm and Jacopini's paper 'Flow diagrams, Turing machines, and languages with only two formation rules' [23] gave the go-ahead signal to those who favored goto-less programming. By elaborately using Turing machines, Böhm and Jacopini had proved a fundamental result in programming which, when recast from Dijkstra's perspective, states that goto-less programming does not come at the expense of computability. In other words, an ALGOL-like language does not lose computational power when discarding the goto statement. Some ALGOL researchers had indirectly been waiting for this theoretical go-ahead signal and it was Dijkstra who reaped the benefit.

The italicized word in the previous passage suggests, however, that Dijkstra, just like Hoare (see Chapter 4), did not study the Böhm-Jacopini paper in detail. Moreover, as stated before, Böhm and Jacopini's theorem follows rather directly from Kleene's Normal Form theorem when the latter is examined with programming in mind. It therefore seems fair to say that several leading researchers in programming were, during the 1960s, typically not well versed in computability theory[54]. From this angle, Dijkstra's application of the unsolvability of the Halting Problem can be viewed as rather unorthodox. Two other examples, presented in later sections, will serve to strengthen this standpoint, as will my discussion with Hoare in Chapter 4.

During the mid-1960s, men like McCarthy, Strachey, Böhm, Jacopini, and Dijkstra were coming to grips with the implications that undecidability has on high-level programming languages. Other leading researchers, having other research agendas, were far less aware of these particular theoretical developments. I have already provided a first example in the introduction of this chapter by citing Grace Hopper. A second example comes from Jean Sammet's 1969 book *Programming Languages: History and Fundamentals* [266].

> Recursive procedures were introduced by ALGOL. They certainly should be considered a significant contribution to the technology, but it is not clear how great a one. The advocates of this facility claim that many important problems cannot be solved without it; on the other hand, people continue to solve numerous important problems without it and even in a few cases manage to handle (sometimes in an awkward way) some of the problems which the recursion proponents claim cannot be done. [266, p.193]

This passage indicates that Sammet and at least part of her large readership were not aware of the practical implications of Böhm and Jacopini's 1966 paper [23]. For, Böhm and Jacopini's theorem implies that recursive procedures are *not* needed in ALGOL60 in order to compute any computable function; composition and iteration suffice[55].

2.3.2 Correct-by-Construction Programming

During the late 1960s, Marvin Minsky contributed greatly to making computability theory more accessible to programmers. In 1967, his popular book *Computation: Finite and Infinite Machines* [197] was published, in which he explained the concept of "effective procedure" by introducing the work of Kleene, Turing, Post and others to the non-logician.

Dijkstra read Minsky's book between 1967 and 1971 because he explicitly referred to it in the second chapter of his 1971 lecture notes *A Short Introduction to the Art of Programming* [72], where he reapplied Cantor's diagonal argument to prove the unsolvability of the Halting Problem. Dijkstra's application of the diagonal argument was not conducted with Turing machines but in the high-level programming language ALGOL60[56], and was, hence, similar to Strachey's proof in CPL (cf. Section 2.2).

In his second chapter, Dijkstra first distinguished between a *proper* algorithm, which halts on all inputs, and an *improper* algorithm, which does not halt on all inputs[57]. Afterward, he explained that it is not possible to algorithmically distinguish between a proper and an improper algorithm, by referring to the unsolvability of the Halting Problem[58]. Dijkstra subsequently proved the unsolvability of the Halting Problem, as mentioned previously, and then interpreted it in his own original way:

> The moral of this story is that it is an intrinsic part of the duty of everyone who professes to compose algorithms to supply a proof that his text indeed represents a proper algorithm. [72, p.16]

The originality of this statement follows by contrasting it with Minsky's interpretation of the unsolvability of the Halting Problem:

> [...] it is impossible to devise a uniform procedure, or computer program, which can look at any computer program and decide whether or not that program will ever terminate. *This means that computation scientists cannot aspire to evolve a completely foolproof 'debugging' program.* [197, p.153, my italics]

Both Dijkstra and Minsky only considered programs that halt on every input to be practically relevant. But, while Minsky stressed a negative implication of the unsolvability of the Halting Problem, Dijkstra provided a more positive conclusion. Minsky stated that it is not possible to completely automate a posteriori verification of an arbitrary program. Dijkstra, on the other hand, aware of this negative result, used it to motivate that programming and correctness proving should go hand in hand, also known today as correct-by-construction programming. According to Dijkstra, the programmer should restrict his programs so much that he can prove that they halt. Dijkstra's approach would become one of the cornerstones of the field of activity called programming methodology (cf. [74, 112]).

2.3.3 Dijkstra's Advice to the DoD

A third and final example of Dijkstra's application of the unsolvability of the Halting Problem starts in 1974 when the US Department of Defense (DoD) embarked on a "common language effort" with the aspiration of having all military departments use a common programming language for the development of their defense systems. This effort would eventually lead to the design and implementation of the ADA programming language. The driving technical and political forces behind this effort were David A. Fisher and Lt. Col. William A. Whitaker, respectively. Fisher wrote most of the language requirements and Whitaker got the DoD services to give up their individual languages and to financially support their movement. Between 1975 and 1980, the DoD published a series of increasingly specific technical reports: Strawman, Woodenman, Tinman, ... Stoneman. Several of these reports were sent to people from industry and academia, including Dijkstra, with the purpose of receiving technical feedback from them (cf. [92, 300]).

Dijkstra's overall dissatisfaction with the technical reports of the DoD was due to a lack of separation of concerns. All too often, according to Dijkstra, the design of the language was mixed up with its implementation (cf. [75]). In an open letter [76] to Whitaker in 1978, Dijkstra tried to dissuade the DoD of defining a programming language in terms of the cleverness of a compiler. He did this by discussing the topic of side effects.

Dijkstra started his letter by conveying the message (which he assumed was in accord with Fisher's intentions) that some procedures with side effects have practical merit and that, therefore, side effects should not be ruled out altogether. To simplify his exposition, he introduced f as an integer procedure without formal parameters. Calling f would result, in general, in a value functionally dependent on the initial values of some of its global variables. He then asked the reader to scrutinize the following statement:

(1)   "the integer procedure f is free from side effects"

In an attempt to capture the meaning of (1), Dijkstra proposed to equate (1) with (2):

(2) (a) Within its scope, the inner block
     (b) *begin integer h*; $h := f$ *end*
     (c) is semantically equivalent to the *empty* statement

Dijkstra justified this choice by remarking that when f is free of side effects in accordance with (2), then the following transformations might be undertaken as harmless by an optimizing compiler:

(i)   transform $y := f * f$ into   *begin integer h*; $h := f$;
                                         $y := h * h$ *end*
(ii) transform b *or* $f = 1$ into   *if b then true else* $f = 1$
(iii) transform $a * f$ into   *if a = 0 then 0 else* $a * f$

Dijkstra was, thus, reasoning about (1) in terms of how a compiler works. By doing so, he was temporarily playing along with those who, in his opinion, did not clearly separate language definition from language implementation. Dijkstra then argued that

> [I]t is impossible for a translator to 'enforce' that the function procedure f is in the above sense free of side effects, as it would require the solution of the halting problem [. . .]

That is, (2)(b) is, in general, not equivalent to the *empty* statement because f computes a partial function. The calling of f, Dijkstra explained, only leads to proper termination provided some condition D, describing its domain, is satisfied. Given the inadequacy of (2), Dijkstra made the following correction:

"the integer procedure f is free of side effects
with respect to condition D"

if and only if

if D
then begin integer h; $h := f$ *end*
else skip

is semantically equivalent to the *empty* statement

Dijkstra furthermore emphasized that it is the user, not the compiler, who has to explicitly state and then guarantee that D is satisfied wherever the function procedure may be invoked [76, p.1–2].

Toward the end of his letter, Dijkstra generalized his findings by distinguishing between a 'legal' program and a 'correct' program. Compilers can reject illegal programs, but they cannot reject all incorrect programs.

> [F]or legal programs the language definition should define the *proof obligations to be met [by the user]* in order to make the legal program also a correct program. [76, p.2, my italics]

Hence, similar to his case against the goto statement and his lecture notes *A Short Introduction to the Art of Programming* [72], Dijkstra emphasized that the programmer's involvement is key in program development.

In summary, Dijkstra applied the unsolvability of the Halting Problem in an attempt to convince the DoD that a clear-cut separation between language definition and implementation was in their best interest, and that automation has its limitations. Whether the DoD understood and agreed with Dijkstra's appeal is another story.

2.4   Final Remarks

As a tribute to Turing and Dijkstra, I have delved into the history of computing in order to explain how the work of the former has indirectly influenced the thinking of the latter. Through this historical journey, several fundamental principles of programming languages have come to the fore. Distilling from what we have seen, Turing's 1936 paper has had at least three different receptions among computer practitioners of the 1950s–1960s. A second take-away message is that Dijkstra applied the unsolvability of the Halting Problem in distinct ways and, in particular, that his case against the goto statement implicitly relied on it. If Dijkstra had thought that every problem could be solved by automation, like Grace Hopper and other leading researchers did, then he would have had much less of an incentive to make a case against the goto statement in the first place, nor to stress the general importance of the programmer's manual involvement in program development. Equally important is Dijkstra's reception of Böhm and Jacopini's 1966 paper [23], contrary to others like Jean Sammet. Even though Dijkstra most likely only read Böhm and Jacopini's paper lightly, he was sufficiently acquainted with computability theory to make the connection between their theoretical result and his practical programming concerns with regard to the goto construct.

The aforementioned messages have, to the best of my knowledge, not been described in the literature before. Again, what has been discussed extensively is whether Von Neumann was influenced by Turing's 1936 paper when working on the EDVAC machine, a question which remains unsettled up till this day.

Instead of plunging into the history of the computing machine, I have pondered Turing's influence on programming and on Dijkstra's thinking in particular. Doing so has, I believe, brought Turing's true legacy to the fore. Turing's 1936 notion of universal machine was recast by logicians like Post, Church, Kleene, and Davis. Eventually and gradually, during the 1950s, recast notions helped some leading switching theorists, hardware engineers, and researchers in automatic programming to see the bigger picture of what they were accomplishing. Later, the undecidability results of Church and Turing, in the form of Davis's Halting Problem or in a form equivalent to it, influenced some experts in the emerging field of high-level programming. Dijkstra was definitely one of them. Other research areas, like artificial intelligence and complexity theory which heavily rely on the recast notion of a Turing machine as well, have yet to be examined.

Finally, I stress that this chapter is synthetic, not analytic. I have tried to paint an outstretched landscape, not an absolute and definite mathematical object. The implication is that, when discussing the work of, say, Carr I have been everything but thorough.

3. Dijkstra's Rallying Cry for Generalization

This chapter is, by permission of Oxford University Press, an improved and extended version of
The Computer Journal (2011) 54 (11): 1756–1772.

Half a century ago, the 31 year old Dutchman Edsger W. Dijkstra was sitting in Rome's "Palazzo dei Congressi" attending the Panel Discussion on 'Philosophies for Efficient Processor Construction' at the *International Symposium of Symbolic Languages in Data Processing* (March, 1962). Together with Naur, Duncan, and Garwick, he was one of the few strong proponents of the recursive procedure in the ALGOL60 programming language. Even though he had become famous more than a year before the symposium by being one of the first to build an ALGOL60 compiler and corresponding runtime system that could handle recursive procedures, a large group of panel members remained skeptical about its usefulness.

Inspection of the proceedings [230] shows that almost every panel member had a slightly different view toward why the recursive procedure should or should not belong to a machine-independent programming language, such as ALGOL60. For instance, and as is explained in greater detail later, Dijkstra heavily supported the recursive procedure for linguistic reasons, even though he did not use it in his ALGOL60 programs[59]. In contrast, Strachey and Samelson claimed that general language constructs, such as the recursive procedure, typically led to inefficient object programs. Strachey wanted to restrict (but not necessarily abolish) the use of recursive procedures [230, p.368,373]. Samelson was primarily concerned with immediate economic considerations: "the final judge in matters of efficiency is money". Samelson wanted to minimize the financial cost of a complete project: designing a programming language, building a compiler, compiling programs, and executing those programs. In his opinion, the efficiency of the running program influenced the total cost the most and, therefore, he preferred to avoid the recursive procedure [230, p.364,372].

The tension between several panel members was apparent [230, p.373]. For instance, Naur's views, which were very similar to those of Dijkstra, were in sharp contrast to Samelson's economic considerations. And, Seegmüller's nasty but loudly applauded comment certainly did not help ease the tension:

> And the question is —to state it once more— that we want to work with this language, really to work and not to play with it, and I hope we don't become a kind of Algol play-boys. [230, p.375]

The comment was directed towards Dijkstra, Naur, and other linguists; i.e. researchers who favored general language constructs.

Not many people during the early 1960s openly claimed the potential usefulness of the recursive procedure as a programming construct. It seems that, in McCarthy's absence, only the Norwegian researcher Garwick did so at the Rome symposium [230, p.369].

In hindsight, limited support for the recursive procedure is not so surprising. ALGOL60's main application domain was numerical analysis[60] and the recursive procedure was not used by numerical analysts during the early 1960s. For instance, only by 1963 did the Swiss mathematician Rutishauser find two examples of recursion for numerical computations which he himself found convincing. He also contrasted his two examples with others[61] in which recursion could, and in his opinion should, be replaced by iteration [263].

The ALGOL60 report [10], published in May 1960, did quickly lead to *non-numerical* applications of the recursive procedure. It enabled Hoare to express his intuitive ideas on sorting and resulted in his now-famous QuickSort [124], which he published as a recursive ALGOL60 program [128, p.145]. Besides the recursive procedure, ALGOL60 was also innovative due to its recursive syntax, formalized in Backus Naur Form (BNF) notation. The formalized recursive syntax, in turn, led several researchers to design their ALGOL60 compilers as a collection of mutually recursive procedures. Grau, for instance, described in a pseudo-ALGOL60 language what we would today call a recursive descent compiler[62]. A similar but later example is Hoare's compiler for the Elliott machine (cf. [128, p.146] and Chapter 4).

If numerical analysts did not use recursive procedures in their work, and if ALGOL60 was primarily designed for numerical computations, why then did ALGOL60's official definition [10] include the recursive procedure as a language construct? Why was it such a controversial topic in Rome in 1962? McCarthy had, based on his experience with recursion in LISP, unsuccessfully attempted to put forward the recursive procedure as an ALGOL60 language construct. Instead, it was the linguistically minded Amsterdamers, Van Wijngaarden and Dijkstra, who had convinced the editor of the ALGOL60 report, Naur, to include recursive procedures in ALGOL60. However, these three men knew that recursive procedures were heavily opposed by other influential ALGOL60 researchers. Why then did the Dutch persevere, given that they did not need it in their programming?

ALGOL60's definition was discussed on the international scene during the late 1950s and it was officially defined in May 1960. Its definition [10] strongly suggests that it had been defined without having a particular machine in mind: its syntax was presented with the help of a formal language (BNF, discussed later) and its semantics were stated without mentioning specific machine features. Placing ALGOL60 in a historical context, however, suggests otherwise. The programming systems prior to ALGOL60 had typically been defined in terms of specific machine features and by several researchers who would later become ALGOL60 actors. It therefore seems rather unlikely that all ALGOL60 actors were indeed reasoning machine independently during the late 1950s and early 1960s. In this chapter, several people (Bauer, Samelson, Strachey, and Wilkes) will be mentioned in this regard as researchers who primarily reasoned in terms of machine efficiency and less so as linguists (à la Van Wijngaarden and Dijkstra) who focused on general language constructs prior to dealing with machine-specific problems.

The shared ambition, among all ALGOL60 actors, was to implement a universal, machine-independent programming language in conformance with the ALGOL60 report [10]. But it was not clear a priori to many ALGOL60 actors whether all of its language constructs were implementable [252, p.12–13]. In practice, various ALGOL60 dialects were implemented, dialects which were influenced by local programming habits and specific machine features. For example, the British researchers Strachey and Wilkes wanted to restrict the official ALGOL60 definition — and the use of the recursive procedure in particular — due to specific features of contemporary machines, as explained in their 1961 article [287] and as heavily criticized by Dijkstra [61, p.16–18][67, p.40–42].

Most early ALGOL60 implementations were not able to handle all language constructs and the recursive procedure in particular[63]. Dijkstra and Zonneveld, by contrast, did succeed in building one of the first ALGOL60 compilers and corresponding runtime system which could handle almost all of the language, including the recursive procedure. Their implementation was completed in August 1960 and impressed several researchers. In Naur's words:

> The first news of the success of the Dutch project, in June 1960,
> fell like a bomb in our group. [205, p.119]

Essential to the Dijkstra-Zonneveld implementation was its runtime stack. Yet, the stack had long been invented by several independent researchers and its runtime usage was not novel either, as Dijkstra also explicitly acknowledged when he described some of the key ideas underlying the Dijkstra-Zonneveld implementation [60, p.313]. On the other hand, it is equally clear that their solution was indeed a technical innovation, as Rosen's comment illustrates:

> Almost everyone involved in writing an Algol compiler has used some of the ideas developed in connection with the Algol Compiler written by professor Dijkstra and his colleagues at the Mathematisch Centre in Amsterdam. [260, p.181]

What, then, made the Dijkstra-Zonneveld implementation[64] so special?

Answers to the aforementioned questions are presented in the sequel of this chapter by describing the work of some key players who were involved in the ALGOL60 effort. By doing so, two main messages are conveyed in this chapter.

The first message is that the early history of programming languages can be viewed as an emerging dichotomy between specialization and generalization. Specialization refers to language restrictions, static (compile time) solutions, and the exploitation of machine-specific facilities — in the interest of efficiency. Generalization refers to general language constructs, dynamic (runtime) solutions, and machine-independent language design — in the interest of correctness and reliability. The dichotomy becomes effective if we keep in mind that most ALGOL60 researchers were neither completely specialists nor generalists, and that they initially did *not* characterize each other as such. Only after 1960 did the dichotomy become increasingly apparent.

The second message conveyed in this chapter is that Dijkstra's continual appeal for generalization led to practical breakthroughs in compiler technology, while some prominent ALGOL60 researchers who favored language restrictions in the interest of obtaining immediate practical results failed in their endeavours. Dijkstra's successes will, however, be put into perspective as well by showing that the dichotomy outlived the ALGOL60 effort, contrary to the claims Dijkstra made in Munich, half a year after the Rome conference [64].

Three disclaimers conclude this introduction. First, a historically accurate narrative, as attempted here, often implies mathematical inaccuracy with respect to the current state of the art. In this chapter, the recursive procedure is described in terms of what computer practitioners of the late 1950s and early 1960s understood by it. Therefore, the recursive procedure is presented informally and without any mention of terminationtermination proofs. Likewise, noting in hindsight that Dijkstra, McCarthy, and others had made mistakes in their pioneering work has practical relevance [189, 284], but lies outside the scope of this book. Second, the history of ideas is much less concerned with "firsts" than it is with the contextual development of ideas [170]. For example, the fact that Grau and Hoare, mentioned above, used `ALGOL60`'s recursive procedure in unanticipated ways is far more important than noting that Grau did so before Hoare. Third, this chapter presents a *synthesis* of Dijkstra's work on `ALGOL60`. It therefore most definitely does not address all of his contributions. When discussing some of his papers, I will often discuss only parts of their contents.

3.1 Specialization versus Generalization

World War II coincided with the beginning of the computer era. As two victors of the war, the USA and the UK were among the first to systematically build computers. Continental Europe, by contrast, was in turmoil. Relying heavily on the Marshall Plan for economic revival, several continental-European researchers traveled to the USA and the UK to acquire knowledge in computing. In 1947, for example, the Dutch mathematician Van Wijngaarden visited the UK and the USA [2, p.102], and in 1949 Rutishauser from Switzerland visited the computer pioneers Aiken at Harvard and Von Neumann at Princeton [269, p.2].

3.1.1 USA

Besides building computing machines, American researchers were also quick in seeking easier ways to instruct their machines. As mentioned in Chapter 2, in May 1954 the American Navy organized a conference in Washington D.C. entitled *Automatic Programming for Digital Computers* [288]. Instead of having a programmer tediously write down machine code, the conference attendees wanted to be able to provide the programmer with a more mathematical notation in which he could express himself more easily. The research challenge was to design a computer program that could automatically translate the mathematical expressions of the programmer into the instructions of the machine. Although most presentations at the 1954 conference covered mathematical notations and automatic-translation programs that only worked for a specific kind of machine, there were two exceptional presentations given by Gorn [108] and Brown & Carr [28]. These three researchers discussed translation techniques that were applicable for any type of machine. To obtain such a general technique, they realized that the mathematical notation (intended for the programmer) had to be independent of any computing machine. That is, the mathematical notation had to be a *machine-independent* language. Furthermore, Gorn, Brown, and Carr sought a *universal* machine-independent language; that is, a language that was close to the universal language of mathematics and, hence, applicable to a large class of mathematical problems.

To appreciate the extreme stance taken by Gorn, Brown, and Carr, two observations are in order. First, the aspired universal, machine-independent language embodied generality in two ways: it was intended for various mathematical problems and a variety of computing machines. Second, given the limited storage sizes and execution speeds of contemporary computing machines, programmers in the 1950s did their utmost best to optimize the efficiency of their programs. That is, they applied special programming tricks in order to obtain programs that were economical in terms of program size and computation time. To apply such tricks, they exploited specific details of the mathematical problem that their computer program was intended to solve and they also exploited specific details of their computing machine. Hence, specialization — in contrast to generalization — was the prime occupation in computing during the 1950s. A general language, such as a universal machine-independent language, was viewed by many as unrealistic, because of the inefficiencies it would incur.

Due to its generality, Brown and Carr acknowledged that their aspired language would, indeed, incur a runtime penalty in efficiency, compared with existing machine-specific programming techniques. But, according to them, this penalty would be outweighed by a decrease in programming time and programming errors. For, by being completely ignorant of what machine would execute his mathematical expressions, the programmer only had to convert his mathematical problem into the mathematical notation of the universal language. He did not have to incorporate machine-specific characteristics in his manual labor. To get this message across, Brown and Carr advocated an overall measure of effectiveness which included the new criteria of programming time and program correctness, along with the more traditional criteria of program size and computation time [28, p.89].

Speedcoding & FORTRAN

Also present at the 1954 conference were Backus and Herrick. They described a high-level *and* machine-dependent system, called Speedcoding. Instead of having to directly program in machine code, the aspiration was that a programmer could solely write down the formulas for the numerical problem at hand (i.e. declaratively). Yet, in order to obtain fast executables, the programmer would also be able to express how the data should be transferred from one storage hierarchy to another [9, p.111–112]. In their own words:

> [T]he question is, can a machine translate a sufficiently rich mathematical language into a sufficiently economical machine program at a sufficiently low cost to make the whole affair feasible? [9, p.112]

To obtain an affirmative answer, Speedcoding and the later FORTRAN were designed for *specific* machines and, hence, at the price of machine portability [260, p.11][266, p.151]. The tendency to specialize also reflects in the program constructs: *do* statements (i.e. *for* loops) had to have static bounds and it was not possible to express potentially unbounded *while–do* loops, nor recursive procedures [266, p.145,159–160].

Backus: from FORTRAN to ALGOL58

After having worked on FORTRAN, Backus joined the ALGOL effort and made a significant contribution [7] by devising a formal notation to describe the syntax of ALGOL58. Backus's notation almost went unnoticed however; it was Naur who grasped its potential and, who, after making some small but important modifications, used it to define ALGOL60's syntax. The notation was originally called Backus Normal Form. In 1964, Knuth pointed out that it wasn't what mathematicians call a normal form and suggested changing the name to Backus Naur Form in honor of both Backus's and Naur's accomplishments while keeping the same acronym (cf. [8], [159], and [212, p.99]).

To appreciate the conceptual leap that Backus took from FORTRAN to ALGOL58, it is important to note that, prior to his contribution, computer practitioners described syntax informally (e.g. in verbose English). For example, consider the definition: A real number is

> any sequence of decimal digits with a decimal point preceding or intervening between any 2 digits or following a sequence of digits, all of this optionally preceded by a plus or minus sign.

$$
\begin{aligned}
<\text{digit}> \quad &:= \quad 0 \mid 1 \mid 2 \mid 3 \mid 4 \mid 5 \mid 6 \mid 7 \mid 8 \mid 9 \\
<\text{integer}> \quad &:= \quad <\text{digit}> \mid <\text{integer}><\text{digit}> \\
<\text{realPart}> \quad &:= \quad .<\text{integer}> \mid <\text{integer}>. \mid \\
&\qquad <\text{integer}>.<\text{integer}> \\
<\text{real}> \quad &:= \quad <\text{realPart}> \mid +<\text{realPart}> \mid \\
&\qquad -<\text{realPart}>
\end{aligned}
$$

Table 3.1: An example in Backus Naur Form.

The previous passage is similar to how a real number was defined in ALGOL58 [239, p.11] in that no mention is made of the finiteness of the machine. By including machine-specific constants, which do express the finite-storage limitations of the machine, the previous definition can be extended to the following condition:

The number must be less than 10^{38} in absolute value and greater than 10^{-38} in absolute value.

The previous two passages, together, constitute the original definition of a real number in FORTRAN[65].

In short, both FORTRAN's and ALGOL58's syntax were defined informally. The syntax of FORTRAN was defined with and that of ALGOL58 was defined without finite-storage limitations in mind. The informal definitions were ambiguous, incomplete, and often lengthy: FORTRAN's and ALGOL58's syntax were very cumbersome to use in practice [19, p.26–27].

Continuing with the real number example, the BNF equivalent of the first passage, presented above, is depicted in Table 3.1. With | denoting *or*, Line 1 expresses that a digit is either 0 or 1 or 2 or ... or 9. Line 2, in turn, *recursively* defines a sequence of digits to be either a digit or an integer concatenated with a digit. Line 3 defines the real part of a real number to either be an integer preceded by or followed by a decimal point or an integer followed by a decimal point and an integer. Finally, Line 4 defines a real number to have no sign, a plus sign, or a minus sign.

Note that Table 3.1 is only the BNF equivalent of the first passage, presented above. The finite-storage limitations of the machine (cf. the second passage) cannot be expressed concisely in BNF notation. Indeed, the syntactic recursion, exemplified in Line 2 in Table 3.1, is what made BNF notation so concise: Line 2 allows an arbitrarily long but finite integer to be written down in ALGOL60 and, hence, also integers that simply could not fit in every computer's memory!

Backus's conceptual leap of abstracting away the computing machine's finite limitations cannot be stressed enough. Unlike his work during the FORTRAN years, where he focused on the design of the translator to obtain efficient machine code, Backus's abstraction allowed him to *solely* focus on the language. On the one hand, Backus was aided by ALGOL58's abstraction of finite storage. On the other hand, as we shall see, many computer practitioners did not let go of machine-specific features while designing and implementing a machine-independent programming language.

List Processing

Not present at the 1954 conference but equally important to mention are Newell, Shaw, and Simon. By 1957, these three men had implemented a list processing system for automatic theorem proving [224, 225]. Their system was called the Logic Theory Machine (LT) and it served the purpose of trying to better understand how effective human problem solving works in reality, such as finding a proof of a mathematical theorem, playing chess, or discovering scientific laws from data [225, p.218–219]. They used their Information Processing Language (IPL) to implement LT [224, p.232].

In contrast to the many numerical programs implemented during the 1950s, LT was symbolic in nature. While numerical programs were primarily static in the sense that, for example, the set of variables and constants to be used at run time could be determined in advance (i.e. prior to program execution), LT was primarily dynamic. The number, kind, and order of logical expressions used in LT were completely variable. Therefore, runtime translation was needed and carried out by an interpreter [224, p.230,231,235].

IPL was a very flexible programming language. A user could express the creation of a list during the course of computation. In addition, a user could create lists that consisted of other lists or lists of lists, etc. Adding, deleting, inserting, and rearranging items in a list was possible at any time. Finally, it was also feasible for an item to appear in any number of lists simultaneously [224, p.231]. In modern terminology, dynamic memory management and aliasing characterized the work of Newell, Shaw, and Simon.

IPL was not only flexible in terms of memory assignments, but also in terms of defining processes. There was no limitation on the size and complexity of hierarchical definitions. Likewise, no restriction was enforced on the number of references in the instructions or on what was referenced. Of particular interest is that processes could be defined implicitly, e.g. by *recursion* [224, p.231]. More generally:

> [T]he programmer should be able to specify any process in whatever way occurs naturally to him in the context of the problem. If the programmer has to 'translate' the specification into a fixed and rigid form, he is doing a preliminary processing of the specifications that could be avoided. [224, p.231]

In short, Newell, Shaw, and Simon focused more on the flexibility of their IPL language than on machine efficiency. Their first pseudo code was developed in a machine-independent way with the purpose of precisely specifying an LT machine. Only *afterward* did they define IPL and in accordance with the RAND JOHNNIAC machine [224, p.232]. Not surprisingly, IPL had some shortcomings in terms of memory space and computation time, shortcomings which were not considered too problematic:

> [F]or it seemed to us that these costs could be brought down by later improvements, after we had learned how to obtain the flexibility we required. [224, p.232]

Hence, the prime concern was the language and the ease of being able to express oneself in that language for the problem at hand.

Likewise, McCarthy was, contrary to the many numerical analysts of the 1950s, trying to use recursion in his programming. He tried to add recursion to FORTRAN, but without success. This led him to develop his own list processing, recursive command language LISP [274, p.27], which was greatly inspired by the work of Newell, Shaw, and Simon [187, p.187].

3.1.2 Western Europe

During part of World War II, Heinz Rutishauser was a PhD student at the Eidgenössische Technische Hochschule in Zurich (ETH). In 1949, Rutishauser visited the computer pioneers Howard Aiken at Harvard and John von Neumann at Princeton, in order to acquire the state of the art in computing of that time. During his stay abroad, Rutishauser's boss, Eduard Stiefel, had managed in Zurich to rent Konrad Zuse's Z4 machine. So, after Rutishauser returned to Zurich, he found himself in a comfortable position. On the one hand, he was well aware of American computer technology and, on the other hand, he had a German computing machine at his disposal [269, p.2].

By 1950, Rutishauser had begun working on numerical methods, i.e. scientific computing. In collaboration with Eduard Stiefel and Ambros Speiser, he wrote a series of four papers in which he covered topics such as possible number systems, fixed vs. floating point and complementation, arithmetic processes, etc.[66]. In 1951, Rutishauser submitted his habilitation at ETH, entitled *Automatische Rechenplanfertigung,* in which he described a machine procedure for handling various portions of an arithmetic formula and how these could be combined to produce machine code [269, p.2–3].

Rutishauser's strong position, in terms of computing machinery and know-how, attracted his neighbours from Munich: Klaus Samelson and Friedrich Bauer. Gradually, during the 1950s, these three men increased their cooperation and friendship [269, p.3]. By the late 1950s, they were internationally respected for their expertise in automatically producing machine code from algebraic expressions[67].

The collaboration between the aforementioned researchers was officially conducted in the Swiss-German ZMD group, with researchers from Zurich, Munich, and Darmstadt [226, p.61]. These three cities collaborated closely in scientific computing but were hindered by the diversity of computing machines: different machines were being built in each of these cities. To overcome this diversity, Rutishauser appealed for a "unified algorithmic notation" in the 1955 GaMM[68] meeting and the ZMD group subsequently became more involved in researching automatic-translation techniques [19, p.5][226, p.61].

In May 1958, a one-week ACM-GaMM meeting was held in Zurich, indicating the start of a collaboration between an American delegation, led by Carr, and the ZMD group [239]. The collective focus was to define a universal, machine-independent programming language. Initially, the chosen name for the language was International Algorithmic Language. Later it was called ALGOL58. By January 1960, the name changed into ALGOL as an abbreviation for Algorithmic Language [19, p.35][238, p.79]. In this book I denote the final language as ALGOL60.

The purpose of ALGOL58 was threefold [239, p.9].

1. The new language should be as close as possible to standard mathematical notation and be readable with little further explanation.

2. It should be possible to use it for the description of computing processes in publications.

3. The new language should be mechanically translatable into machine programs.

Besides the Swiss and West-Germans, also others such as the Dutch, Danes, and British were actively involved in computing during the 1950s. In Amsterdam, for instance, Van Wijngaarden led a team at the 'Mathematisch Centrum' (Mathematical Center). Contrary to Rutishauser, who had a rented computing machine at his disposal as early as 1950 [158, p.24–25][280, p.41–50], the Amsterdamers had to build their own machine before being able to experiment with programming techniques. It took until January 1954, with the advent of their ARRAII machine, for the Amsterdamers to possess a working computer [2, p.124]. Only in 1959, with their X1 machine, did the Amsterdamers actively participate in advancing the art of automatic translation by joining the ALGOL60 effort. Surprisingly however, the Amsterdamers Dijkstra and Zonneveld succeeded very quickly in implementing ALGOL60 by August, 1960. By doing so, Amsterdam instantly became an internationally renowned city for those involved in the ALGOL60 effort [2, p.125].

During the second half of the 1950s, the Swiss-German ZMD group extended and changed its name into ALCOR (ALgol COnverteR). Research teams from Copenhagen and Vienna had joined the ALCOR initiative [265, p.210]. Each ALCOR team had its own unique computing machine, but shared the same aspiration: an easy mathematically-oriented programming language (initially ALGOL58, later ALGOL60). Similar to the Gorn-Brown-Carr philosophy, the ALCOR members wanted to be able to write a program once in ALGOL58 and then be able to automatically translate it into the instructions of any ALCOR machine. Furthermore, the ALCOR members wanted efficient translators *and* efficient machine programs [265, p.210]. The latter ambition, however, conflicted with their quest for a universal machine-independent language. For, recall from Brown and Carr's work that efficient machine programs and machine independence did not mix well, as Bauer and Samelson's own words from 1962 also seem to indicate:

> The [ALCOR] group was in agreement from the beginning, partly as a result of the experiment in machine design, to devise a [universal, machine independent] language and translator as an efficient programming tool *using available machine facilities to the fullest extent possible.* [265, p.210, my italics]

As we shall see later, Dijkstra, by contrast, designed a language after having first abstracted away from the machine. A similar remark holds concerning the design of the Dijkstra-Zonneveld compiler and runtime system.

3.1.3   The Recursive Procedure Enters ALGOL60

As part of the ALGOL60 effort, a subcommittee in November 1959 (consisting of Rutishauser, Ehrling, Woodger, and Paul) recommended that certain restrictions be put in place with respect to the parameters of a procedure, thereby automatically preventing recursive activation through a parameter. According to Perlis, recursion in general was therefore not explicitly forbidden [238, p.86]. According to Naur, however, it was:

> We should also mention that this procedure concept of the old language introduced for every procedure body a completely closed universe of names. There was no communication to the outer world except through parameters. In this way of course, recursive activations were ruled out by the language itself. [212, p.151,154]

In August 1959, McCarthy wrote a letter in which he openly advocated recursive procedures [184], based on the experience he had acquired with his own language LISP [284, p.302,304]. In January 1960, at the final ALGOL60 Paris conference, McCarthy suggested to add recursive procedures to the ALGOL60 language [238, p.86][274, p.30]. With regard to McCarthy's proposal to add recursive procedures, an American representative to the ALGOL60 conference proposed to add the delimiter *recursive* to the language, to be used in the context *recursive procedure*. The American's proposal was voted down by a narrow margin [212, p.112]. According to some this rejection was interpreted to mean that recursive procedures should not be added to the ALGOL60 language; others, however, interpreted it to mean that recursive procedures should not be distinguished syntactically from non-recursive procedures by means of the proposed delimiter [212, p.160]. The latter category of people, therefore, did assume that recursive procedures (introduced by McCarthy) belonged to the ALGOL60 language, while the former category of people — including Naur and McCarthy [212, p.159–160] — assumed that recursive procedures did not belong to the language. In short, and in Perlis's words: "it is not clear what the votes meant!" [212, p.160].

The voting took place before other issues, concerning the (informal) semantics of procedures, had been clarified [212, p.160–161]. After the voting, and after several modifications were made to the semantics of procedures, the defined language, from Naur's perspective, contradicted the November 1959 proposal to prohibit recursion [212, p.112]. For, Van Wijngaarden and Dijkstra had stumbled upon the possibility to syntactically express recursive procedure activations. Not sure whether recursion was indeed intended semantically, they contacted the ALGOL editor, Naur, by telephone on approximately 10 February 1960 to convey this ambiguity [212, p.112]. After consulting Dijkstra, Van Wijngaarden suggested to Naur to add the following clarification to the ALGOL report:

> Any other occurrence of the procedure identifier within the procedure body denotes activation of the procedure. [10, p.311]

Hence, this made explicit that recursive procedures could be expressed in ALGOL60. The fact that the alternative, of preventing recursive procedure activations by means of several language restrictions, would be cumbersome, was also mentioned by Van Wijngaarden[69]. It is, in hindsight, clear that Van Wijngaarden and Dijkstra were primarily reasoning along linguistic lines and *not* in terms of specific machine features[70]. As we shall see, simplicity for them meant less language restrictions.

Naur had initially been in favor of ALCOR's efficiency driven philosophy. But he became charmed by the one-sentence clarification of the Dutch and added it to the ALGOL60 report. According to Naur's 1978 recollections:

> I got charmed with the boldness and simplicity of this [one-sentence] suggestion and decided to follow it in spite of the risk of subsequent trouble over the question (cf. Appendix 5, Bauer's point 2.8 and the oral presentation). [212, p.112–113]

Naur's reference to Bauer shows that he was well aware of ALCOR's strong will to prohibit introducing recursive procedures in the language, in accordance with the November 1959 meeting[71].

3.2 Dijkstra's Continual Appeal for Generalization

Van Wijngaarden's team in Amsterdam spent most of the 1950s building computing machines and corresponding machine languages. The programmer Dijkstra typically had to construct the machine's software on paper, awaiting for the machine to be built by his colleagues Loopstra, Scholten, and Blaauw [2, p.111]. Only in 1959, did the Amsterdamers join the ALGOL60 effort by actively pursuing a definition of the ALGOL60 language and a corresponding translation technique. In hindsight, the Amsterdamers' lack of expertise in translation technology and machine-independent languages may have been a blessing in disguise, as Dijkstra's words from 1980 indicate:

> The combination of no prior experience in compiler writing and a new machine [the X1] without established ways of use greatly assisted us in approaching the problem of implementing ALGOL60 with a fresh mind. [77, p.572]

Van Wijngaarden and Dijkstra viewed a programming language, such as ALGOL60, as a mathematical object. If certain aesthetic criteria were met, they would consider the language to be elegant and, hence, relevant. Only after such a language was defined, did they seek an automatic-translation technique. Their working style differed radically from the efficiency driven approach followed by Bauer, Samelson, Strachey, Wilkes, and others.

3.2.1   In Search for a Simple Language

An important aesthetic criterion for the Dutch was generality: any unnecessary language restriction had to be avoided at all costs, in the interest of obtaining a simple language. Dijkstra clarified this point in a later publication [67] by making an analogy between ALGOL60 and the English language. He suggested considering any English text that respects five restrictions:

1. Words of more than 15 letters are forbidden.

2. The total number of letters of three consecutive words may not be greater than 40.

3. Sentences of more than 60 words are not allowed.

4. In one and the same sentence, the same word may not be used twice as a subject.

5. A list of 2000 words is given and each word in that list may not be used.

Dijkstra remarked that the readability of any text respecting restrictions 1–5 is not necessarily hindered and one can read such a text while being completely ignorant of the restrictions. But, constructing a correct English text in conformance with restrictions 1–5 is problematic, due to a lack of intuition when trying to comprehend the restrictions. In the interest of clarity and program correctness, Dijkstra did not want a language such as ALGOL60 to contain restrictions similar to 1–5 either. For instance, a procedure that can call another procedure but not itself was an unnecessary language restriction for Dijkstra. By discarding it, a more general and hence simpler language was obtained; i.e. a language which could handle recursive procedures.

In his paper 'On the design of machine independent programming languages' [67], Dijkstra applied his ideology to ALGOL60 by advocating *dynamic* instead of static constructs, since they make the language more systematic and powerful. One of Dijkstra's examples was based on the switch and procedure declarations in ALGOL60. The switch is a vector of statement labels, declared at the beginning of a block. Its declaration looks syntactically like an assignment statement. For example, a source program containing the statement *switch S := S1, S2, S3* is equivalent to the same program in which the previous statement is replaced by the following:

> *procedure S(n); value n; integer n;*
> *if n = 1 then goto S1*
> *else if n = 2 then goto S2*
> *else goto S3*

and where correspondingly *goto S[i]* in the source program is replaced by *S(i)* in the target program.

Both the switch and procedure declaration have a hybrid nature, which is an undesirable property according to Dijkstra. On the one hand, the switch and procedure declarations both reserve an identifier for a special sort of object and that object is defined statically, i.e. immediately. In this sense, both the switch and procedure declarations are similar to the 'constant' declaration. On the other hand, however, while a constant number can be used in an assignment statement which dynamically assigns a value, a switch or procedure declaration cannot be used in such a dynamic manner. Dijkstra therefore suggested to extend the concept of 'assignment of a value' so that lists, statements, etc. can also act as assigned values. This, in turn, would allow one to remove the value-defining function of the switch and procedure declarations. The result would then be that the declarators *switch* and *procedure* would only be followed by a list of identifiers, to which suitable assignments would eventually be made at run time; that is, during program execution [67, p.35–36]. According to Dijkstra:

> [Such a modification] is an improvement: the language then becomes more systematic and more powerful at the same time, as *all value-relations* have now become *dynamic*. [67, p.36, my italics]

Dijkstra's emphasis on general language constructs and corresponding dynamic implementations would, as many observed, have an adverse effect on computation time. In Strachey's words:

> I think the question of simplifying or reducing a language in order
> to make the object program more efficient is extremely important.
> I disagree fundamentally with Dijkstra, about the necessity of
> having everything as general as possible in all possible occasions
> as I think that this is a purely theoretical approach [...][72]

It is therefore no surprise that Dijkstra and his fellow linguists were the
laughing stock of Seegmüller's well-received comment at the 1962 Rome
symposium. Indeed, for most people at the symposium efficiency was *the*
prime concern.

A closer look at Dijkstra's ideology, however, shows that his agenda was
not to neglect efficiency issues *per se*, but to focus on the more general
objective of increasing programming comfort. In Dijkstra's words:

> In order to get as clear a picture as possible of the real needs of
> the programmer, I intend to pay, for a while, no attention to the
> well-known criteria 'space and time'. Those who on the ground of
> this remark now doubt the honest fervour with which the following
> is written, should remember that, in the last instance, a machine
> serves one of its highest purposes when its activities significantly
> contribute to our *comfort*. [67, p.30, my italics]

In other words, to better understand the real underlying problems of
programming, Dijkstra suggested to temporarily ignore (i.e. abstract
away) machine-specific features. While a decrease in execution time or
memory footprint may, indeed, contribute to an increase in programming
comfort, other criteria, such as program correctness, could contribute
much more. According to Dijkstra:

> I am convinced that these problems [of program correctness] will
> prove to be much more urgent than, for example, the exhaustive
> exploitation of specific machine features, if not now, then at any
> rate in the near future. [67, p.30]

As a final example, by countering Strachey and Wilkes's efficiency driven
proposal to explicitly delimit the use of recursive procedures, Dijkstra
clearly explained where he stood on these matters:

> [Strachey and Wilkes] make an appeal to the fact that "... a
> recursive procedure is both longer and slower than a non-recursive
> one." But the recursive procedure is such a neat and elegant
> concept that I can hardly imagine that it will not have a marked
> influence on the design of new machines in the near future. And

this influence could quite easily be so considerable, that the possible gain in efficiency that can still be booked by excluding recursiveness, will become negligible. [61, p.17][67, p.41]

To clarify, Strachey and Wilkes were in favor of static solutions enforced by language restrictions in the interest of machine efficiency. They viewed the requirement that all ALGOL60 procedures could potentially be recursive as an example of "unnecessary generality" [61, p.16][67, p.40]. Instead, they wanted all procedures to be non-recursive by default and only recursive if explicitly delimited by the programmer. By doing so, it would be possible to write compilers that could generate far more efficient machine code. Dijkstra, by contrast, wanted to avoid such case distinctions in order to obtain a simple language and implementation technique. To accomplish this, he advocated general language constructs and corresponding dynamic solutions. Dijkstra acknowledged that his general recursive programming approach led to inefficient machine code, but he also stressed that this would probably be resolved in the near future (cf. citation above and his abstract in [60]). In hindsight, it seems that Dijkstra was anticipating the advent of the stack-machine architecture.

To conclude, Dijkstra's philosophy is in many ways similar to the Gorn-Brown-Carr philosophy of 1954. His appeal for dynamic constructs is, albeit for very different reasons, similar to the work of Newell, Shaw, and Simon. Furthermore, Dijkstra believed that efficiency problems would be resolved in the near future, or at least become negligible. According to Dijkstra, generalization of a programming language allowed for simplification in compiler building and this would in the long term prevail over the short-term engineering problems that concerned people such as Bauer, Samelson, Strachey, and Wilkes.

3.2.2 An Analogy Between Mathematics and Programming

In his technical report of October 1961 [61], Dijkstra also used an analogy between mathematics and programming in order to explain why he viewed a good programming language to be one of a small number of very general concepts.

Dijkstra described a programming language "as a means of feeding programs into a machine" and openly wondered what it means for a programming language to promote "good use of a machine". He noted, as described above, that leading British and West-German researchers viewed good use of a machine in terms of machine efficiency; he contrasted this with his own view that a programming language should primarily be a tool to achieve program correctness.

On the assumption that program correctness is vital, Dijkstra subsequently pondered about the criteria to be used in programming language design in order to alleviate programming errors. The question to be answered was: Which criteria should be used in defining (and implementing) a programming language such that it helps the programmer write correct programs? To address this question, Dijkstra first elaborated on the notion of correctness, wondering what it means in the field of mathematics as opposed to programming. In his words:

> [I]t is impossible to prove a mathematical theorem completely, because when one thinks that one has done so, one still has the duty to prove that the first proof was flawless, and so on, ad infinitum. [...] One can never guarantee that a proof is correct, the best one can say is "I have not discovered any mistakes."

In response to the above concern, Dijkstra provided two reasons why mathematical theorems, nevertheless, do have a high degree of plausibility. Both reasons are sociological in nature.

1. "[S]o many people have, each in their own way, derived these theorems, that there is a non-negligible probability that they do indeed follow from the axioms."

2. "[T]he pretended conclusions are subject to conditions so orderly that the user's task of showing that he has applied the theorem correctly is not too cumbersome."

It is the second reason which I will elaborate on here. It states that a theorem is useful only if it is applied under a minimum number of clear conditions. For example, a statement that distinguishes between prime numbers and composite numbers is useful, but a statement that distinguishes between seven different cases is much less useful. Hence, the first statement, after being proved, is considered by many mathematicians to be a theorem while this is not necessarily the case for the second statement.

Now comes the analogy. Dijkstra noted that, just like the mathematician, "the programmer is in exactly the same position" for, he too, cannot prove the absolute correctness of his programs. The mathematician has theorems, the programmer has subroutines. If a theorem is only useful if it is applied under a minimum number of clear conditions, then — if

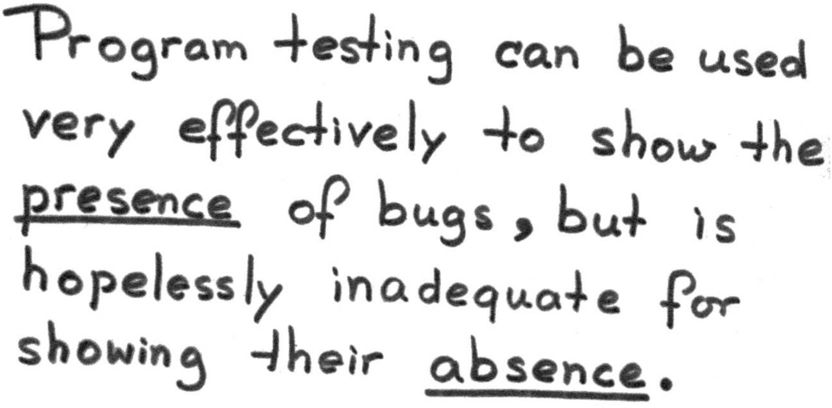

Program testing can be used very effectively to show the presence of bugs, but is hopelessly inadequate for showing their absence.

Figure 3.1: The limitations of program testing expressed in Dijkstra's own handwriting.

the analogy is effective — a similar remark holds for a subroutine. In Dijkstra's words:

> [T]he usefulness of a subroutine (or, in a language, a grammatical instruction) increases as the chance decreases, that it will be used incorrectly.

Extending the analogy further, the language designer has grammatical instructions and, for similar reasons, it is in his interest to have a small number of language concepts. These concepts, while few in number, are great in generality. This, in brief, captures Dijkstra's 1961 notion of elegance in his fields of expertise: imperative programming and language design.[73]

The previous exposition shows that, already in 1961, Dijkstra was much in favor of mathematical reasoning. In later years, he would become an ardent supporter of correct-by-construction programming (cf. Section 2.3.2). Figure 3.1 presents one of Dijkstra's visuals which he used at a conference in Geneva in 1973.

3.2.3 Generalizations of the Stack Principle

Dijkstra's urge to generalize was not only felt at the level of language definition. Also in the Dijkstra-Zonneveld implementation of ALGOL60 did he seek general principles. For example, Dijkstra generalized the

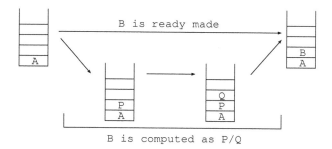

B is computed as P/Q

Figure 3.2: Generalizing the functionality of the stack.

manner in which a stack was used in two essential ways. First, he showed how the functionality of the stack can be further generalized in time, by not only using it to evaluate arithmetic expressions but also expressions containing procedure calls. That is, procedures were treated like arithmetic expressions by means of some additional bookkeeping [60]. Second, he showed how several different kinds of items (operators, operands, states, priorities, etc.) can be stored on one general stack, instead of using multiple specialized stacks for each kind of item [65].

Further Generalization in Time

By the late 1950s, the stack had been invented over and over again by several independent researchers[74]. It was the "stack principle" of Bauer and Samelson [16] which Dijkstra referred to in his now-famous 1960 article 'Recursive Programming' [60] in which he elaborated on how to use the stack as a runtime object; that is, as an object during program execution.

Figure 3.2 helps to illustrate the concepts underlying Dijkstra's generalization. The top-most horizontal arrow shows how B is placed on the stack, assuming that B is ready made. If, however, B is not ready made but, instead, has to be calculated by means of the formula $B = P/Q$, then the alternative sequence of arrows in the figure is applicable: P and Q are placed on the stack and eventually removed from the stack in order to compute P/Q.

The generalization lies in the fact that a stack can be used for both scenarios: whether B is ready made or has to be computed, by temporarily using a number of next stack locations, the net result remains the same. More generally, and not explicitly shown in Figure 3.2, B may just as well be computed by means of a call to a procedure which contains the expression P/Q. In Dijkstra's words:

> [I]t is immaterial to the 'surroundings' in which the value B is used, whether the value B can be found ready-made in the memory, or whether it is necessary to make temporary use of a number of the next stack locations for its evaluation. When a function occurs instead of B and this function is to be evaluated by means of a subroutine, the above [illustration] provides a strong argument for arranging the subroutine in such a way that it operates in the first free places of the stack, in just the same way as a compound term written out in full. [60, p.314]

To arrange the procedure in such a way that it operates in the first free places of the stack, Dijkstra subsequently, in his paper, explained how *one* runtime stack could do the job[75]. As a *byproduct* of Dijkstra's generalization, recursive procedure activations became feasible:

> The subroutine only has to appear in the memory once, but it may then have more than one simultaneous 'incarnation' from a dynamic point of view: the 'inner-most' activation causes the same piece of text to work in a higher part of the stack. Thus the subroutine has developed into a defining element that can be used completely recursively. [60, p.317]

Dijkstra's generalized stack was able to store parameters and local variables of activated procedures. To make these elements accessible Dijkstra had devised a mechanism to delve deep down in his stack, a mechanism which was not needed for the evaluation of simple arithmetic expressions.

Dijkstra was not the first implementor of recursive activations[76]. The relatively simple recursive mechanisms of the list processing languages IPL and LISP had already been implemented by means of a stack[77]. Rutishauser, in his 1963 paper [263, p.50], credited not only Dijkstra as the inventor of a technique to implement recursion for ALGOL60, but also the Americans Sattley and Ingerman (cf. [268]), who had worked closely with Floyd, Irons, and Feurzeig (see e.g. [148]). Furthermore, Turing had, by 1945, already thought through the idea of using a stack for recursive activations but had not implemented it[78]. Bauer has confirmed Turing's contributions and has also mentioned Rutishauser[79], Van der Poel, and Huskey as researchers who had implemented recursive activations prior to 1960 [14, p.39][15].

It is Dijkstra's generalizing style which stands out when a comparison is made with the work of his contemporaries. Rutishauser, for example, had limited the order of his procedure activations in his runtime system [295], while Dijkstra had no such restriction. Floyd's work [94, p.42–43] relied on three specialized "yo-yo" lists (i.e. stacks) instead of one general stack. Likewise, the MAD translator [4, p.28] used several specialized tables. Also, and most importantly, the ALCOR compilers were severely restricted in that they could not handle several ALGOL60 language constructs, including the recursive procedure (cf. Section 3.2.5). Finally, although the Irons-Feurzeig system [148] *did* implement recursive procedure activations *and* by means of one general runtime stack, it was, in the interest of efficiency, sophisticated in its runtime capabilities and, hence, unlike the runtime system of the Dijkstra-Zonneveld implementation of ALGOL60 (cf. Section 3.3.2).

Further Generalization in Space

To further illustrate Dijkstra's appeal for generalization, I summarize the essential ideas [62] underlying the paper he presented in Rome 1962, entitled 'Unifying Concepts of Serial Program Execution' [65]. In his paper, Dijkstra described what he called the condensation of his meditations after having implemented ALGOL60. He presented a language of a stack-based machine which was "of a perverse inefficiency" [62, p.1]. For, again, Dijkstra's main objective was to pursue "extreme simplicity and elegance" [62, p.1] by devising a uniform way in which his machine could perform different operations. Some examples from his paper are presented below.

Consider the program

$$5 \ + \ 39 \ / \ (\ 7 \ + \ 2 \ * \ 3 \ ) \ - \ 6 \ ;$$

Its corresponding postfix notation is

$$5 \ 39 \ 7 \ 2 \ 3 \ * \ + \ / \ + \ 6 \ -$$

which is read from left to right by the stack-based machine in the following manner. When it encounters a number, it is copied to the top of the stack. When it encounters an operator, the corresponding operation is performed at the top of the stack.

Dijkstra remarked that the function of an operator is, thus, a double one. On the one hand, it indicates that copying words to the stack has to be interrupted. On the other hand, it also specifies the operation that has to be performed at the top of the stack. Dijkstra suggested to separate these two functions by treating arithmetic operators *in the same way* as numbers: the operator should *also* be copied onto the stack, and its evaluation should be performed by a new and separate word E

(for Evaluate). In accordance with these new conventions, the postfix notation would then be

$$5 \quad 39 \quad 7 \quad 2 \quad 3 \quad * \quad E \quad + \quad E \quad / \quad E \quad + \quad E \quad 6 \quad - \quad E$$

Whenever the word read is unequal to E, the word is copied onto the stack. Whenever the word read is equal to E, it is not copied; instead, the operation on the top of the stack is performed. As the reader can check, such an execution would finally result in the number 2 being the top element of the stack, as desired.

Further on in his paper, Dijkstra introduced variables which could be placed on the stack as well. For instance, the expression

$$x \quad + \quad 4 \quad ;$$

corresponds to the post-fix notation

$$x \quad E \quad 4 \quad + \quad E$$

Upon execution, x would first be placed on top of the stack. After encountering the first occurrence of E, the variable x would be substituted by the value it denotes, which depends on the state of the process at that moment. For example, the top element of the stack, x, could be substituted by 3, implying that the final result would be a stack with as top element the value 7. In short, Dijkstra treated variables as operators and, as explained previously, he treated operators as numbers.

Dijkstra's further generalization was led by the observation that a number is only a special kind of expression. That is, while in the previous examples the final addition to the stack was merely a number, it should, more generally, be possible to devise examples in which the final result is a general expression. To achieve this generalization, Dijkstra allowed the word E to be placed on the stack as well by introducing a new word P (for Postponement). Upon evaluation of P, it would be replaced by the word E. As an example, consider the following text with three variables x, y, and *plinus*:

$$x \quad P \quad E \quad y \quad P \quad E \quad plinus \quad E \quad P \quad E$$

Upon execution, the top of the stack would show in succession

```
...   x
...   x   P
...   x   E
...   x   E   y
...   x   E   y   P
...   x   E   y   E
...   x   E   y   E   plinus
...   x   E   y   E    +
...   x   E   y   E    +    P
...   x   E   y   E    +    E
```

The last line in the previous illustration contains the string of words which, when read as a piece of program, would effectuate the evaluation of the expression $x + y$. Likewise, if the value of the variable *plinus* had been $-$, then the resulting string of words would have corresponded to the expression $x - y$. In other words, the net effect of the previous illustration is that the expression x *plinus* y has been partially evaluated with as result *another expression*.

Dijkstra continued in his paper by showing that the distinction between numbers and instructions was superfluous as well. His generalizations furthermore led him to introduce a second stack, which he called the stack of activations. In his words:

> We could try to merge our two stacks into one. This merging would present itself in a completely natural fashion if the two should expand and shrink "in phase" with one another. In general, however, this is not the case and trying to merge the two stacks into a single one would give a highly unnatural construction. [65, p.247]

In summary, while Dijkstra had only needed one stack to implement ALGOL60, he needed two stacks to implement his more general stack-based programming language of 1962. In both cases it was his quest to generalize which stands out.

3.2.4 Machine-Independent Object Language

Dijkstra's single most important ALGOL60-related contribution, in terms of generalization, is without doubt his design of an intermediate *machine-independent* object language[80]. That is, a language which serves the purpose of describing the behavior of a general stack-based machine and *not* the X1 machine in particular. Dijkstra situated this language in between ALGOL60 and the machine instructions of the X1, and thereby created what we would today call a separation of concerns, which drastically simplified the implementation of ALGOL60.

The separation of concerns is twofold: a translation stage followed by an interpretation stage. The translation, from ALGOL60 to the object language, is accomplished in a machine-independent manner and, hence, without any appeal to machine efficiency. Candidates for this translation stage are jobs that can be done once and for all, i.e. jobs that are independent of the execution of the program and, hence, are intrinsically static. An example is determining which brackets in an ALGOL60 program form pairs [66, p.349]. In the second stage, the runtime stage, the obtained object program is processed by an interpreter written in the machine code of the X1. Only at this stage does dynamic physical memory management come into play. An important example is mapping the runtime software stack onto X1's memory [66, p.336].

It is Dijkstra's top-down perspective, from ALGOL60 to the machine, which stands out in comparison with the machine-specific approaches of Bauer, Samelson, and others[81]. In Dijkstra's own words:

> [W]e are completely free to determine how the computer should be used, this in contrast with machines for which considerations of efficiency force us in practice to a special manner of use, that is, force us to take account of specific properties and peculiarities of the machine. [66, p.330]

> [T]he making of an ALGOL translator is a relatively simple job if the translator may formulate the object program in operations cut out for the problem. [66, p.344]

To design his object language, Dijkstra made several abstractions. For instance, he assumed the presence of a sufficiently large homogeneous store, and thereby abstracted away from X1's heterogeneous memory, i.e. the presence of a fast, small store and a slow, large store. Likewise, he assumed X1's arithmetic unit to be extremely fast, thereby allowing him to extensively use subroutines without being concerned with computation time [66, p.330].

Similar to Brown and Carr in 1954 and as mentioned before, Dijkstra was fully aware of the prolonged computation times introduced by his abstractions. Moreover, he acknowledged the short-term limitations of his solution:

> We are fully aware of [...] a certain prolongation of the calculating time, and we can imagine that for some computer which is still in

use today one cannot accept this delay. There are twofold reasons why we nevertheless made this choice, one of principle and one practical [...] [66, p.330]

3.2.5   Reception of Dijkstra's Ideas

Dijkstra and Zonneveld succeeded very quickly in implementing ALGOL60. Their success did not go unnoticed, as the British researcher Randell recollects:

> [One] week of discussions with Dijkstra were spent [...] These discussions we documented in a lengthy report [251] [...]. For the next few years Dijkstra used our report to defend himself from the numerous further requests he was getting from people who wanted to visit him and find out about the X1 compiler. [250, p.3]

Dijkstra's generalizing style had clearly influenced subsequent practical developments in compiler technology during the 1960s — as explicitly confirmed by Naur [211, p.105]. By breaking away from the efficiency regime, Dijkstra and Zonneveld had succeeded in building a general and fast ALGOL60 compiler and a corresponding runtime system for a relatively small computer, the X1.

Contrary to the Amsterdam team, several ALCOR members already had functional translation technology available before the recursive procedure entered the ALGOL60 definition (cf. telephone call between Van Wijngaarden and Naur) [212, p.129][265, p.210]. In the interest of machine efficiency, ALCOR had decided to minimize their runtime system as much as possible by following a static approach: each procedure was allocated a fixed working space prior to program execution, not unlike the FORTRAN approach described in Chapter 1. This meant that procedures could not be activated more than once during program execution and, hence, that recursive procedure activations in particular were ruled out. At the 1962 Rome symposium, however, Bauer and Samelson expressed their regret in choosing a static solution:

> [I]t was decided, to assign static data storage to each procedure separately within the block containing the procedure, which of course rules out recursive procedures. The waste of static storage, in conflict with our original cellar [i.e. stack] principle, was considered *regrettable*. [265, p.214, my italics]

These words are ironic because ALCOR was a strong proponent of practical engineering-based solutions. Some ALCOR members, such as Seegmüller, had openly distanced themselves from Dijkstra, Van Wijngaarden, and Naur who did not seem to care much about machine efficiency, but instead strove for a general algorithmic language. The irony, thus, lies in the fact that ALCOR's approach had failed, even though they had restricted the use of the programming language, while Dijkstra, for instance, had not.

Naur's team in Copenhagen had initially joined ALCOR and, hence, had followed an efficiency driven philosophy as well [205, p.118]. Even after having started a close collaboration with the Amsterdam team in March 1960, the Danes remained reluctant in subscribing to the Amsterdam approach. In Naur's words:

> [In March 1960, t]he Dutch group impressed us greatly by their very general approach. However, although they were prepared to put their solution of the problem of recursive procedures at our disposal we decided to stick to the more modest approach which *we had already developed* to some extent. The reasons for this reluctance were practical. [...A]t the time we feared the loss of running speed of a system which included recursive procedures (a fear we now know was unfounded). [205, p.118–119, my italics]

Hence, the Danes were initially not able to handle recursive procedures. In line with ALCOR's doctrine, they had chosen static solutions [151, p.441]. Furthermore, the Danes had explicitly allowed information transfers between core store and drum to be expressed in their ALGOL60 programs [151, p.441]. Such machine-specific programming was in sharp contrast to the Dijkstra-Zonneveld approach and was very similar to the work of Strachey and Wilkes [287, p.491] and Backus's Speedcoding (cf. Section 3.1).

In their later 1962 GIER system, however, the Danes did follow "the Amsterdam school" and therefore were able to handle recursive procedures[82]. The ALCOR group would need some more years before they too would finally adopt the Amsterdam approach, as exemplified by the compiler described in 1965 by Gries et al. [113].

3.3 The Dichotomy Outlived the ALGOL60 Effort

As a successful ALGOL60 implementor, Dijkstra was invited to give a keynote address in Munich during the autumn of 1962. In his presentation entitled 'Some meditations on advanced programming', he made a sharp contrast between reliability and optimization and, unsurprisingly, championed the former. In his words:

> In deciding between reliability of the translation process on the one hand, and the production of an efficient object program on the other hand, the choice often has been decided in favour of the latter. But I have the impression that the pendulum is now swinging backwards. [64, p.537]

Subsequently, Dijkstra mentioned that there are two ways one can use a new and more powerful computer. The classical reaction, he said, is to use the new machine as efficiently as possible. The alternative, however, is to recognize that the new machine is indeed faster and that, hence, time does not matter so much any more; that is, the cost per operation in the new machine is less than in the old machine. Hence, it becomes more realistic to invest some of the machine's speed in other things than sheer production, such as programming comfort, elegance, and reliability [64, p.537].

Dijkstra viewed optimizations, on the one hand, and reliability and trustworthiness, on the other hand, as opposing goals. He described optimizing as "taking advantage of a special situation" (cf. specialization). According to him, the construction of an optimizing translator is "nasty", in comparison to "straightforward but reliable and trustworthy" translator technology[83].

Afterward, Dijkstra described ALGOL60 as a "great promotor of non-optimizing translators", a remark which I shall return to shortly, when discussing the work of Irons and Feurzeig. Dijkstra continued by contrasting the Dijkstra-Zonneveld implementation to the many other ALGOL60 implementations which were based on language restrictions:

> The fact is that the language, as it stands, is certainly not an open invitation for optimization efforts. For those who thought that they knew how to write optimizing translators — be it for less flexible languages — this has been one of the reasons for rejecting ALGOL60 as a serious tool. In my opinion these people bet on the wrong horse. [64, p.538]

The last sentence misleadingly suggests that the dichotomy between specialization and generalization was equally obvious to other researchers, as it presumably was to Dijkstra himself in 1959 and 1960. On the other hand, however, the dichotomy did indeed become more apparent *after* 1960, as is illustrated by the comments of Galler [100, p.525], Gallie [102], and Randell's 1964 recollections[84].

3.3.1 Twin Approach

While the Dijkstra-Zonneveld compiler (and corresponding runtime system) was closely mimicked by Randell and his colleagues in Leicester, it is equally important to note that the British did not follow Dijkstra all the way. For, in later years, the Leicester team had two fully functional ALGOL60 compilers at their disposal: the Whetstone compiler and the Kidsgrove compiler. While the former closely resembled the Dijkstra-Zonneveld compiler and was, therefore, fast in translating ALGOL60 programs but poor in generating fast programs, the latter compiler showed little resemblance to the Dijkstra-Zonneveld compiler and was a slow compiler that produced very fast programs. The practical approach taken by the Leicester team was twofold. A new ALGOL60 program was first quickly compiled by the Whetstone compiler and tested. After the programmer became convinced of the correctness of his program, he would subsequently use the Kidsgrove compiler to recompile his ALGOL60 program in order to obtain fast machine code. The Leicester team had thus come up with a "twin approach" in which Dijkstra's philosophy was embodied in one compiler and the efficiency regime was embodied in the other compiler[85]. Hence, in a very practical sense, the dichotomy outlived the ALGOL60 effort, thereby partly contradicting Dijkstra's keynote address in Munich 1962.

3.3.2 Runtime Optimizations

Though Dijkstra viewed ALGOL60 as a "great promotor of non-optimizing translators", it is interesting to note that in 1960, in the same year in which Dijkstra's paper on recursion [60] was published, Irons and Feurzeig had also come up with an implementation technique for recursive procedures [148]. Unlike Dijkstra and Zonneveld's runtime system, however, the Irons-Feurzeig runtime system applied *optimizations*; that is, during the execution of the program.

By means of some additional bookkeeping, the Irons-Feurzeig system detected during program execution whether the procedure under investigation was involved in recursion or not; that is, the system *specialized at run time* by distinguishing between recursive and non-recursive procedure activations, and treating each kind of activation separately. As a result, only the truly recursive procedures were slowed down and taxed in terms of storage allocation while in the runtime system of Dijkstra and Zonneveld *all* procedures were handled conservatively.

The Irons-Feurzeig system is best described as a hybrid system, located in between two extremes: the very static solution of Bauer and Samelson on the one hand and the very dynamic solution of Dijkstra and Zonneveld on the other hand. In the Bauer-Samelson approach, fixed storage was assigned to each procedure prior to program execution by the compiler. This was very much in line with tradition and with FORTRAN compiler technology in particular. In the Dijkstra-Zonneveld approach, all data was handled dynamically by means of one general runtime stack. Hence, the data for *both* recursive and non-recursive procedures was placed on the stack when called upon during program execution.

The Irons-Feurzeig approach was hybrid in that it followed Bauer and Samelson's compilation strategy for each procedure but, when, during program execution, their runtime system detected that a procedure was called upon for a second time, then that procedure would be treated dynamically; that is, its data would be placed on the general runtime stack in line with the Dijkstra-Zonneveld approach.

Dijkstra and Zonneveld's runtime system, by contrast, made no check during program execution to determine whether an activated procedure P was called a second time or not; that is, was recursive or not. Therefore, whenever P was to call another procedure Q, the conservative assumption was made that P was recursive and, hence, would be called again later. As a result, all the local variables and arrays of P had to be placed on the software stack prior to calling Q such that they could retain a unique identity for the special recursive case that the procedure were to be called again. In the runtime system of Irons and Feurzeig, such expensive stack management was only carried out *after* it was determined that P would be called more than once.

Irons and Feurzeig's runtime specialization was implemented by using several case distinctions. A first example is of course the aforementioned distinction that their runtime system made between recursive and non-recursive procedures. A second example is the distinction between blocks and procedures. In the words of Irons and Feurzeig:

> Since a block cannot be entered more than one time without an intervening exit, unless it is contained in a recursive procedure, it suffices to maintain a counter only for each procedure, rather than for all blocks as well. [148, p.67]

If Dijkstra would have been forced to apply runtime optimizations, then he would have treated procedures and blocks in a unifying manner, not distinguishing between the two even if this came at the price of machine efficiency. A third example concerns the distinction between self-recursive procedures and procedures that are indirectly recursive. Irons and Feurzeig noted that by making this distinction, further optimizations could be achieved in terms of machine efficiency [148, p.69].

The several case distinctions in the Irons-Feurzeig runtime system were, from Dijkstra's point of view, unneeded sophistication. From an efficiency driven perspective, however, the Irons-Feurzeig approach was outstanding in that it not only provided fast ALGOL60 programs, but it also did so *without* having to restrict the ALGOL60 language. In retrospect, then, the dichotomy between specialization and generalization does not hold in the case of Irons and Feurzeig. Their solution implied that *specializations* were made during program execution *and* for the ALGOL60 language in full *generality*.

The runtime specializations of Irons and Feurzeig did, however, still stand in sharp contrast to the general implementation technique that Dijkstra and Zonneveld used in their own runtime system. Viewed in this broader context of *both* compile time and run time, the dichotomy persisted; that is, part of Dijkstra's keynote address in Munich 1962 remained valid in that the runtime efficiency pursued by Irons and Feurzeig still opposed the runtime simplicity Dijkstra wanted in the interest of correctness and reliability.

3.4   Final Remarks

Several researchers have written about the history of computing (e.g. [35, 36, 39, 50, 181, 192]) and, in particular, about the history of programming languages (e.g. [158, 163, 246, 260, 266, 298]). Also, an increasing number of students are interested in past developments (e.g. [19, 140, 164, 229]). Nevertheless, in accordance with Mahoney's words, I believe more research is needed:

> [Historians] remain largely ignorant about the origins and development of the dynamic processes running on [computers], the processes that determine what we do with computers and how we think about what we do. The histories of computing will involve many aspects, but primarily they will be histories of software. [181, p.127]

The recursive procedure is an example par excellence of such a dynamic process. To the best of my knowledge, it has not been treated technically in any previous historical account. Nor has the history of software been written by contrasting Dijkstra's views with those of his contemporaries, as I have attempted both in this chapter and in the previous one.

Research contributions of Gödel, Carnap, Turing, and Tarski have been studied and documented over and over again by logicians and philosophers themselves. Researchers in computing, by contrast, have yet to commence with similar work concerning the ideas of their fathers: Dijkstra, McCarthy, Hoare, and others. This, in turn, explains my motivation to write this book.

More historical accounts, written by other researchers, are however needed in order to further improve our understanding of Dijkstra's contributions. Based on an earlier draft of this chapter, I have received the comment that Dijkstra's ideas on programming language design, elaborated on in Section 3.2.1, were only meant for theoretical purposes and that I have thus misinterpreted Dijkstra to some extent by connecting his abstract thoughts with his practical work. A similar remark has been made concerning Dijkstra's abstract machine, explained in Section 3.2.3.

Based on my understanding of Dijkstra as a man who did not want to distinguish between theory and practice, as a man who practiced what he preached, I view the two aforementioned remarks as ill-founded. The remarks remind me of Seegmüller's and Strachey's criticism to Dijkstra, claiming that the latter's work was purely theoretical. Not so! Dijkstra's abstract ideas clearly reflect in his applications. For example, Dijkstra's temporary abstraction of efficiency, while discussing the quality of a programming language [61, p.10][67, p.35], is directly reflected in the two-stage design of the Dijkstra-Zonneveld implementation of ALGOL60. Likewise, his thoughts on abstract-machine languages is clearly related to the stack-based object language which he introduced to simplify the implementation of ALGOL60. Finally, Dijkstra used one universal stack to implement ALGOL60 while many of his contemporaries used multiple specialized stacks, and he used two stacks in his later work presented in Rome in 1962. Is it a coincidence that most first generation stack machines, which were designed to execute ALGOL-like languages, only had a single stack [164, p.36], and that second generation stack computers separated evaluation and control flow by means of two stacks [164, p.10]? I would not be surprised if Dijkstra's abstract thoughts, again, had a direct bearing on such practical matters.

Several other questions concerning Dijkstra's career have yet to be investigated. To give one detailed example, I refer to the following suggestion made by Henriksson [121]: Dijkstra may have become acquainted with Turing's work on 'Reversion Storage' (i.e. Turing's stack principle) via Huskey who had visited Van Wijngaarden and Dijkstra in Amsterdam in the summer of 1959. In fact, at the end of his 1960 paper [60], Dijkstra explicitly thanked Huskey for the *inspiring* conversations that he had had with him in Amsterdam. Twenty years later, however, Dijkstra's recollections were quite the opposite:

> Harry D. Huskey had just spent a few sabbatical months at the Mathematical Center, working on an algebraic compiler, but his style of work differed so radically from mine that, personally, I could not even use his work as a source of inspiration; the somewhat painful discussion with my boss [i.e. Van Wijngaarden], when I had to transmit to him that disappointing message, is remembered as one of the rare occasions at which I banged with my fist on the table. [77, p.572]

More research is thus needed to understand how Huskey did or did not influence Dijkstra in implementing ALGOL60. But it is important to stress that, during the 1950s, the USA and the UK were technologically advanced compared with the Netherlands (cf. Section 3.1). The American Huskey may well have played an important role in terms of technology transfer from Turing to Dijkstra by visiting Amsterdam in 1959.

On the one hand, Huskey's style seems to have been very much at odds with Dijkstra's quest to generalize, as follows from Huskey's negative comments on general language constructs in [230, p.379–380] and his various specialized lists in [141, 144]. In retrospect then, the previous quote may not be so surprising after all[86].

On the other hand, however, Keese and Huskey's 1962 compiler technique [152] is very similar to that of Dijkstra and Zonneveld. It has an intermediate machine-independent object language, and dynamic storage assignment and recursive procedures are processed by the assembler. Had Huskey learned these techniques from Dijkstra or vice versa? Or did the ideas of both men converge to a similar solution? As the historian Mahoney has noted, "even when we can't know the answers, it is important to see the questions. They too form part of our understanding. If you cannot answer them now, you can alert future historians to them" [180, p.832].

Finally, it should be remarked that, due to focusing on Dijkstra and ALGOL60, several important researchers have been mentioned only briefly or not at all in this chapter. Examples are Zuse, Hopper, Laning, and Zierler. Likewise, concerning nationalities, also French (e.g. Vauquois), Norwegian (e.g. Garwick) and British (e.g. Woodger) researchers actively participated in defining ALGOL60. Other important topics, such as syntax-directed compilation, have only been mentioned in passing and deserve more attention in future work.

Conclusions

Two messages lie at the heart of this chapter: (i) the early history of programming languages, and the `ALGOL60` effort in particular, can be perceived as an emerging dichotomy between specialization and generalization, and (ii) Dijkstra's continual appeal for generalization led to practical breakthroughs in compiler technology. Specialization, as promoted by Bauer, Samelson, Strachey, and Wilkes, refers to language restrictions, static solutions, and the exploitation of machine-specific facilities — in the interest of efficiency. Generalization, as promoted by Van Wijngaarden and Dijkstra, refers to general language constructs, dynamic solutions, and machine-independent language design — in the interest of correctness and reliability.

In Western Europe, Van Wijngaarden and Dijkstra's linguistic reasoning seems to have been the exception rather than the rule. Dijkstra in 1961 devoted an entire report [61] to countering the language restrictions that Strachey, Wilkes, and others had proposed in the interest of machine efficiency. Here the battle between generalists and specialists is vividly illustrated in Dijkstra's own words. Likewise, the panel discussion [230] at the Rome 1962 conference shows the tensions created by the dichotomy.

Dijkstra's simple solutions, due to his generalizing style, stand out in comparison with the work of his contemporaries and it is this what made the Dijkstra-Zonneveld implementation of `ALGOL60` shine. Furthermore, it was his quest to unify which led him, together with Van Wijngaarden, to promote the recursive procedure in the first place, and to find a corresponding implementation technique. For, just like many of his contemporaries, he did not see any real necessity in using the recursive procedure to solve practical programming problems. In his own words in 1962:

> One of our great features of our compiler is that it happens to turn out that it is very easy to have a good recursive function in it. [...] They are hardly used by customers. [...] [T]hey give us possibilities that make the tool inspiring. So I am perfectly willing to incorporate a further thing like recursive procedures which are never used [...] [230, p.368]

> In practical computations these [general] features are not too frequently used, but the bare fact that the programmers could use them if they wanted to made the language very appealing. [63, p.127]

Though Dijkstra had succeeded, together with Zonneveld, in implementing `ALGOL60` with recursive procedures, many participants at the Rome

1962 symposium remained very skeptical about Dijkstra's emphasis on general language constructs and corresponding dynamic implementation techniques. These techniques had, as many observed, an adverse effect on computation time. Not surprisingly then, Dijkstra was perceived as someone who totally neglected efficiency issues, while most people at the symposium considered efficiency to be of prime importance. It seems, however, that Dijkstra was anticipating some of the enormous advances that would soon follow in electronic technology.

Contrary to the Amsterdam team, the ALCOR group already had a lot of technical experience with ALGOL58 when the international community turned toward defining the ALGOL60 language in 1959 and 1960. Led by an efficiency driven philosophy, they eschewed the recursive procedure and other dynamic language constructs. Van Wijngaarden and Dijkstra, on the other hand, were in search of a general language. They were led more by language aesthetics than by practical limitations of actual computing machines. Again, only as a result of such a philosophy, did they become proponents of the recursive procedure.

Dijkstra's appeal for generalization resulted in practical breakthroughs in compiler technology, with British, Danes, West-Germans, and others copying parts of his unifying work and, in particular, his top-down compiler-design approach and runtime system. Such immense success and recognition led Dijkstra to present his rather bold views on compiler technology in his keynote address in Munich 1962. Clearly aware of a dichotomy between specialization and generalization, he championed the latter and viewed ALGOL60 as a "great promotor of non-optimizing translators". However, as the work of Randell, Irons, Feurzeig, and others illustrate, Dijkstra's generalizing style, while indeed influential, did not override the efficiency regime. In fact, in a very practical sense, the dichotomy outlived the ALGOL60 effort.

4. Tony Hoare and Mathematical Logic

This chapter has been accepted for publication in the
Journal of Logic and Computation
(Oxford University Press).

Though logic has permeated through several fields in computing during the past decades, it is not clear exactly how and to what extent it has done so. To document logic's role in the history of programming languages (and software engineering in general), I have conducted a discussion with the computing scientist Tony Hoare who, during the late 1960s, used ideas from mathematical logic to define programming language semantics. The discussion's transcript is presented in this chapter. It differs from previously published interviews with Hoare in that several of the topics raised are directly related to mathematical logic and computability theory in particular.

The discussions with Wirth, Liskov, and Naur are presented in three subsequent chapters. Just like Hoare, these three researchers contributed to the field of programming languages. Unlike Hoare, mathematical logic did not attract them very much. This observation is noteworthy by itself in that it helps us grasp the extent to which logic influenced first-generation programmers. It should also be noted here that, unlike my discussion with Hoare, the discussions with Wirth, Liskov, and Naur have yet to be put into historical perspective.

4.1 Introduction

In November 2010, a two-day symposium *The Future of Software Engineering* was held in Zurich. Both days ended with a panel discussion between those who had presented their work earlier during the day. It is interesting to note that both panels contained lengthy debates about the applicability of ideas from mathematical logic. One of the questions posed in the first panel concerned the practical merit of treating software requirements as one large predicate. In the second panel, the mentioning of the Halting Problem by somebody from the audience led to a long discussion about the practical implications of the undecidable problem of program correctness. The panel members in Zurich were divided. Some heavily defended the overall importance of logic in software engineering, such as Yuri Gurevich who is a mathematical logician by education. Others questioned that proposition. The full transcript of both panels is available as an easily digested booklet [56].

Many logically minded computing researchers today emphasize, even over-emphasize, the importance of mathematical logic in computing while others strongly oppose any kind of formalization whatsoever. That is the impression I have obtained during the past twelve years as a former software engineer in industry and as a student in logic. Extending this standpoint further, I hypothesize that the gap between these two camps has widened from 1960 and onwards[87]. Support in favor of this hypothesis can be found in Peter Naur's 1975 paper 'Programming Languages, Natural Languages, and Mathematics' [209], my extensive discussion with him [55], and in Hoare's 1996 paper 'How Did Software Get So Reliable Without Proof?' [131, p.13]. Both Naur and Hoare acknowledge a widening gap but only Naur views the gap to be problematical. Hoare considers the gap to be useful as will follow from my discussion with him in this chapter.

Further support for the aforementioned gap was provided in the previous chapter where I described the *emerging* dichotomy of the early 1960s between mathematical aesthetics and hard-core engineering by elaborating on the differences between the work of the "generalists" and "specialists" in the field of imperative programming. The generalists were scientists, like Dijkstra, who would later become ardent supporters of formalization in computing. The specialists were the down-to-earth engineers who, to a noticeable extent, were still following the FORTRAN tradition of programming.

As a second hypothesis about the history of computing, I believe several ideas from mathematical logic that influenced first-generation computer programmers were primarily received indirectly and without full comprehension. Not thoroughly grasping the borrowed literature may, in fact, have been a prerequisite in some cases to advancing the state of the art in computing. In many other cases, lack of comprehension clearly slowed down the progress of research. In this regard, I refer to Stoyan's historical accounts of McCarthy's work on LISP and, in particular, McCarthy's limited reception of Church's λ-calculus [284, 285]. Other examples are presented in this chapter with regard to Hoare's reception of mathematical logic.

The discussion with Hoare in this chapter and the discussions with Wirth, Liskov, and Naur in subsequent chapters are first and foremost about their careers and their research contributions. For instance, my discussion with Hoare is primarily centered around some ideas which he obtained from the mathematical logic literature. On the other hand, the reader will notice that several questions posed by me are directly related to my own personal views and, in particular, to the two hypotheses just mentioned. For example, in my discussion with Hoare, receptions of Turing's paper come to the fore, along with my insistence to discuss the Halting Problem and the 1972 paper entitled 'Incomputability', authored by Hoare and Allison [133]. As another example, my questions related to Hoare's ALGOL60 compiler and, in particular, the implementation of the recursive procedure are relevant when studying the advent of recursion in imperative programming, as elaborated on in Chapter 3. Finally, as a third example, the potential dichotomy between efficiency and goto-less programming, as commented on from Hoare's perspective, is especially of interest to those who are researching the history of programming methodology.

Like any oral history, the discussion with Hoare has to be taken with a grain of salt in terms of objectivity for it presents a very personal — and, naturally, a biased — perspective of the past. Nevertheless, oral histories can be instructive when the subject himself mentions that he did *not* understand or was not able to do something in the course of history. Hoare has on several occasions during my discussion with him, explicitly and sometimes spontaneously mentioned the limited extent to which he had grasped the work of Quine, Turing, Kleene, Davis and others. By documenting these specific recollections of Hoare, this chapter contributes to showing how logic has *and* has not permeated through computing. In fact, Hoare's explicit denial of having studied Böhm and Jacopini's theoretical 1966 paper [23] in detail has been of great value in preparing Chapter 2, as has been his remarks concerning his limited reception of Kleene's Normal Form theorem.

A Personal Incentive

My reason to study logic's influence in computing is related to the fact that, all too often, I have met researchers who either completely dismiss industrial practice or disapprove of any kind of formalization whatsoever. In an attempt to understand why these researchers have such strong opinions, I often receive what I believe are ill-founded remarks, such as: "Mathematical rigor is not useful in practice" and "It is an insult to ask me to consider the practical implications of my work". I question these remarks because when one studies the contributions of Hoare, Wirth, Liskov, Naur, and Dijkstra in some detail, one will quickly notice that these actors have either worked in or with industry[88]. The real and honest answer, I believe, is that it takes considerable effort today (i.e. years of investment) on behalf of the researcher to understand *both* the practical and theoretical implications of his work and that external constraints naturally refrain him from making that effort.

It is only to be expected that some researchers promote their work and their ideals in as many ways as they can muster[89]. However, when a leading researcher in, for example, a keynote address portrays an idealized account of historical events in order to advertise his research field, things become problematical. Not only is such an account misleading, it is harmful to those who actually want to conduct research *across* disciplinary borders, especially when the borders separate the "theoretical" from the "practical", as is often the case in computing today[90]. For, what should such an ambitious student say when the leading researcher falsely proclaims that the history of his field has always been one of either pure science or pure engineering?

Meeting Tony Hoare

My discussion with Hoare took place on 25 May 2010 in his office at Microsoft Research, Cambridge, UK. Its digital recordings were transcribed by me and subsequently lightly edited by the historian Gerard Alberts and myself. Afterwards, Hoare and I edited the transcript two more times. In particular, endnotes were added and some passages were shortened in the interest of clarity. The discussion, presented in the sequel, has been edited further, based on input from anonymous reviewers of the Journal of Logic and Computation.

The oral history is strictly speaking not an interview, because on several occasions I have expressed my own thoughts and elaborately discussed these with Hoare[91]. Furthermore, by focusing on mathematical logic and computability theory in particular, my discussion with Hoare is also content-wise very different from previously published interviews, including those conducted by Frana [99], Drobi [85], and Bowen [26].

Short Biography of Tony Hoare

Sir Charles Antony Richard Hoare was born on 11 January 1934 in Colombo, Sri Lanka to English parents. He received a Bachelor's degree in Classics from the University of Oxford (Merton College, 1956), was enrolled in the National Service in the Royal Navy (1956–1958), followed by graduate-level statistics at Oxford (1958–1959), and studied computer translation of human languages at Moscow State University (1959–1960). During the period 1960–1968, Hoare held a number of positions with Elliott Brothers, Ltd., England. Between 1968 and 1977, he was Professor of Computing Science at The Queen's University in Belfast, Ireland. In 1973 he was a visiting Professor at Stanford University, USA. In the period 1977–1999, he was Professor of Computing at the University of Oxford where he led the Programming Research Group of the Oxford University Computing Laboratory. From 1999 onwards, he is Principal Researcher at Microsoft Research Ltd., in Cambridge, England.

Hoare received several awards, such as the A.M. Turing Award in 1980 for "his fundamental contributions to the definition and design of programming languages" and the Kyoto Prize for Information Science in 2000. He was elected Fellow of the Royal Society and of the Royal Academy of Engineering in 1982 and 2005, respectively. In 2000 he was knighted for services to education and computer science.

4.2   A Discussion with Hoare

My discussion with Hoare is divided into six parts: (1) Hoare's reception of some of the literature on mathematical logic, (2) his college days in Oxford, (3) his involvement with the `ALGOL60` programming language, (4) his 1969 paper, 'An Axiomatic Basis for Computer Programming', (5) his research on incomputability, and (6) his views on academic versus applied research.

4.2.1 Literature on Mathematical Logic

Before I met Hoare in person, he mentioned by email some of the books and articles, related to mathematical logic, which he recalls having read by the mentioned dates:

- Russell's *Principles of Mathematics* (1952)

- Quine's *Mathematical Logic* (1954)

- Fraenkel's *Set Theory* (1956)

- Böhm's 'CUCH' –an article based on Church's lambda-calculus (1964)

- Presburger's *Decision Procedure* (1969)

- Kleene's *Introduction to Metamathematics* [no date mentioned]

- Tarski's *Relational Calculus* (1977)

- *Category Theory* (e.g., Sanders McLane and others) (1983)

In response, I showed some of those books to Hoare during the first part of our discussion.

Daylight: That's Russell's book *The Principles of Mathematics* [262]. Then I have *Mathematical Logic* [247].

Hoare: Oh that. Yes, yes! You brought the original dust cover? That's the revised edition. Aaah. I lost my dust cover which is very sad because it has a most wonderful sentence in it. [Pause, Hoare studies Quine's book.] Well, "this revised edition in which an inconsistency and some other shortcomings have been put to rights" [cited from the book's front flap]. An inconsistency isn't normally regarded as a shortcoming. It is a not-being-there-at-all coming. [H&D: Laughter]

Daylight: This is the third book, *Introduction to Metamathematics* [155].

Hoare: Yes, I've got a copy of that down there I think. [Takes his copy of *Metamathematics* and his copy of Quine from his shelves.] That's my copy of Quine which I had at university. And that's my copy [of *Metamathematics*] which, probably, dates from around that time. Yes, 1952. OK, I never got very far in Kleene. The first section is about the paradoxes. But the rest of it is [sigh]. It is a bit technical.

Daylight: So you read Russell's book before you read Quine's book?

Hoare: Yes. I can't remember absolutely. It is possible that what I read included the other book [of Russell], the *Introduction to Mathematical Philosophy*. This one seems to be a little more technical than I remember it to be. What's the date of publication? [Looks through Russell's book.] Hmm. Did you mark those?

Daylight: No, these are second hand.

Hoare: Oh right. Yes. Yes. OK, well from one source or another I probably would find that relatively easy to read.

4.2.2 College Days in Oxford

Daylight: Starting with your college days in Oxford, from what I read from your Turing Award lecture [128], you were very much inspired by Quine's book. As a young student, actually studying with your neighbours on mathematics?

Hoare: Yes, when I went to my college in Oxford, I met up with a mathematician, a second-year mathematician in the same staircase, in the quad. I suppose at roughly weekly intervals we used to gather in his room at ten o'clock, say, after we had all finished our working or drinking for the day. And, study a book by Quine which I think was probably *Methods of Logic*, not that one [points to *Mathematical Logic*] because that didn't come out till later. But, at some stage, I was inspired to buy the book and I read it quite thoroughly, up to a certain point any way. In fact a colleague and friend who was also a year behind me at Merton also studying Classics and Philosophy. I used to teach him out of that book and he went into computing as well. He's now still a very distinguished computer scientist. He was elected to the Royal Academy of Engineering the same year as me.

Daylight: And who is this person?

Hoare: Michael Jackson.

Daylight: Is it correct that when you were studying Quine you had no affiliation yet with computing?

Hoare: That is correct. Yes.

Daylight: So nothing with programming or even just physical computing machines? You were out of touch at that point?

Hoare: In 1952 there wasn't much to be in touch with. The first job I applied for, this must have been 1956, was with a company I think called United Steel in which a cybernetics unit was led by Stafford Beer. Also a notorious enthusiast for computers. That was an automation job, automating a steel mill, computer-controlled rolling mills. So that was a contact with computers in 1956. Before that I had another friend at Merton who was interested in making logical machines, little relay circuits inside a cigar box that would compute logical functions.

I think probably my final year my tutor was John Lucas who was a well-known philosopher of science in computing, or subsequently became so. And he set me to read — I may be misremembering this but — I did have an opportunity to read Turing's article 'On Computable Numbers' [291] in the Radcliffe Science library. I was so fascinated by it that I missed my lunch without noticing. [H: Laughter]

Daylight: Do you recall the year?

Hoare: Probably '56; '55 probably.

Daylight: You say you missed your lunch. Can I just ask how did you read such a paper? Did you literally copy it by hand? Or did you just read it a couple of times?

Hoare: I think I just read it as carefully as I could, a couple of times. I don't think I understood it. [H: Laughter] But I had to write an essay about it.

Daylight: That's very interesting.

Hoare: Now I come to think of it. It wasn't John Lucas who set me that assignment. It was my other philosophy tutor, Professor Walsh.

Daylight: Turing's paper was purely on logic; he was solving a logical problem. Today we use the phrases "Turing machines" and "general-purpose computers", but Turing's paper does not contain a link to computing machines.[92]

Hoare: Well, no. [H: Laughter]

Daylight: So when you read it in '55/'56, I assume it was also because you were fascinated by logical problems, right?

Hoare: No, I think it was a genuine interest in computing. For instance, when I went back to Oxford in 1958, I took a book out on incomputability [47] by Martin Davis which, again, I probably didn't understand, but ... I think I understood Turing machines better after I read Martin Davis's book.

4.2.3 ALGOL60

Daylight: OK. So we're still in the college days. I am just going back to Quine's book because that influenced you a lot. It will be important for later because we will of course talk about your 1969 article 'An Axiomatic Basis for Computer Programming' [125] in which you actually presented an axiomatic approach to programming semantics. Already in the early 1950s, by reading Quine's book, you became very much interested in the axiomatic approach. What I would like to understand, as we progress in the discussion, is when you actually connected Quine's work to computing?

Hoare: In 1964 I think. I was working on the ALGOL compiler for Elliott. I read the ALGOL60 report [10] and was very impressed by the syntax, and very keen to solve the problem of semantics in a similar way. In particular, in a machine-independent way. I attended a conference in Vienna called *Formal language description languages*[93]. I wasn't a speaker but people like Strachey and Landin, McCarthy, and others were speakers. They were mostly talking about what I would call interpreters; defining a language by its interpreter. By giving it what we now call its operational semantics. There was even a proposal by Jan Garwick to define the language by its translator plus a machine. But I thought that the purpose of a formal definition is to give a definition which is independent of implementation. Certainly, there would be general agreement that it should be independent of any particular implementation, say on an IBM computer (because it wouldn't have been an Elliott computer). But, I thought, really, we want it to be completely independent of all implementations. You just wanted to give enough information about the meaning of the language. You want to describe the language in a way that is independent of the implementation. And, which is sufficiently strong to guide the implementation and at the same time sufficiently strong to write useful programs. So the axioms serve as an interface between the implementor and the user of the language.

Daylight: After your college days in Oxford but before 1964, one of your first tasks when you were working with computing machines was to write library subroutines at Elliott, right?

Hoare: That's right, yes.

Daylight: What I again see in your recollections is that efficiency was very important for you or your managers, right?

Hoare: Ah well, certainly, I agree. The speed of the machine was 2000 instructions a second.

Daylight: So you were writing machine code? [H: Yes] Were you, when trying to optimize your machine code, in any way thinking about what you had learned about logic?

Hoare: No. I mean apart from Boolean algebra obviously, it was important for doing machine code. One of the tasks I was given was writing a device routine for a magnetic tape system and I toyed with the idea of deriving the conceptual framework for the device routines from Turing machines which of course have a tape. But I very quickly came to the conclusion this wasn't the way that our customers would want to use a tape. [H&D: Laughter]

Daylight: Your superiors asked you to devise or design a new language. They were not happy with machine language.

Hoare: That's right.

Daylight: Why, what was actually going on there? What did they ask you? Did they have a clear idea what they wanted?

Hoare: Well, they were embarking on a hardware design for a much faster computer. The first transistor computer they built was the 802. There was what was called an autocode for the 802, which is sort of a bit less powerful than FORTRAN. It's just a three-code address coding system, similar to Mercury Autocode, a precursor of a higher-level language. The autocode was actually designed and implemented by my wife to be, before I arrived. So the model was "oh a new machine, we are going to need a new autocode". I looked at the ALGOL60 report as a guide, an inspiration for ideas to put into the language, but I thought it was far too complicated for general programmers to understand and so I was simplifying it. It wasn't until some later stage, in '62 or '61, my boss and the sales manager of the division and my wife-to-be and me went to a course on ALGOL60 given in Brighton for a few days.

Daylight: Easter 1961.

Hoare: Easter '61 was it already? Yes, I think that's right. I had only joined the company in October '60. I had written a sorting program and that magnetic tape routine. In the car on the way back from the Brighton course, I asked "So why don't we just do ALGOL60?" And they said "yes".

Daylight: You just mentioned your sorting routine, this was before you had become acquainted with ALGOL60, right? You already had an idea on how to implement it?

Hoare: Yes, I had written a machine-code sorting routine, based on what was called Shell sort [275].

Daylight: Coming back to Easter '61 in Brighton. Peter Naur, Edsger Dijkstra, and Peter Landin were there as tutors. I am very intrigued by these three people. What impression did they give you? Were they very different people? Did they have a different style of programming in ALGOL60 or did they all present the same style? Do you have any recollections on that? [H: Laughter]

Hoare: No I don't. I do remember that I didn't remember Dijkstra at all. He didn't have a beard. Peter Landin was the first person to look at QuickSort, which I was doing instead of the set exercise. So I rather shyly showed it to him, and he looked a bit puzzled to begin with, but soon he said "Oh, oh I see" and he called Peter Naur to come and have a look as well.

Daylight: Were there any examples of recursion that they had presented? Because ALGOL60 was famous, controversial for the recursive procedure.

Hoare: Yes. Well I can't quite remember. I had been reading the ALGOL60 report quite intensively a little time before the course. I knew about recursion, I think basically from that. There was also an issue of the Communications of the ACM on ALGOL60 which I looked at again recently. But it may not have been out by the time we went on that course.

Daylight: Using recursion is really not so easy. It requires a conceptual leap for students in school to learn.

Hoare: Indeed, yes.

Daylight: You said you had already implemented QuickSort in machine code?

Hoare: No, not in machine code. I thought of the idea of the algorithm when I was studying at Moscow State University in 1959–60. But I couldn't manage to program the organization of the subtasks in Mercury Autocode which was the only language I knew at that time — I had attended a course on the Mercury Autocode in 1959 at Oxford. Somehow, when I read the ALGOL60 report, I must have understood that famous sentence[94] and seen that this was the solution to the idea of organizing a divide-and-conquer algorithm.

Daylight: How did you at that time, as a programmer, compare yourself with other programmers? This is kind of a strange question but, were you looking from the machine-language up to recursion or to ALGOL? Because later on you were clearly looking down, top-down. I would like to know when that changed, or were you in the beginning already inclined to look at it rather differently than many of your colleagues?

Hoare: I think, my progression of my own understanding of computer science has followed a trajectory of always trying to start higher than last time. More abstractly, more generally. Programming, really in any language, but of course particularly in machine code, is intensely intricate, down to the bit-level detail thinking. It takes a long time to realize that one can think effectively about the same subject more generally by exploiting abstraction. So I still think that bottom-up is the way you have to educate people. Each abstraction should be a discovery and delight that students enjoy after stubbing their toes on a lot of low level detail. Unfortunately [H: Laughter], it is sometimes quite the reverse.

Daylight: Concerning the Elliott `ALGOL60` compiler, you mentioned it was structured as a collection of mutually recursive procedures [128, p.146], so based on the recursive syntax of `ALGOL60`. In a sense this is then probably your second example of recursion that you already applied in practice?

Hoare: Yes. In fact, I designed the overall structure and some of the details of the compiler by writing the algorithms in a sort of pseudo `ALGOL`. The implementors, Jeff Hillmore and Jill my wife, translated it into machine code.

Daylight: With an explicit stack for recursion?

Hoare: Yes, that's right.

Daylight: But the subset of `ALGOL60` which you were implementing, that initially did not yet contain the recursive procedure?

Hoare: Well, I think it was always written with recursion in mind. The initial delivered version had recursion, I am pretty sure. So I think recursion was in there from very early on.

Daylight: So in the middle of 1963 your first version of the compiler was delivered? That's what I have here from your Turing Award lecture, I think.

Hoare: Right, there will probably be documentary evidence for that.

Daylight: What about the runtime system of your `ALGOL60` implementation? When I compare the work of Dijkstra, Naur, and Bauer & Samelson, I notice that the implementation styles are very different in terms of compile-time and runtime translation. Do you recall whether your first ALGOL60 implementation was static in that a lot was accomplished at compile time, in the interest of efficiency? Or was it dynamic?

Hoare: Oh, definitely very static. Yes. The basic administration of the stack and the recursion was minimal. I think I wrote it myself. It was not the usual method of Dijkstra's display, using index registers to point to activation records of enclosing blocks. The thing we had to do at run time was to test the bounds of the subscripts, which was a significant inefficiency. But, otherwise, the main limitation was on the length of the code. We had rather small stores in those days. The first internal versions of the compiler ran on 4000 words of store, of 39 bits each, so we are talking about 16 KB. The compiler ran on that, and the object programs had to run on that too. So space was very much at a premium.

Daylight: If your runtime system was very limited in the interest of space, or efficiency[95] actually, do you recall how many stacks your runtime system had?

Hoare: One.

Daylight: One, OK.

Hoare: Or no, maybe two, at both ends.

Daylight: Because in the US there were approaches where they had very many stacks, very specialized stacks, and Dijkstra had just one stack. So, there's a big difference. The West-Germans preferred not to have a runtime stack in the beginning with ALCOR[96].

Hoare: Oh right, yes.

Daylight: Were you aware of the Dijkstra compiler, how it worked, when you were working with Elliott?

Hoare: I don't think so. [Pause] No, the main source of information was the issue of the Communications of the ACM, which may have been April 1960 or '61, some time around there. Dijkstra had an article in it on, what's it called, the cellar principle and used it in the compilation of arithmetic expressions[97]. But, I used recursion in my ALGOL version which of course had to be implemented as a stack.

Daylight: So, now we are in the middle of the '60s. You've read Quine. I mean you had this interest in logic from your days at college. When you started programming, when you were working on the ALGOL compiler, is it fair to say that your interest in logic was in the back of your mind but you were not really active on that, you were trying to build a compiler?

Hoare: Yes, that's fair, clearly.

4.2.4   An Axiomatic Basis for Computer Programming (1969)

Daylight: At some point, you were, just like many of your colleagues, unhappy with the semantics of ALGOL. I mean it was defined in natural language. So you wanted to address that problem. You knew some researchers, like Landin and Strachey, who did it operationally and you were actually unhappy with that approach. Did you have discussions with these people? Did you know Dijkstra at that time well?

Hoare: No.

Daylight: With perhaps other people? Did you discuss the fact that the operational approach is probably not the way to go?

Hoare: Oh well, a major remark at that conference, which you can probably look up. It said something like "the more I hear of what's going on at this conference, the more I realize that the essential thing is to leave parts of the language undefined."[98] And that's what I claimed the axiomatic method would do.

Daylight: You also mentioned Bob Floyd's article [96] as a source of inspiration.

Hoare: I didn't see that until after I'd moved to Belfast in 1968. In fact I found a mimeographed offprint in the boxes of books that I carried with me. I did have an employment between Elliott and Belfast. I went to work for the national computing center in Manchester. I was only there for three months. Which was rather unkind. But there I wrote a paper on the axiomatic method of language definition, which was mimeographed. Saw it again, recently, and I thought, I don't understand this. [H: Laughter] It seemed just as bad as the operational.

Daylight: How was your paper received among your contemporaries who were reasoning operationally? Now it's a famous paper, but was it at that time difficult for people to understand, let alone appreciate it?

Hoare: The people I was talking to then were logicians and programming methodologists. People interested in specification. Well I didn't expect a great deal of reaction. When I talked about it, the logicians objected: "But you can't just write axioms, you've got to have a model", and I couldn't see what the fuss was about. I think because I understood the implementation. I was confident that I knew how to implement it. The whole point was that it wasn't dependent on the implementation. Now at last I have realized they were right. All my work since then has been model building. You can't really understand axioms without having a model to think about, an example, otherwise it's just symbols on a page.

Daylight: Let me just cite you here from your 2009 article:

> My hope was to find axioms that would be strong enough to enable programmers to discharge their responsibility to write correct and efficient programs. Yet I wanted them to be weak enough to permit a variety of efficient implementation strategies, suited to the particular characteristics of the widely varying hardware architectures prevalent at the time. [132, first page]

Now it is really going top-down, right? You have your machine-independent axioms and then in a later stage somebody adds one or two machine-dependent axioms of his choice, depending on his machine, right? [H: Yes] And, he would become interested in efficiency issues, because he knows the machine. [H: Yes] So is it correct that you have actually put efficiency second, while simplicity and correctness come first?

Hoare: Yes, this was really following the example of Dijkstra. He was a great advocate of constructive methods of correctness proving. To develop the proof and the program at the same time.

Daylight: But in all fairness Dijkstra has also very often been criticized because he wanted to keep efficiency as much as possible out of the story. So, it would be correct and simple, but it wouldn't necessarily be the most efficient implementation that he would obtain by working in that manner, while you still have an efficiency part in the trajectory, in the top-down trajectory.

Hoare: And so did Dijkstra. Very much so. I think his point of view was to cultivate your ability to consider these things separately as well as bringing them together. That of course is the secret of science and engineering, to be able to do that.

Daylight: Continuing this discussion about correctness and efficiency, when I read Knuth's 1974 paper 'Structured Programming with go to Statements' [161] and also your 1975 paper 'Recursive data structures' [127], I have the impression that they are two of the same kind: both authors want to work structured — so I mean it has to be clear, the clarity has to be there — but both authors are also interested in efficiency.

Hoare: I wouldn't have put those two papers as an interesting comparison.

Daylight: I would say they are both similar actually.

Hoare: There were no goto's in the 'data structures' paper.

Daylight: Knuth's paper is indeed about goto's, but it is, in general, also about structured programming. He was trying to obtain efficient implementations by means of transformations on the initial structured code. [H: Right.] And he was inspired by you when you were in Stanford. He says he had a mental block about optimization:

> For some reason we all (especially me) had a mental block about optimization, namely that we always regarded it as a behind-the-scenes activity, to be done in the machine language, which the programmer isn't supposed to know. This veil was first lifted from my eyes in the Fall of 1973 when I ran across a remark by Hoare [126] that, ideally, a language should be designed so that an optimizing compiler can describe its optimizations in the source language. [161, p.283]

And then for example the Darlington & Burstall paper [46] from 1973 is a nice example of that[99]. But, well, as I try to understand these papers, Knuth says efficiency has always been something that he was not supposed to touch, or at least only later at the machine-code level.

Hoare: Right, yes, yes.

Daylight: He was not allowed to do that up front, because this would very often ruin the structure of his program.

Hoare: Indeed.

Daylight: So, is it fair to stay that in the '60s and '70s, when structured programming was becoming broadly applied, it was not clear how to fit efficiency into the structured-programming paradigm?

Hoare: The enthusiasts for goto's, I am sure, were using efficiency as an excuse, as we would now say. I think they eventually realized that the amount of optimization you get by writing a goto is very limited. It is not worth really going to the stake about it. So structured programming is more widely accepted. Mind you, there are still a lot of jumps all around the place. I did later write a paper about how to prove correctness about programs with jumps. Now, I think understanding theories has developed well enough to see that jumps are really not an issue as far as verification is concerned. So the issue has become a non-issue as far as both the theory and probably the practice as well.

4.2.5 Incomputability

After a short coffee break, we continued our discussion.

Hoare: I didn't think I have anything very important to say about incomputability but fire away.

Daylight: Well you already explained when you became acquainted with Alan Turing's work. And you wrote your 'Incomputability' paper [133] in '72 with Allison. Could you perhaps say a bit more about Allison?

Hoare: Donald Allison was a lecturer in my department in the Queen's University, Belfast. He was originally, and I think continued to be, a numerical mathematician. Of course he became a computer scientist and taught the subject in the department at Queen's University.

Daylight: Content-wise, in this paper on 'Incomputability' you present proof-by-contradiction and essentially also address the Halting Problem, to some extent.

Hoare: That was the subject of the paper, yes.

Daylight: But you don't use the words "Halting Problem" in that paper.

Hoare: No ... Yes, I don't.

Daylight: So these words must have come in later — now they are used frequently. You referred to Strachey's 1965 letter 'An Impossible Program' [286]. [H: Yes] Did you talk to Strachey about this or were you at two different ends of the world? Well, you were both in Great Britain, but, did you see him regularly?

Hoare: I did know him and I saw him occasionally but not regularly. We certainly didn't talk about this.

Daylight: Right. So, this section on incomputability, I actually have three main questions. On the one hand, it's your reception of Turing's paper, which we have talked about. Yet, it is still interesting to note that in your paper on 'Incomputability' you actually referred to Davis's 1958 book [47] but not directly to Turing's 1936 paper [291].

Hoare: Right.

Daylight: Just as a historian, again, interesting to see how these ideas propagate. And then the Böhm-Jacopini 1966 paper [23] with their theorem. You say something interesting with respect to structured programming and the reception of the Böhm-Jacopini theorem. So now I am quoting you:

> This showed that an arbitrary program with jumps could be executed by an interpreter written without any jumps at all; [...]

This theorem was needed to convince senior managers of the company that no harm would come from adopting structured programming as a company policy; and project managers needed it to protect themselves from having to show their programmers how to do it [. . .] [131, twelfth page]

Hoare: This was a story I think I heard when I was interacting with IBM.

Daylight: Oh OK. Because this Böhm-Jacopini paper, when I read it, it is extremely technical. It also relies on Turing machines again. But, I wonder, did you for example or did your colleague Allison study this paper in depth?

Hoare: Probably neither of us, I certainly didn't, no sorry.

Daylight: Were these two people actually well known after the '60s? Did you see them in conferences?

Hoare: Never met Jacopini. I did meet Böhm, very nice man. But he was at the time working on a programming language based on Church's lambda calculus, called the CUCH[100], which I was very impressed by.

Daylight: Yes, you have referred to that one as well [cf. the literature list in the beginning of the discussion]. What about the reception of Kleene's work, *Introduction to Metamathematics*? Kleene had a Normal Form theorem. [H: Laughter] Does that ring a bell?

Hoare: Yes, I did read his work on the Turing model of computation. But, [H: Sigh] again, I can't recall ever having understood it. [H: Laughter]

Daylight: Because when I read the Böhm-Jacopini paper; well, when I look at the theorem that they have proved, it is actually also a result of the Kleene Normal Form theorem.

Hoare: Yes. No, I didn't follow that connection because I didn't really know about Kleene normal forms.

Daylight: Right. But, on the other hand, if I then go back to your 'Incomputability' paper [133], you introduce a procedure mu somewhere in the paper — on page 175 actually — and you explain the potential unboundedness of the procedure mu. I have the paper with me.

Hoare: Oh right, that might need reminding me. [Daylight points to procedure mu on page 175.] Oh yes, yes yes. That I have met in Kleene [*Introduction to Metamathematics*]. Because it is one of the definitions of computability. A Turing-complete language is one that includes this as a function.

Daylight: So that actually comes very close to his Normal Form theorem. [H: Yes] The potential unboundedness of the mu operator.

Now given these theoretical connections: the Böhm-Jacopini theorem, Kleene's Normal Form theorem, or to some extent this book [*Introduction to Metamathematics*], and also Turing's paper. One of the big questions in computer science during the '60s was whether the recursive procedure of ALGOL60 was actually needed to compute any computable function. There was a whole discussion going on. If I may cite Sammet from her '69 book:

> Recursive procedures were introduced by ALGOL. They certainly should be considered a significant contribution to the technology [H: Laughter], but it is not clear how great a one. The advocates of this facility claim that many important problems cannot be solved without it; on the other hand, people continue to solve numerous important problems without it and even in a few cases manage to handle (sometimes in an awkward way) some of the problems which the recursion proponents claim cannot be done. [266, p.193].

Daylight: She wrote this in 1969, reflecting back on the previous decade. Also when I look in the proceedings of Rome'62 [230], there were heavy debates going on about whether they should have this recursive procedure in the ALGOL60 definition or not.

Hoare: Oh yes yes.

Daylight: Were you part of this debate?

Hoare: No, I came in at the end and heard some after-shocks of it. [H: Laughter] Yes. Because I hadn't found much difficulty. Recursion wasn't a desperately inefficient thing.

Daylight: But the theoretical question whether it should belong to ALGOL60 because you need it to compute any computable function.

Hoare: I haven't heard any body say that . . . Because it's not true.

Daylight: In fact, that it is not true follows from Böhm-Jacopini's paper immediately. They prove that

> [E]very Turing Machine is [. . .] equivalent to, a program written in a language which admits as formation rules only composition and iteration. [23, p.366]

You actually don't even need procedures. You can program everything in one procedure, theoretically speaking.

Hoare: Quite. I think the implications of some of the things Sammet says are ... I can't remember any serious claim that recursion was needed in order to make things computable. However, there is one problem. You might have to violate the typing system in order to get a uniform procedure for eliminating recursion. Because the types of the variables that you would have to store in the stack are different and the language doesn't allow that. But if you didn't use types, then you wouldn't need recursion, because everything would then have to be an integer or a boolean. That would certainly not be a very good way of writing large programs.

4.2.6 Academic vs. Applied Research

Daylight: Last topic: academic vs. applied industrial research. You write there is a large gap between theory and practice and that this is indeed a good thing, and then you explain:

> [I]t would be crazy for industry to try to keep pace with the latest results of pure research. If the research fails, the industry fails with it; and if the research continues to succeed, the industry which is first to innovate runs the risk of being overtaken by competitors who reap the benefits of the later improvements. For these reasons, it would be grossly improper to recommend industry on immediate implementation of results of their own research that is still in progress. [131, thirteenth page]

Hoare: I think that still represents my views.

Daylight: I just quoted you from your 1996 paper 'How did software get so reliable without proof?' [131].

Hoare: I came in for a lot of flack for that paper.

But, the person who first started me on this idea was Sir Richard Doll, the cancer and smoking researcher. When I first went to Oxford, I attended a public lecture by him on the results of some recalculation of the damage done by the nuclear bombs at Hiroshima and Nagasaki. He participated in a statistical analysis of subsequent illness and death, which led to a revision of the estimates of the acceptable maximum exposure rate for a population of radioactivity: the rate had to be halved. At the end of the lecture, someone got up and asked him "What advice would you give to the government for action to take on the basis of your findings?" He said "I refuse to answer that question". And then he explained "The basic principle of my scientific research is that I never give advice on actions that need to be taken on the basis of my current research. Because, if I do that, I lose my most precious attribute, which is scientific objectivity. The rest of my research project would be trying to show that my advice was correct, while real science is all about showing that things are wrong." So he stops being a scientist at once. And that seems such a devastating argument. He said "I am willing to give advice about the application of other people's research, and I am prepared to give advice on applications or results of research I did twenty years ago." Aah, I thought, this man is a real scientist. I have been telling people to use the results in my research, because I more or less had to, in order to get research grants. And, it's all wrong. You see the same mistake being made over and over again. By people who think that a scientist can judge the impact of his own research. Absolutely impossible. Nobody can judge the impact of research. Most people can't judge the impact of anything. And the politicians are among the worst offenders. But the attempt to assess the impact of research before it is done is going to destroy research completely. I am glad to say that Microsoft Research has consistently adopted a policy of absolutely banning that. They will engage in research because it is interesting, because it's about computing, and because it might produce results that will be applicable in unexpected ways. [H: Sigh] This is a real breath of fresh air not to have to continue to make claims about potential consequences of your own research, other than in the most general terms. I mean, it is possible that in twenty years time, our research will have had an influence. Microsoft is prepared to support good research with almost arbitrary time frames.

Daylight: I also have, again, a paper from Knuth [160], in which he expresses his reservations about asymptotic analysis in complexity theory. He claims that, very often, if you base yourself on asymptotic complexity results, you will have to take an algorithm which is actually not the best one to take in practice. Also for automata-theoretic results he expresses his reservations. He is, I believe, one of the few researchers who puts such reservations in writing. In a sense, he is cautioning, or asking for more scrutiny of pure theoretical research. Very often, when a student asks a theoretician in a university what the practical pay off is of the theoretician's work, the student will get the answer "I am not interested in practical results". And then there is nothing the student can do because the theoretician could be right, his work could be applicable in twenty, fifty years.

Hoare: Exactly.

Daylight: But he could also be wrong, obviously. Maybe only a small percentage of these theoretical results will actually make it into practice.

Hoare: That's right too.

Daylight: So how would you advise students to deal with this situation? The student is willing to invest in both practical and theoretical work but also wants to take the right path. That is, a path leading to academic success. Because it's not very easy.

Hoare: [H: Laughter] It certainly isn't. I think it is important to know what you are doing. To make your own decision, as to what your time scales are. If you want to have an impact, you can characterize it in broader terms, the area of a possible impact that you could have. My feeling is that you, if you are asking for money to support research — and let's face it, research doesn't come for free any way — you should have a potential application area, but not either commit yourself to it or predict the time scales or any commercial returns or whatever, unless you want to work more on the development side. So, basically throughout your research career, your objectives and your time scales will change. And that's all to the good, it keeps life interesting.

Daylight: Concerning, in general, this approach of structured programming, the formal top-down approach, with a specification going to an implementation, proving correctness, etc. When I read papers of Peter Naur or others, I have the impression they have taken a step back from that approach and criticized it[101]. Peter Naur has, by the way, also written about Turing: he gave Turing's paper to his students and asked them to study it and apparently got very different results[102].

Hoare: [H: Laughter] Exactly.

Daylight: So, one of Naur's claims is that, very often, a formal method is not really scrutinized. A lot of researchers fall in love with their formalism. Again, I am just trying to contrast this now with the scientist who should actually try to be as objective as possible — while somebody in industry has other goals, so that's clear — but a scientist who wants to conduct mathematics and wants to have an objective view is in a sense very often barking up a tree where he is just defending his formalism.

Hoare: I have done it myself, so I know it very well. Towards the end of my academic career, and now as well, I've got very interested in unifying theories. That seems to me to be a common goal of all branches of science. Show what used to be five laws is really expressible only as three. Or that a range of possibilities are really only special cases of a more general law. And, that the various presentations of theories that people defend as their own throughout their research career are indeed members of the same family. I think one of the things that science or theoretical mathematically based science can do, with benefit which is directly contributed to engineering, is to explore the full range of choices and possibilities that can be implemented by an engineer for a particular purpose or a range of purposes. An engineer would like to know at the beginning of the project that there are only five ways of doing this. Quite deep mathematics can be needed to show that there really are only five ways. The great unification in computability theory shows many examples and then conjectures that all definitions of computability are really the same, that is a unifying theorem, which prevented a lot of logicians from controversy, from advocating a particular style of presentation over another. This is very important. I was reading a book about Paul Dirac, the quantum theorist. He invented his own presentation of quantum theory and so did Heisenberg and so did Schrödinger. They'd all approached it from a different mathematical presentation. They shared the Nobel Prize for this. But what Dirac did was to show that all three presentations were the same; he unified the theories. So I think his achievement was the greatest. It had a very important effect. It meant that you never got any controversy about the foundations and the presentation of the subject. Everybody knew that you would never find an experiment that would differentiate them. So how much was the contribution? First, he has avoided people wasting their substance on fruitless controversy, splitting the whole field into rival schools of notations which differ only in presentational matters. He has prevented a completely fruitless search for counter examples, for experiments that will differentiate them. The combination of a religious fervour with scientifically unresolvable controversy at the foundations of the subject actually kills the subject, because a good scientist will avoid that subject, that topic, completely. It is the province of bigots, in which issues look irresolvable. So to have unified that theory really made quantum theory possible, and got it accepted and applied in the whole of the rest of physics. Completely transformative. Yet it was a pure theoretical discovery, made by use of mathematics alone, no experiments, no nothing. So unifying theories, I think is what computer science needs. We don't need more theories.

Daylight: Thank you very much.

Hoare: Thank you.

4.3   Final Remarks

My discussion with Hoare has, I believe, shed light on the two hypotheses stated at the beginning of this chapter. Starting with the second hypothesis, Hoare has mentioned several times during the discussion that some ideas from mathematical logic influenced him without full comprehension. A first example is Kleene's Normal Form theorem and the mu operator in particular. A second concerns the lack of using models in his early research on axiomatic based semantics. A third example is his lightweight reading of the Böhm-Jacopini paper. Finally, as a fourth example, Hoare mentioned that he tried to comprehend Turing's 1936 paper during the early 1950s, but with difficulty. To understand it better, he later read Davis's 1958 book *Computability and Unsolvability* [47], but also without full comprehension.

Though Hoare did not study the details of the Böhm-Jacopini paper, his reception of that paper should not be underestimated. When presenting Sammet's 1969 question to Hoare concerning the logical superfluousness of the recursive procedure in ALGOL60, it became apparent to me how different his research agenda was from Sammet's. That is, while the practical implications of the Böhm-Jacopini paper in terms of programming had reached Hoare and his close colleagues like Dijkstra (see Chapter 2), they had clearly not reached the many others like Sammet who were advocating very different programming languages, such as FORTRAN and COBOL.

I now have the impression that, in many cases, Hoare simply did not make the effort to grasp the mathematical logic literature in detail. In some other cases (e.g. Turing's paper), he did make the effort but with difficulty. Furthermore, not understanding all of Turing's paper may well have been an advantage to Hoare and other first-generation programmers. His research was, after all, related to programming and not to the foundations of mathematics. Grasping all of Turing's work may, in my opinion, have separated him too much from his programming concerns. On the other hand, Hoare did suggest that his disregard toward using models in his early research on axiomatic systems did slow him down.

In retrospect, the observations just made are only to be expected. A researcher who wishes to advance one research field by borrowing ideas from another will encounter ups and downs. Some problems which were originally hard to solve can become surprisingly easy. But, not thoroughly understanding the origins of a new technique can obviously imply that not all problems are solved correctly!

The observations just made may be trivial but are nevertheless important to state explicitly. If correct, then they support my original unstated conviction that Hoare's research was *across* the practical-theoretical divide. Although I thought I had anticipated Hoare's practical incentive to introduce his axiomatic method, I was surprised by its force when discussing the matter with him. Hoare was not a mathematical logician perusing axiomatic based systems, he was first and foremost a computer practitioner in industry who wanted to solve a practical problem. His education in Classics and his work in industry had paved the way for him to eventually write his 1969 paper 'An Axiomatic Basis for Computer Programming' [125]. His bottom-up teaching of programming illustrates further his practical inclination toward computing.

The contradistinction between practical and theoretical thus does not seem to have played a large role in Hoare's research of the 1960s. In later years, however, after having joined academia, this contradistinction — and the role of mathematics in software engineering in particular — became a prime topic of discussion in his research papers [129–132]. It is his 1996 paper 'How did software get so reliable without proof?' [131] which I discussed with Hoare and which brings me back to my first hypothesis: many logically minded computing researchers today emphasize, even over-emphasize, the importance of mathematical logic in computing while others strongly oppose any kind of formalization whatsoever. Having been a strong proponent of formalization during the 1970s and 1980s, Hoare supported both sides of an admittingly widening gap between practice and theory in his 1996 paper. As confirmed in the last part of our discussion, Hoare believes there is plenty of room for both practical and theoretical work in computing, both are important, and the gap is necessary and useful.

In retrospect, after having reflected on our discussion and after having restudied Hoare's research papers, I cannot quite get over the feeling that Hoare has, since the late 1960s, remained first and foremost a strong advocate of formalization in the name of science and rationality. For example, in our discussion he stressed that "quite deep mathematics can be needed" and that "a pure theoretical discovery, made by use of mathematics alone, no experiments, no nothing" can be of great benefit to the engineer. Likewise, in his 1996 paper, he stated that a proper response to the gap between theory and practice is not only to congratulate the practitioners but also the theorists "for it is they who have achieved research results that are twenty years ahead of the field of practice" [131]. That is, though the work of the engineers is important, it are the theoreticians who "lead" and who have to put themselves in an "uncomfortable" position:

> It is not their failing but rather their duty to achieve and maintain such an uncomfortable lead, and to spread it over a broad front across a wide range of theories. [131]

Unsurprisingly, then, Hoare's standpoint has been described as modernistic [178, 258], a view that mathematics and science are the only vehicles for true progress.

It would be interesting to contrast in depth Hoare's standpoint to that of, for example, the late Alan J. Perlis and Peter Naur, i.e. two Turing Award winners with a more empirical philosophy toward computing. According to them, most "scientists" in computing put themselves in a comfortable position, not an uncomfortable one in that they completely abstract away the real, informal world in which we operate. "Scientists" do not "lead" a group of practitioners but are merely symbol chauvinists who firmly believe that mathematical structures prevail over material ones (cf. [55, 195, 217]).

5. Niklaus Wirth and Software Engineering

To better understand the history of programming languages, I have conducted a discussion with Niklaus Wirth, the 1984 Turing Award winner. Wirth was educated as an electrical engineer and became a successful programming language designer. He is the inventor of the programming languages EULER, ALGOL-W, Pascal, Modula, and Oberon.

The discussion's transcript presented in this chapter shows that during the 1960s Wirth was well aware of the dichotomy between mathematical elegance and machine efficiency. He chose the former to communicate and teach effectively but also stressed that he was first and foremost an engineer wanting real machinery running. The dichotomy will become apparent when Wirth recollects his preference for the simple solution of using one runtime stack even if it came at the price of machine efficiency. Also his appeal for a machine-independent object language for portability of Pascal programs is very similar to Dijkstra's work on ALGOL60.

During the early 1970s, Wirth became interested in Hoare's 1969 paper 'An Axiomatic Basis for Computer Programming' [125] and collaborated with Hoare in an attempt to apply the latter's axiom-based semantics on the former's programming language Pascal. In later years, in the aftermath of his early successes, he conceded that such formalization endeavours had limited practical merit and that "most programmers are not pure mathematicians". In his later writings, he clearly reacted to the tidal wave of formalization in computing of the 1960s and later. Also today, he views the gap between practice and theory to be widening. In his words:

> [T]he way theoreticians have developed [analytic methods for program verification] is like an academic cloud that moves away from the place where it is supposed to be. [See Section 5.2.2]

Other topics discussed with Wirth concern the Software Crisis of 1968 and embedded software.

Meeting Niklaus Wirth

My discussion with Wirth took place on 9 November 2010 in the RZ building, Clausiusstrase 59 at ETH Zurich, Switzerland. Its digital recordings were transcribed by me and subsequently lightly edited by Wirth and myself.

Short Biography of Niklaus Wirth

Niklaus Wirth was born in 1934 in Winterthur, Switzerland. He received a Master's degree in electrical engineering from the Eidgenössische Technische Hochschule (ETH) Zurich in 1958, subsequently worked for a short time as a teaching assistant at Laval University in Quebec, and then went on to pursue a PhD in programming languages under the supervision of professor Harry D. Huskey at the University of California at Berkeley (1960–1963). Wirth was an assistant professor at Stanford University (1963–1967) at the newly founded computer science department, and returned to Zurich in 1967 where he shortly thereafter co-founded the Department of Computer Science at ETH. He spent sabbaticals at Xerox (1976–1977 and 1984–1985) and retired in March 1999 as professor at ETH. Wirth received several awards throughout his career, including the IEEE Emanuel Piore Prize (1983), the ACM Turing Award (1984), and the IEEE Computer Pioneer Award (1988).

5.1 Engineering: from Hobby to Profession

Daylight: Niklaus Wirth, you were born in 1934 in Winterthur. Is this in the German-speaking part of Switzerland?

Wirth: Yes, it's about 30 kilometers north from Zurich.

Daylight: Do you still live there now?

Wirth: No. But I spent the first 25 years of my life there. During my studies at ETH I commuted from Winterthur about 20 minutes by train.

Daylight: Do you recall the second World War? Switzerland wasn't involved in the war was it?

Wirth: Formally not, but it was affected.

Daylight: In what ways did it affect you?

Wirth: Well, of course, I was a young boy. But still I could sense that there was tension in the air. My father was for very much time in the service border guard, and so I lived with my mother alone. Food was rationed and it was relatively scarce. We had to plant vegetables in the garden, things like that. Of course we heard the airplanes going across, day and night, during the latter part of the war. That was very upsetting.

5.1.1   An Early Passion for Engineering

Daylight: At the end of the war you were eleven years old. What about the years immediately after the war, did you have another passion first like football and did you gradually become interested in engineering?

Wirth: No, I was in a way a clear-cut case. From early childhood I was always interested in machinery and toys, I had Meccano. A bit later I studied physics and chemistry books, which I had found in the book shelves of my dad. My interests were clearly in the technical sciences.

Daylight: Did you have brothers or sisters?

Wirth: No, I was alone. I had to learn to keep myself busy.

Daylight: How did you study those books, did you just read them?

Wirth: I always liked to experiment. As a young boy I was interested in trains. I lived at a house where four train tracks passed by, so I often watched them and put together schedules. I hoped I would get a model railway which I didn't, and later I became interested in model airplanes. I became very active in this, starting at age 12. I first build model airplanes from kits and then, more interestingly, I started to design them myself. At the age of 15 I was in the national team being sent to England for an international competition. That was a very busy time for me. I wonder, in retrospect, how I managed to get through high school which I did without much trouble. When following chemistry courses in school, I built a chemistry lab in the cellar at home. So that was the chemical period. Then came remote-control systems for airplanes. I got one of the first in Switzerland, ordered it from England. Of course my attempts always failed and that's how I was forced to study electronics. I had gotten a book on electronics from somebody in town. Finally, the time approached when I had to decide what to study. Naturally, I chose electronics because it's what I needed immediately. That's why I ended up studying electrical engineering at the ETH in Zurich for four years.

Daylight: That was until 1958?

Wirth: Right.

5.1.2 Emigration to North America

Daylight: After your studies at ETH, you went to Quebec.

Wirth: Yes. My father had advised me to go abroad after my studies. He recommended I go for at least a year or two to see something of the world. Remember, the borders had been closed during the war and they were just slowly opening. So I took his advice. He convinced me to do it right after having finished my studies at ETH. Otherwise I would probably take up a job in Switzerland, start a family, and get glued down. So I did as he said and I emigrated to Canada in the intent of finding a job as an engineer. It was kind of a depression at the time so I didn't find one, but I could get a teaching assistantship at Laval University. That's how I ended up in Quebec more or less by chance. I thought to myself, if I don't like it there, then I can look for another job from the place itself.

Daylight: How did you, after your stay at Laval University, end up with Huskey in California?

Wirth: Well, I had initially planned to work as an engineer, but during that year at Laval University I was encouraged by co-students to go on for a PhD. They said that a Master's degree shouldn't be the terminal point for me. By the way, we were six graduate students only: one Chinese, one Pakistani, one Brazilian, one French, one Canadian, and myself. At the beginning I didn't like the idea of a PhD, I had had enough of studying. But then, after some reflections, I decided to apply. I think I applied for a PhD program at five American universities. The position would have had to include an assistantship, because I had to get some income. I was accepted by four of them, among which the university of California at Berkeley. There I was given an assistantship with a professor in information theory. Now, that wasn't really my cup of tea, it was purely mathematical. So already during the first half year I started looking around. Then I found that a position in computing was going to be available under professor Huskey, and computing happened to be one of the topics I was interested in, though not the only one. That's how I ended up with Huskey.

Daylight: How would you describe Huskey? By that time he had already travelled a lot, he had for instance worked with Alan Turing. Was he a visionary man? Did he influence you a lot?

Wirth: He was rather a quiet man. His fame, I think, was mainly from working at the early computer developed in Los Angeles, Whirlwind I believe. Later he worked at Bendix designing the G15 machine (which was the first one I programmed). But he was a busy man too. He was president of ACM and other organizations. So if I may be very frank, no he didn't influence me very much. The man who took his role in this sense was Aad van Wijngaarden who came to spend a sabbatical semester at Berkeley. I got in touch with him because I had found a group of three doctoral students who worked in a small corner downstairs in the mathematics building — I had to go there because the computer center was there. They did something which looked very strange but which I found very interesting. They programmed — and I was just learning to program the 704 with `FORTRAN` — and they wrote a program that could process a programming language, its own language. It was a compiler, now we know how these things are called, a compiler for `NELIAC` which was an early dialect of `ALGOL58`. It was professor Huskey who had introduced that programming language from some naval research base. That's how I had become involved with programming and software. I had actually come to Berkeley under Huskey to learn about hardware and how computers were built, how they operated. But it was not the right time any more to build computers at universities. They had just finished building a huge computer. So, I drifted into software instead.

5.1.3 Compilers

Daylight: Lets talk about different ways of defining the semantics of a programming language. Aad Van Wijngaarden was using a very dynamic approach which would eventually lead to `ALGOL68`. But at that time, when both of you were at Berkeley, did he already have a very machine-independent way of looking at a programming language? Was that something he was already working on? Or did you get some other impression from him?

Wirth: Yes, yes. I remember his work published then, called 'Generalized `ALGOL`' [301].

Daylight: I think that was 1962.

Wirth: Probably even 1961. That's when he visited Berkeley and when we discussed these matters. By that time I had already learned how to design compilers. Seeing that the `NELIAC` compiler was a huge mess, a program that only one person could understand (that was Carol Conn), I thought to myself that bringing more order into the process of compiler design would be a marvelous PhD topic for me. Van

Wijngaarden influenced me with his reduced ALGOL, his generalized ALGOL. His approach entailed fewer but more general rules. So both things flowed into each other. Recall that I was first and foremost an engineer: I didn't want to write a paper, I wanted a machinery running. Thus, I not only designed a language which I called EULER and which was much along the lines of Generalized ALGOL, but I also implemented it. Implementing EULER was important because only then it would have a real existence for me. That work resulted in my dissertation in 1963 at Berkeley. But the definition of EULER was, essentially, still in the old mechanistic way, though I didn't say (like other people at the time) that the definition lied in it's implementation. Instead, I had devised a mechanism of defining semantics in terms of a much simpler machine which was then used to run an interpreter for the language. It was, however, not a satisfactory solution, I have to concede that, though at the time I knew nothing better.

Daylight: It was your Phrase Structure System [312], right?

Wirth: Yes, I also worked on syntax parsing. That was a very hot topic at the time and is of course the basis for making a compiler more systematic.

Daylight: Right, because then we have your Phrase Structure Programming Language [312]. Please correct me if I'm wrong, but isn't this directly related to what you called an Hypothetical Stack Computer [270, p.88]?

Wirth: Yes, that was then the simpler machine which I referred to.

Daylight: Where did that idea come from? Was it your invention? Or was it hanging in the air?

Wirth: I wouldn't want to call this my invention. I mean, the idea of a stack was just around. But maybe I was the first to define a language in terms of a much simpler language — though, in retrospect, this was an obvious idea. I reused the idea later for Pascal P code and Modula M code.

Daylight: Huskey also wrote about machine-independent intermediate languages, in 1962 [142, 152]. He was also expert in compilers I would think.

Wirth: No, he was really a hardware man.

Daylight: I see. Did Van Wijngaarden talk to you about Dijkstra's compiler work for ALGOL60 when he visited Berkeley?

Wirth: [Pause] No. [Pause] When did I get to know Dijkstra? I met Dijkstra for the first time at the IFIP congress in Munich, 1962. I knew about him through this little group of three people who worked on the NELIAC compiler. [Daylight shows the NELIAC paper [143] to Wirth.] Oh you have it right here: Huskey, Love and Wirth are the authors of this paper, but the person primarily involved in the compiler was Carol Conn. And there was Bill Kees. These people held a seminar and the very influential thing there was the ALGOL60 report [10]; that was in early 1961. I had come to Berkeley in the fall of 1960. So we started analyzing ALGOL60 and through that effort I got to hear about Dijkstra, and then there was the IFIP congress in Munich 1962. I took this opportunity to go to Munich and also meet Dijkstra. He held a paper [64] there, a very influential one. But no, Van Wijngaarden himself did not talk much about Dijkstra's compiler work when he visited us at Berkeley.

Daylight: Do you think this is maybe because Van Wijngaarden was not as much involved in compiler building as were Dijkstra and Zonneveld?

Wirth: Yes, I went to Amsterdam in 1965 and spent two months there at the mathematical centre. Dijkstra wasn't there any more. Zonneveld I think was, and I also recall Nederkoorn.

Daylight: What surprises me is that Dijkstra and Zonneveld, with their ALGOL60 compiler, also introduced an intermediate object language with one universal stack, very similar to the later P code. So I think this technique must have originated at several different places simultaneously.

Wirth: It could well be. I think it was an obvious idea. I wouldn't want to claim ownership of it. But I don't remember that I learned it from someone.

Daylight: There were not many who did that very early on.

Wirth: Well, the computers were so slow. Nowadays having interpreters is no problem. Pascal P came of course a bit later, but it was a method of having, so to say, a portable object that would help people port Pascal compilers to their machines.

Daylight: Do you remember, in the case of Pascal, whether your intermediate machine had one stack or many stacks?

Wirth: One.

Daylight: Why, was this essential to you? Was it a must to have just one stack?

Wirth: Well, I never saw a need for a second stack, and when it comes to this I always go for the simpler solution.

Daylight: Because later on for `Lilith`, as explained in 'Lean Systems in an Intrinsically Complex World' [270, p.88], you went for two stacks.

Wirth: Yes, but that's a different kind of stack. There was the normal stack for procedure-activation records and the additional stack for expression evaluation. The second stack, implemented as 16 registers, was dictated by the hardware. You can view it as being the top extension of the normal stack.

Daylight: It is very nice, this striving for simplicity. Dijkstra also had just one stack. But then when I look at what most others did, they seem to have had several specialized stacks. Even "seven stacks in the SDL virtual machine in the interest of performance but at the price of simplicity" [270, p.89–90]. When striving for a uniform stack, did you sometimes pay a price in performance?

Wirth: You know [W: Laughter] at one point I will say that any way. I always was a teacher and as a teacher you have to explain things to people. You are very grateful if the things you have to explain are simple enough, because then they get much more easily across. I have realized this again and again, even in programming people normally program for machines so that their programs run. I think that at universities people should program so that other people can learn from their programs. This is of course an academic idea. Also here at ETH most people can't program in the sense I understand it, making it explicable to others. So I always felt that we should make our machines, our languages, our operating systems as simple as possible.

Daylight: So then I would imagine that, when you met Dijkstra for the first time, you must have felt aligned with his way of thinking. Did you talk to him in Munich 1962?

Wirth: Very much so, yes. Also from his writings of course. Yes, I met him very briefly in Munich. My work on **EULER** was of course known to Van Wijngaarden, so he invited me to participate in the IFIP working group. I accepted the invitation and attended the group meeting in Europe for the first time in March 1964 in Tutzing near Munich, and that's where I then met these people.

Daylight: Also Tony Hoare for the first time?

Wirth: Yes, absolutely.

5.1.4 Semantics

Daylight: In your paper 'EULER: A Generalization of ALGOL, and its Formal Definition: Part I' [312] you described some of the various approaches that people were trying out in order to define programming language semantics. You mentioned Böhm [22] and Landin [165, 166], who were much inspired by the λ-calculus. You also explained Van Wijngaarden's dynamic approach [301, 302] and Garwick's approach [104].

Wirth: Where did I do that?

Daylight: This paper. [Daylight shows [312]].

Wirth: Ah, OK. [W: Laughter] It's a long time ago.

Daylight: It's a nice overview. You for instance mentioned the applicability and evaluation scans in Van Wijngaarden's approach.

Wirth: You give me some reason for rereading my work. [W&D: Laughter]

Daylight: And then there's Garwick, who seemed to suggest a very operational approach.

Wirth: Very, extremely. Garwick was of course, I remember him very vividly, an energetic man, very much stuck in his mechanistic definition. With my own experience of explaining a language in terms of a simpler language, I felt that couldn't be the end of the story. So the axiomatic approach, which I think Floyd and then Hoare propagated, was really a much more promising way.

Daylight: That came after your work on EULER?

Wirth: Yes, the EULER work was conducted between 1963 and 1966.

Daylight: Floyd and Hoare came with a totally different approach compared with the λ-calculus. You worked very closely with Hoare to axiomatize Pascal, right?

Wirth: Yes. I had had discussions with Hoare about his axiomatic definitions and I found that to be a much better approach. I suggested to him to try his method on Pascal and so we sat together, worked together, and wrote a paper on the axiomatic definition of Pascal. I was also looking for it yesterday and I couldn't find it[103]. But to tell you the truth, we didn't really finish the job. There were some parts which we didn't know how to handle, particularly *var* parameters, the problem of aliases. The goto's were also a nasty thing. And, frankly, you can't define the goto axiomatically without not really making progress, in contrast to loops like the *while* statement which can have this very nice form. So, in my following languages, there was no goto statement any more. [W: Laughter]

Daylight: Thus the formalism, in a sense, forces you to keep the good concepts.

Wirth: To eject those which do not fit.

Daylight: What about the λ-calculus? There was a lot of interest — I would almost say an obsession — by some people to use the λ-calculus. Where did that come from? Did they have a practical incentive to do this or was it mainly in the interest of mathematical elegance?

Wirth: It came from people who had a strong mathematical inclination. It was originated by John McCarthy, also a paper from the IFIP congress in Munich 1962, a very interesting paper entitled 'Towards a Mathematical Science of Computation' [186]. There too, no reference is made to a machinery. But, since everything is defined in terms of function calls with recursion, the question is: What do you gain? With simple programs it's fine, but not so with complicated problems. McCarthy's paper was the origin of the school of functional programming languages. Strangely enough, that school remained very much the domain of the British, mainly the Scottish. Edinburgh is the high seed of functional programming languages. Names that come to my mind are Milner and Strachey.

5.1.5 Recursion

Daylight: You just mentioned recursion, which was controversial in the ALGOL60 definition [10]. A sensitive question during the early 1960s was whether ALGOL60 compilers should implement recursion or not. In fact, you yourself mentioned that with respect to Pascal:

> [A] ban against recursion had been lifted: recursivity of procedures was to be the normal case. [307, p.99]

Wirth: You see, I was trained as an engineer. I felt that Pascal should be implemented so that people would be keen on using it. This meant that it had to be implemented efficiently. I remember that for many many years, until the late 1970s, FORTRAN set the standards for efficient implementations, and I knew that another language could only gain wide acceptance if its programs would run as efficiently as FORTRAN programs. One of the main stumbling blocks against efficiency was recursion, because it required a stack which, by the way, is also good for other reasons. People who only programmed in FORTRAN didn't see any advantage in using a stack. Later, particularly when writing compilers with recursive descent, I realized myself that recursion was, indeed, a very essential feature. By that time I had also learned that it is not so difficult to implement, particularly because computers had become available with base addressing through registers, which is of course key.

Daylight: With respect to ALGOL60, Dijkstra and Zonneveld were one of the first to implement recursion with their compiler. In August 1960 their compiler was already running. This feat surprised Peter Naur and, well actually, whole Europe if I may say so. For example, some British researchers went to Amsterdam to learn from Dijkstra on how to build an ALGOL60 compiler that could handle recursion. Dijkstra had implemented recursion with one runtime stack, but he had also acknowledged that his ALGOL60 programs were not very efficient in terms of runtime execution. He was looking forward to the day when computers would be fast enough. I think he was referring to the hardware stack. Dijkstra said "look it may not work efficiently today, but it will in the long run". He explained all of this in his keynote speech [64] at Munich 1962.

Wirth: Yes, machines at that time were not really suitable for good languages. They were built for FORTRAN. [W: Laughter] But then machines came up, in particular in 1964 with the IBM System 360, which had an array of registers. They could be used as index registers (all of them) and base registers and that opened the door for efficient implementations of recursion.

Daylight: Was it only because of efficiency reasons that people did not want recursion? Or was it also because they simply did not see how it could be useful in programming?

Wirth: Yes, definitely.

Daylight: Bauer and Samelson had not implemented recursion with their ALCOR compilers.

Wirth: Right.

Daylight: They were very sensitive to the fact that the Amsterdamers *were* doing it. That gives the impression that this was not just a technical dispute.[104] It was also one of . . .

Wirth: Philosophy. [W: Laughter] Which is all the more surprising, because Bauer was also a mathematician. But if you talk about linear algebra, matrix computations and things like that, recursion is not really important. They were thinking in terms of a flat memory. But, of course, as computers became more important there were more applications and more applications where recursion proved to be useful, and compilers were one of the early ones. By the way, if I may insert a comment here, this technique of recursive descent was I think first used by Hoare.

Daylight: Also Grau [111] and Irons [147].

Wirth: Grau, could be. And then there was this new idea, instead of top-down use bottom-up parsing. I continued working on Floyd's idea of precedence grammars, one of the reasons was that then you would not need recursion: everything was a table of syntax data and they had an interpreter running on that. But after the `ALGOL-W` compiler, I abandoned all that work and went back to the recursive descent, which is so much more transparent.

Daylight: Did you work closely with Floyd?

Wirth: No, he was I think in Pittsburgh. Knuth came to Stanford a year after I left or just in the year I left, and he made it the condition for the acceptance of his professorship that also Floyd would be appointed as professor. So Floyd got to Stanford the year after I left.

5.2 The 1970s in Retrospect

Daylight: During the 1960s, electronic technology was advancing drastically. By the end of the 1960s, there seems to have been a major shift in focus among academics: extensibility and maintainability became very important, machine efficiency became much less important. Your own words from a 1988 paper emphasize this:

> [P]rogramming is extending a given system.

> Extensibility is the cornerstone for system development, for it allows us to build new systems on the basis of existing ones and to avoid starting each endeavor from scratch. [305, p.204, my italics]

In order to discuss this shift in focus, I suggest we start with the Software Crisis, discussed at Garmisch 1968. Did the participants, such as yourself, really experience 1968 as a climax, i.e. as a crisis?

5.2.1 Software Crisis – 1968

Wirth: Well, first of all, I must say that I was not at that 1968 conference. But, there was a strong feeling that something had to be done against this fast growing complexity and the inability to produce systems that were bug free. Remember, it was the time when big companies tried to implement time-sharing systems, while our huge machines were used to batch processing only. It was McCarthy who had come up with the idea of time sharing; i.e. multi-processing and multi-user systems. Companies jumped on the idea and announced them long before they had them running. As a result, the implementors were under a terrible pressure while not being prepared for the difficulties which are inherent in multi-programming. That was a real crisis coming up. IBM, for instance, had thousands of programmers working on OS/360 alone. I think the merit of the conference you mentioned is that it brought this word crisis into the open. It was the first time that high-ranking people in these companies confessed that they were in deep trouble, because before that they had kept it under the rug. They didn't want to lose customers to whom they had promised great things. So yes it was a real problem.

Daylight: In the follow-up conference, in 1969, Dijkstra presented his ideas on Structured Programming [71]. That was a reaction to the Software Crisis, wasn't it?

Wirth: Yes, as always, Dijkstra was ahead of the crowd. [W: Laughter] I remember, it must have been in 1965, when I got a monograph of his, 'Notes on Structured Programming'[105]. That was a very revealing writing to me. I mean, I had had all these ideas too, but not really expressed and brought down in clear form on paper. In a way, `Pascal` was my reaction to it. I said to myself "these are great ideas but we must make them available to the programmers, not just in the form of papers, but in a language which incorporated this discipline". That was the idea of `Pascal`.

Daylight: `Pascal` was not only an embodiment of structured programming, it also served Hoare's appeal for axiomatic based semantics.

Wirth: Yes, Hoare's approach was only applicable to a language which had a good phrase structure, and `Pascal` was suitable for that.

5.2.2 Formalisms: Past and Present

Daylight: Continuing with Hoare's axiom-based approach, you have mentioned that:

> The 1970s were also the years when, in the same vein, it was believed that formal development of correctness proofs for programs was the ultimate goal. C.A.R. Hoare had postulated axioms and

> rules of inference about programming notations (it later became
> known as Hoare-logic). He and I undertook the task of defining
> Pascal's semantics formally using this logic. However, we had to
> concede that a number of features had to be omitted from the
> formal definition (e.g., pointers)[106] [307, p.108]

I have the impression that you definitely wanted to try this axiomatic
based approach. But, in a recent paper you wrote:

> Ultimately, analytic verification and correctness proofs were
> supposed to replace testing, but that has not happened. [311,
> p.32]

I believe you also have your reservations about programming languages
that are formally defined in very lengthy documents. Is it correct that
you have a more sober view on formal methods today?

Wirth: Absolutely. You know, actually in just two weeks from now there
is a small conference here, bringing in people from many places about
program verification to celebrate Bertrand Meyer's 60th birthday [56,
201]. They asked me to give a talk and I said yes. And the reason is that
I have a chance to express my reservations. [W: Laughter] They have
kind of flown off in an academic cloud, with high mathematical concepts.
Now, most programmers are not pure mathematicians. With these formal
methods you just put more difficulties in their way instead of removing
them. Program verification, this analytic method of assertions (Hoare's
assertions or Dijkstra's predicate transformers) worked fine for selected
small examples, but not for the big systems. The assertions you can still
use, but formally proving them is another question. I think it is useful
work for teaching programming, carrying a proof with your design is an
important idea. But, the way theoreticians have developed it is like an
academic cloud that moves away from the place where it is supposed to
be.

Daylight: It is very interesting because Dijkstra was not working so
formally in the 1960s. He had to wait until Hoare and others before he
became convinced of the formal approach. But in the second half of his
career, his work was extremely formal.

Wirth: Yes. But I tell you, I am sorry about that. He had left the world
of programmers. In his last ten years of his life he didn't do any computer
science any more, he did mathematics and of course mathematical pearls
and problems. The world of computing felt kind of more and more
distanced from him and didn't take him serious any more. That's too
bad, but an explicable result.

Daylight: I wanted to show you this book, entitled *The School of Niklaus Wirth: the Art of Simplicity* [24]. [W&D: Laughter]

Wirth: That was really great.

Daylight: Then I look at Dijkstra's chapter in this book, in hand writing. [W&D: Laughter] Very formal.

Wirth: Quite something isn't it? [W&D: Laughter]

Daylight: It doesn't really mix with the other contributions in the book.

Wirth: No, and not just because of the hand writing. [W&D: Laughter]

5.2.3 Post-modern Academics

Daylight: This shift in focus during the 1970s was due to the drastic advancement of electronic technology. Also today, efficiency comes in second place, while correctness and simplicity come in first place, right?

Wirth: You should think so, but in practice, does it? I don't know.

Daylight: OK, but I mean in academia.

Wirth: Yes, you are right. But, and we may be drifting off now, how many of the computer science professors do still program? Very few. Of course they say "I can do it and I leave it to my assistants now, I don't need to do it myself", which is of course completely wrong. Because, only if you do it yourself, and I do not mean little Dijkstra examples but real systems (compilers and operating systems), then you see where the troubles lie and that often you yourself do not follow all the high advice that is around. The fact that professors do not do it themselves results in them losing touch and not teaching the important things any more. They drift off to theoretical (intellectually pleasing) things, whereas Parnas wrote that students go into the industry as engineers. Have you seen this paper of his? It's entitled 'Education for Computing Professionals' [235].

Daylight: Not this one, but I have read many of his papers. I would also like to add something to what you just said. You are talking about academics who don't program any more, certainly not operating systems or compilers. If I look at my own education as a software engineer, I was never required to actually build a small compiler or operating system. On the one hand, this is completely understandable, it can even be viewed as scientific progress: abstracting away lower level details allows us to focus solely on the application domain. On the other hand, achievements of first-generation programmers, such as Dijkstra's early contributions, are often not understood by new generations of programmers.

Wirth: Right. We can't change this trend. But we can at least work a little bit against it. For instance, I taught a course on compiler design for several years, and never did I use these thick classical books which contain everything you can possibly know about compilers. Instead, I devised a language called `Pascal-0`. It has just the most basic constructs in it, and then I let the students write a compiler for that language. I gave them so-called skeletons of the modules. First I let them do just the syntax analysis (recursive descent). Then came the part of processing declarations, building the data structures and representing the variables and so on. Finally, code generation. At the end of the 12 or 14 weeks they had succeeded in building their own little compiler. They were always very grateful and said "Ah, now I understand". They could go out to industry and build difficult compilers for difficult languages — they had learned something basic, something which you cannot learn from just reading books. I think we need to teach more and more in this way, but it's only possible if the teacher has done it himself. I always did things first myself, I would have felt too insecure otherwise.

Daylight: You have also used the term post-modern in your writings:

> [I]n this *post-modern* academic environment the professor has long ago ceased to be the wise, learned man, penetrating deeper and deeper into his beloved subject in his quiet study. The modern professor is the manager of a large research team of researchers, the keen fund raiser maintaining close relationships with the key funding agencies, and the untiring author of exciting project proposals and astonishing success stories. [310, p.2, my italics]

But this also immediately explains that, even if the academic would want to work on operating systems, he would have a hard time trying to sell it as something new. The typical reaction would be "oh, we already know all we ought to know about operating systems, don't look at that, do something else".

Wirth: Right. We have too much innovation in our field and too little work towards perfection. Engineers cannot do something on the first shot and get everything right. They usually do something and then improve and tune, and that's not done in software where programmers just have to write more code. After all, nobody knows how much software there is, only the computer!

Daylight: Tony Hoare says something which I find a bit ironic. He says that he actually has more freedom at Microsoft Research and hence in industry, compared to when he worked at university. Of course, this is also partly due to his status. But still, Microsoft and Google have more money for fundamental research than academia.

Wirth: Far more money. They are the only ones who can fund such senior research positions and say "Do whatever you please, we don't care. You do something good, we know your reputation." Universities don't do that any more. A typical professor is expected to bring in a lot more money than he earns himself. But that's beside the point. [W&D: Laughter]

Daylight: Universities today have to focus on what sells. In your own words:

> Universities have traditionally been exempt from this commercial focus. Universities were places where people were expected to ponder about what matters in the long run. [311, p.38]

It is interesting to note that during the 1940s and 1950s computers were being built at universities. Later, computer manufacturing moved entirely to industry. During the 1950s and 1960s, several new programming languages were being designed by academics. Later, industry chose its favourite languages such as C, C++, and Java. As a result, academia, to a large extent stopped designing new languages. To obtain research funds, academics are now required to work with these languages, even though there are much better languages available, as you have often remarked in your writings. I don't know how this trend will continue. But, perhaps the real scholar, who also wants to read books — in fact, most professors don't even have the time to read any more — should just not work at university. Trying to counter this forceful trend doesn't seem like a good idea.

Wirth: Yes, it has become impossible. Languages like C were developed in industry, at research institutes of AT&T. Also C++ was developed there. Java at Sun and C# at Microsoft. Now we have Go at Google. Everyone wants to have his own language except they are very much the same. The time of language definitions, I'm afraid, has gone by. Everybody, when they talk about language, they mainly talk about the syntax and that's world-wide C, whether you like it or not. Once something has established itself, it is very hard to go against it. You have to have very good reasons. The same holds for computer architectures. Intel was the first to bring out the 8080. Only half a year later came Motorola 6800, which was really much better. Later on Intel came out with the 8086, and I think half a year later Motorola brought out the 68000, which was again a much better design. But nobody talks about Motorola any more.

Intel is the only one that still exists. So, on the one hand, there is a lot of inertia in the user community. On the second hand, the first thing that establishes itself is hard to remove.

Daylight: So the time has passed for academics to define new programming languages.

Wirth: Yes, even though better programming languages are badly needed, it doesn't happen. `Pascal` made a big step from `FORTRAN`. `ALGOL` was not known except in Europe in some places, and for everything that followed the step was smaller. In order to introduce something new the step must be sizable to warrant a change.

5.2.4 Bloated Software

Daylight: Another development since the 1960s is that:

> Programs and systems have become increasingly complex and almost impossible for a single individual to fully understand. [311]

Moreover, you say:

> Our limitations in designing complex systems are no longer determined by slow hardware, but *by our own intellectual capability*. From experience, we know that most programs could be significantly improved, made more reliable, more economical, and easier to use. [311, p.32, my italics]

What I am trying to get at is Martin Reiser's law which you have referred to. It states that:

> Software is getting slower faster than hardware is getting faster. [306, p.64]

Coming then to my question about Microsoft's software: it has become so complicated that not a single person can understand the whole system. Is it correct that Microsoft programmers are basically forced to just add new functionality to their software, thereby creating fat software.

Wirth: Yes.

Daylight: What exactly does fat software mean? How do you recognize it?

Wirth: People also call it bloated. Blown up to big size, because you don't have the time to think it over and make a structure which allows it to be dense.

Daylight: Do you think the people who are involved are aware of this problem?

Wirth: Oh yes, most of them, probably not every one. And certainly at Microsoft they are.

Daylight: But isn't that then a motivation for them to start from scratch?

Wirth: I tell you a story. I had an excellent PhD student here in the 1980s who later went to America. He tried to found his own little company there but that didn't work very well. So I recommended him to join Microsoft. He designed for `Lilith` the font systems. I had visited him around 1994, and I said "Well look, you are known as a very competent man who keeps things straight and understands things. You are working on this Word system, it's obviously grown far too big and complex. In my opinion, starting from scratch would be the right thing. Why don't you try to do that?" And he said "Well, I have." Several years before he had had that very idea. He had subsequently climbed up the ladder to Bill Gates and presented his proposal to him. He was so convincing that Gates said "Yes, let's do that. You start with your group." And they worked busily on this. Their software was supposedly very good, and then Microsoft sent out sales people into the field to ask the customers what they would think of it. Everybody said "Oh thank God, yes, we are so tired of this unreliable Word system. We will be very happy to adopt it under one condition: it has to be able to process all our texts and it has to be upward compatible", essentially saying "We have invested so much in learning to use this system that we don't want to lose this investment". So, he went back and said "Well, if we have to be fully compatible, then we have to have specifications of the Word system. Where are the specifications?" The answer was "In the code". The result was that the whole thing was scrapped because you could only copy the Word system. The moral of the story is that one has to be careful in blaming big companies for this stand still. It's the customers who don't want to move. That's not only for the Word system, it's for many other things too.

5.3   Embedded Systems

Daylight: Bloated software can lead to even bigger problems when dealing with embedded systems. Do you know Chuck Moore, the inventor of the **Forth** programming language? He talks misgivingly about layers of fat and is an expert in real-time embedded systems. The following words capture his thoughts[107]:

> Computers today are typically deployed with a large amount of software, supplying a hierarchy of languages. The assembler defines the language for describing the compiler and supervisor. The supervisor defines the language for job control. The compiler defines the language for application programs. An application program defines the language for its input. "The user may not know, or know of, all these languages but they are there. They stand between him and his computer, imposing restrictions on what he can do and what it will cost. And cost it does, for this vast hierarchy of languages requires a huge investment of man and machine time to produce, and an equally large effort to maintain. The cost of documenting these programs and of reading the documentation is enormous. And after all this effort the programs are still full of bugs, awkward to use and satisfying to no one."

As a remedy, Chuck Moore suggests to replace the vast hierarchy of languages with just a single layer. It's an extreme approach, but that's what he does with his **Forth** system. He works in industry, more as a consultant pushing technology, than as someone who has to abide by a market-pull strategy. That is, he doesn't have to listen to Microsoft or others, he is his own boss and, in fact, very successful. For embedded systems he seems to have his own niche, presumably because the bloated-software approach does not work here. In short, he recommends to get rid of all these layers of fat. Not only because they contain many bugs, but also, if you want to talk about real time, there's a lot of . . .

Wirth: Overhead.

Daylight: Yes, you have unpredictability due to all these software layers. Coming to your **Oberon**, I see similarities there, in the philosophy.

Wirth: Yes. I think for system building, we should try at a single language. There is absolutely no reason not to do so, as we have shown. We have described the whole system from device drivers to graphic editors, application programs in a single language (**Oberon**) which is *much* simpler than **Java** and all this. So I could support that statement. It is also much easier if you only have one language. No "integration" is necessary. On the other hand, if there is a future in designing newer languages, it's languages for particular application areas. For instance, an accountant only needs mirroring his accounting rules and processes. Or a machine designer has to have a language abstracting his machines. For specifically application-oriented tasks, I could see much more need for tailored languages. But, as far as system software is concerned, I agree with him. `Oberon` is of course an indirect descendant from `Pascal` or `ALGOL` if you want, with `Modula` in between. Just like `Pascal` embodied the ideas of structured programming, `Modula` took up the ideas of modularisation and separate compilation, and `Oberon` all these together with object orientation. So the languages really are just the tools to formulate the ideas and to support a discipline, never an end in themselves.

Daylight: `Oberon` is also a tool for extensibility; this is something you say often. [W: Yes] And also for real-time systems.

Wirth: Not specifically.

Daylight: But it can also be used for that.

Wirth: Right, it has no obstacles against it. Let's put it this way.

5.3.1   Extensibility versus Performance

Daylight: Which I find very interesting, because I always thought that striving for extensibility would lead to fat layers of software. But apparently that need not be the case: it is possible to have extensible systems which are also thin and workable in real time.

Wirth: Yes, that's of course the key.   Not to involve any heavy mechanisms.

Daylight: It's even possible to have an object-oriented real-time system, because you explain in one of your papers how you steered model helicopters [309].

Wirth: Yes, although object orientation hardly played a role there. But, object orientation and extensibility, in my view, are more or less the same thing.   Or, if you like, object orientation is an implementation of extensibility. The object orientation lets you extend existing data structures without changing what exists. You can specialize certain data structures for specific applications by attaching new attributes and attach the operators to the data structures. That's the corner stone of extensibility.

Daylight: But what if this extensibility would imply that you have to do a lot of runtime checking?

Wirth: Well that's the key, that you design your system that you do *not* have to do that.

Daylight: That's the crux of `Oberon`.

Wirth: You cannot reduce runtime checking to zero if you want a safe system together with type flexibility. My idea has always been, starting from `ALGOL` and `Pascal`, that you have a safe type system and static type checking done by the compiler, not burdening the runtime system. As soon as you have object orientation, and if an extension is always compatible with its base type, then you cannot get around some runtime checks. The key is to make them as cheap as possible. In `Oberon` this amounts to essentially one compare instruction, so the checking overhead is negligible.

It's the same thing with subroutines. You pay a little bit of overhead for the calling and the returning and for parameterization of the indirect addressing and so on. The question is always: is it worth that extra effort? If the effort is small enough, as it is for procedures and parameterizations now, if it's that small on modern computers, people don't think about it any more.

This type checking is definitely a great advantage and helps a lot. To implement it so efficiently, even for extensible systems, I think that was the most important implementation achievement I did in `Oberon`. If you have static typing, you can forget about it after the compiler is through. In the case of the extensible systems where runtime checking is required, we have so efficient processors now, that the runtime overhead is not the foremost concern at all any more.

We have other inefficiencies which are a thousand times more affective. If you look at Windows or Unix systems, the same package is present a hundred times in the various application packages, which may be encoded at the same time because it wasn't resolved in the right way. (In `Oberon` you have no module more than once.) These systems use megabytes, first of all because the megabytes are available, and second because they are not well thought through. But since the megabytes are available, nobody thinks of better solutions.

5.3.2   Starting from Scratch

Daylight: Sticking to real-time embedded systems, you have, like Chuck Moore, thrown functionality over board too. You wrote:

> The next decision was to eliminate the RT-OS [Real-Time Operating System], as it seemed possible to do essentially without concurrent processes in the form of threads. [309, p.489]

Wirth: You are talking about my helicopter project now. [W: Laughter] Now we are moving more into the present time.

Daylight: Or the cache and pipelining. You threw those over board as well.

Wirth: Yes. I got in touch with that group that had built the model helicopters because I had heard of their success in a competition. I wanted to have a look at their work and asked myself "what have they done?". They explained things to me, they had the dual 486 processor configuration and real-time operating system and so on and so on. I looked at this more closely and I found that they had so much machinery underneath a little algorithm. First of all, I said you don't need that. So, we got rid of that real-time operating system. Remember, they were mechanical engineers, relying on commercial software. The second thing was to get rid of the processors. Instead of a big box, I did everything on one small board with a new low-power ARM. It needed about a twentieth of the power that they needed before. This meant that the battery could be much smaller and lighter, and the flight duration much longer. The algorithm was so simple that I did not need an operating system at all. That was actually the surprising thing. If you think through it, carefully, possibilities for simplification emerge. Because you have no creation of processes and no deletion. You have essentially just two processes, you could boil down everything to that.

Daylight: The reason why operating systems were introduced historically was because multiple users wanted to run their own programs on the same expensive computer. But if you look in this context, you just don't need it. Isn't this then again an example where people are just blindly reusing past solutions and then somebody who is very experienced says "wait, you can throw it away, you don't need it"? The same holds for the cache which you threw over board as well. Blindly reusing functionality has its price. Breaking the encapsulations between the modules can result in factors less physical memory accesses and, hence, in far less energy consumption. This is important for a battery-driven mobile phone.

Wirth: You pay a price for all those things which you don't know are there. Good engineering avoids producing superfluous things. But, of course, I understand the mechanical engineers, they had heard about languages, operating systems and real time, and thought to themselves "well that will solve our problem". They should have realized that they didn't need it, but they were so involved in their own problem domain of control systems that they didn't look at the real-time operating system. That was just a black box for them.

Daylight: The reaction I often get when discussing this with others is that the systems have become so complicated that it is not possible any more for a single person to understand the whole system: "We cannot know everything." But if we are talking about real-time systems like the model helicopters, you say:

> The designer of embedded systems should be a mechanical, electrical, and software engineer all in one. [309, p.491]

Henzinger & Sifakis have said something very similar:

> [T]he powerful separation of computation (software) from physicality (platform and environment) — traditionally, a central enabling concept in computer science — *does not work for embedded systems.* Instead, embedded systems design requires a more *holistic* approach that integrates essential paradigms from hardware and software design and control theory. [122, p.33, my italics]

Wirth: Yes, you should have at least one person in the team who has the bird's eye view. If you don't, you have to be very careful not to acquire more things than you really need. They should have known how much space the real-time operating system uses, how much overhead it produces. That is, they should have known the specifications of the services offered by the system and then analyzed which parts of the services they really needed. They didn't do a careful analysis.

Daylight: So having talked about these bloated systems, I would like to go back to Dijkstra and his work on the THE operating system. He designed that system by introducing several program layers [117, p.11]. The lowest layers dealt with processors and physical memory, thereby allowing the higher layers to abstract away from them. I can understand that these abstractions are very useful for building a general-purpose operating system. But, if we are dealing with a real-time operating system, where experts say that you need to be aware of the physical mechanics of the system, isn't it then possible that people are blindly reusing Dijkstra's design approach in unintended ways? [W: Laughter] For the helicopter system you threw away the interrupt concept, right?

Wirth: I used exactly one interrupt and that's a milli-second clock which drives the mechanism that gathers the sensor data and outputs the servo data at a fixed rate. But there are many applications where that is not good enough, I am fully aware of that. But I concentrated on this application. It's always a nice concept of abstracting, it's very helpful, but you should not exaggerate. You should not abstract so far from your application that you don't know any more where it is. Here I asked myself, you have these many real-time processes going on. What is really the basic need? I found that just this one-cycle clock would suffice, it's enough.

5.3.3 ADA

Daylight: A related topic is the ADA programming language. Many academics were asked to scrutinize ADA.

Wirth: Including Hoare. [W: Laughter]

Daylight: You, Hoare, Dijkstra, and others. Not only academics, though. The Department of Defense (DoD) really tried to get the best expertise from the international computing community. So they sent language designs in many revisions to several people, but eventually the academics simply didn't like it. In your own words:

> ADA was devised according to a large document of requirements that the designers could not control. These requirements were difficult, extensive, partly *inconsistent*, and some were even *contradictory*. As a result, its complexity grew beyond what I considered acceptable. [308, p.117, my italics]

And I also found this again in Dijkstra's writings. Do you recall some examples? Do you think there are also some good features in ADA or is it all bad?

Wirth: Certainly there are some good features, they took over the whole idea of structured programming and data structures. If you want, from Pascal or Modula. Actually, Tony Hoare and I were called to California for a whole week of consulting when there were four proposals to be submitted to the DoD and we consulted for Stanford Research Institute. We didn't do a good job for them, because we said: "get rid of this, get rid of that, oh that's superfluous too, make it simpler". That's not what the DoD wanted. Hoare once said: "look, what I could recommend to you most is to use Pascal, it exists, we know what it is". But they wanted their own big language, and of course what happened is what we also saw at that consulting week: it became a big thing. That always happens when you have committees, everyone tries to bring in his own idea. At the end you have the union instead of the intersection of ideas. [W: Laughter] If I have one reservation about ADA, it is that it has become too big, too cloggy, too cumbersome, which holds just as well for Java and C#. They break down under their own weight. I am sorry, it is a recurring story. It was the same thing the first time with PL/I. We all experienced that in the mid-60s, and the same thing happened with ALGOL68, I am afraid.

5.4   Epilogue: a Depressing State of Affairs

Daylight: When I read your work along with that of Hoare and Dijkstra, I cannot fail to notice that you are really crying for the intellect, for common sense. [W: Yes] I am just curious how many academics today are still hearing this cry. Or have they become indoctrinated by the Microsoft/Google kind of research?

Wirth: I am afraid so. Yes, I am a bit discouraged. Depressed some times. I was very sorry when Dijkstra died. I immediately realized that an important voice had been lost. It hasn't been replaced. Some people said nobody can take him seriously any more, but still the voice was important. He was just brilliant in formulating ideas.

Daylight: Instead of scrutinizing popular programming languages, we could just as well discuss hardware-design languages, such as Verilog and VHDL.

Wirth: If you look at them closely, Verilog represents the American way of doing hardware design in C. Verilog has adopted the syntax of C. And VHDL has ADA syntax. I don't want to really criticize or compare the two, but one thing is that both systems have become very heavy things. Of course, compiling a software program and compiling a hardware program into a circuit are two very different things. The latter is much more complicated because you have to produce layouts and do a lot of optimization. Nevertheless, I feel we are thrown back at the 1960s. For example, when I do some corrections in my program or my circuit and then push the compile button, I have to wait half an hour for it to recompile! And that for a program that is only four pages long. In the meantime I have to drink coffee or devote my attention to some other problems. Moreover, it has happened more than once that, although compilation ends with "successfully completed", I find that something doesn't run properly after all. Based on further testing I then find the error in my program, an error which could easily have been detected by a simple type check. When I once forgot to specify the correct dimension of a variable, it didn't warn me. Instead, it gave me 200 other warnings — so many that one ignores them. Or once I forgot to declare a variable, again a mistake which I had to detect by myself. The variable had to correspond to an array of 16 bits, but the system put in a single bit. The system didn't tell me "forgot to declare" instead, it "helped" by substituting its own declaration. This in 2010, it is incredible! Often it seems like these people have completely ignored what computer scientists have experienced during the last 40 years.

Daylight: I don't think they look at the literature, because, again, everybody is so busy. When you do show them a technical paper containing a solution, they say "oh, it's just mathematics".

Wirth: They always find an excuse.

Daylight: The programming language papers presented at top conferences are very formal using, for instance, formalized type systems. But, the techniques have to work on C or on C++. It is a bit ironic because as a researcher you thus have to work a posteriori: start with the bad languages and then try to make good.

Wirth: And preserve upward compatibility, which means that the type system may detect errors or it may not.

Daylight: It's discouraging to get into software. [W&D: Laughter]

Wirth: Yes it is. I'm afraid it is.

Daylight: Niklaus Wirth, thank you very much for this interview.

Wirth: You're welcome.

6. Barbara Liskov and Data Abstraction

To help document the history of software engineering, I have conducted a discussion with Barbara Liskov, the 2008 Turing Award winner. Topics of interest are her pioneering work on layered operating system design and her ideas on abstraction which she mainly developed during the 1970s. On the one hand, Turing's work and mathematical logic are only mentioned in passing because Liskov did not rely on it much to advance her research. Dijkstra's and Wirth's work on structured programming, on the other hand, are discussed in detail. Both receptions are, nevertheless, noteworthy. Documenting the first reception albeit briefly is as important as documenting the second because it helps capture the extent of Turing's influence on software engineering.

Meeting Barbara Liskov

My discussion with Liskov took place on 15 December 2010 in the Stata Center, 9th-floor, Vassar Street 32, MIT, Cambridge, MA, USA. Its digital recordings were transcribed by me and subsequently edited by Liskov and myself. The picture of Liskov and me on the back cover of this book was taken after our discussion right outside her office.

Short Biography of Barbara Liskov

Barbara Liskov was born on 7 November 1939 in Los Angeles and grew up in San Francisco. She received a BA in mathematics in 1961 from the University of California at Berkeley and subsequently took up a job as computer programmer at the Mitre Corporation in Boston and later at Harvard University. Afterwards, she was John McCarthy's PhD student at Stanford University, researching chess endgames (1963–1968). She then returned to the Mitre Corporation to work on systems programming as a research-staff member. Four years later, in 1972, she joined the faculty at MIT and has remained there since. Liskov has received several awards for her research, including the Society of Women Engineers Achievement Award (1996), IEEE's John von Neumann Medal (2004), ACM SIGPLAN's Programming Language Achievement Award (2008), and ACM's Turing Award (2008).

6.1 Early Years

Daylight: Barbara Liskov, you were born on 7 November 1939 in Los Angeles and became the first of four children "in a family that greatly valued education" [114]. What does that mean?

Liskov: My father was a lawyer and my mother was a house wife with a college education. The path to success was education, so it was expected that I would go to college; everybody in our family was going to go to college. My brother is nine years younger. So maybe I got more encouragement because that's a pretty common pattern in a family where there is a girl standing in for a boy. I was always encouraged to do very well in school. There wasn't any specific encouragement to be interested in math or science; it was just in general doing well in everything.

Daylight: You were five years old when World War II ended. Do you remember anything?

Liskov: Not much of course, but I do recall them shooting off fire works to celebrate victory.

Daylight: How would you describe the 1950s? The USA had won the war. So I would assume that in this part of the world it must have been a really good period.

Liskov: Well, of course I was a kid so I had nothing to compare it with. But it seems to me it was a period of great prosperity. The USA was well thought of in the world, sort of leading culturally. Whatever happened in the USA spread to Europe. From the point of view of what was going on with women, it wasn't such a great time. All the women were sent home from the factory as soon as the men came back from World War II. The 1950s was I think a time of great conformity, where there was this ideal family with the wife at home while the husband in his suit was at work. And the new car every year, it was very materialistic. My family was a little unusual because we didn't do that. My father was very aware of this kind of thing. We used to talk about how silly it was.

Daylight: Were your parents Americans?

Liskov: My father's parents immigrated from Europe. He was a first generation. My mother's parents were born in the USA. My mother's mother was born in San Francisco, so on my mother's side we were multiple generation San Franciscans. But my father's family came from Poland or Russia and settled in Portland, Maine which is on the east coast.

Daylight: Did you have any hobbies or were you already very much into science?

Liskov: I had a lot of hobbies in my youth and I did folk dancing at college. I had friends who were climbers so I used to go along on these trips but I didn't like it because I have no head for heights. I was also dating, so it wasn't like I was working all the time. I was living a fairly normal life for a young woman except for the fact that I was majoring in math and later went on to get a PhD which was not so typical.

Daylight: You finished your BA in mathematics in 1961. And then you applied for graduate mathematics programs at Berkeley and Princeton?

Liskov: Yes, I can't really remember where else I applied. I was thinking of going to graduate school, I applied to a few places, and then I decided it would be better not to go to school right away. So I went and got a job instead.

Daylight: Which was all the way in Boston.

Liskov: That was because my father's family came from Boston, so I thought it would be interesting to see what it was like living there.

Daylight: How would you explain to a European the difference between the west and east of the USA?

Liskov: Well, it was a bigger difference then than it is now. There were airplanes then too but it was much more of a deal to take a plane ride. Now people do it all the time. Nevertheless, it's 3000 miles away. The way that Silicon Valley has developed is certainly a phenomenon. That wasn't in evidence at the time that we are talking about, because that hadn't started yet. Certainly, LA has always been different because that was the movie capital. So that's kind of different from every place else. I actually think the west and east are not that dissimilar, what's different is the south, the central part of the country — and you can see that by looking at the election maps, which allow you to sense what the political climate of the country is. I think maybe Europeans don't understand how heterogeneous the USA is. They tend to think of it as one country like they have.

In my case it's just that my father's family came from the east and I had relatives there that I didn't know very well. I had been there a couple of times, and I had a friend who was interested in doing the same thing, so we decided to do it together. It was like an adventure.

Daylight: You worked in Boston at the Mitre Corporation.

Liskov: For a year. Mitre is a company that works primarily on government contracts. It does a fair amount of research as well as development and of course, at that time, I was just working as a programmer. So I was writing code.

Daylight: In which language did you do that?

Liskov: FORTRAN. My first day on the job they handed me a FORTRAN manual and they gave me a little problem to write a program for. So, I was entirely self taught.

Daylight: Afterwards you went to Stanford to study, right?

Liskov: Well, actually I worked at Mitre for a year and then I worked at Harvard for a year. At Harvard I worked on the language translation project as a programmer. There I was writing code in assembler and maintaining a huge program written in assembler. I made that switch primarily because, again, it was something new to try plus I was living in Cambridge so it was much more convenient. They were working on English and the program I was maintaining was trying to parse English sentences. But the goal of the project was to translate between different languages.

Daylight: The name that comes to my mind is Chomsky. But of course that doesn't mean you were working with him.

Liskov: No, Chomsky wasn't at Harvard. I was working with Tony Oettinger and Susumo Kuno was, I think, a research associate working with him. I didn't know Oettinger well. I didn't interact with him much because I was just a programmer. But he was the leader of the project. I had much more interaction with Susumo whom I have not seen since. But, remember, I wasn't even a graduate student, while they were faculty members. So there was a big divide there.

Daylight: After that you went to Stanford, which did not have a computer science department at that time. Did you see Wirth, Knuth, or Floyd there?

Liskov: When I got there in 1963 none of them was there yet, John McCarthy was and I started to work with him. Niklaus Wirth showed up

— I'm not sure exactly when — maybe in 1965. Knuth didn't come until after I had left. He might have been there as a visitor but I don't really remember, because the AI lab where I did most of my work was not on campus, it was up in the hills. So by the time I was in my third year and working mostly on research, I was almost never down in the main buildings. Therefore, I didn't get to interact very much. I had Niklaus Wirth for a course, probably in my second year, so I was definitely still on campus when he arrived.

Daylight: Apparently you met McCarthy the first day you were at Stanford [114]. Is this correct?

Liskov: Well this is my recollection but I couldn't swear that it's accurate. We were both walking up the stairs and I asked him if he could support me. Now, in retrospect, this seems like a highly unlikely story, so I really don't know exactly what happened. But certainly I met him very early on because I did start to work with him almost immediately.

Daylight: Did you know who he was before you were there?

Liskov: No.

Daylight: How would you describe him at that time and were you a shy person or were you at that point in your life very confident, knowing where you were heading?

Liskov: No no, I was pretty shy and pretty unconfident I would say. As far as McCarthy was concerned, again, I felt there was a huge gulf. It wasn't like I knew him on any sort of personal level. As an advisor he was pretty hands off. He wasn't somebody who interacted with his students on a regular basis, nor did he have any sort of student organization where the students talked to each other about their work. Everybody was kind of working independently on their own projects.

Daylight: Was that typical for that time or was it typically John McCarthy?

Liskov: I think it has a lot to do with the particular advisor. I think each advisor has a style.

Daylight: Your PhD was about chess endgames. Could you elaborate a bit on that?

Liskov: The thesis was about the endgames that are solvable. For example, king and queen against king is a solvable endgame. The purpose of the thesis was to figure out the strategies that would enable the program to always win these games. John McCarthy thought I would be a good person to do this thesis because I wasn't a chess player and he felt that if you were a chess player you would already have your ideas about how to do it, but what he wanted was to go back to the books and look how the books said you should do it and then translate that into code. Now, in those days chess was a big challenge. Nowadays, of course, it's not much of a challenge and people use very deep searches to figure out what's going on. But back then you couldn't afford to do deep search, you had to be more clever about how to prune the tree so that you could do productive things without searching very much.

Daylight: In what language did you program that?

Liskov: LISP. And I must have learned — I'm trying to remember — did I learn Pascal? I'm not sure Pascal existed then. I learned some language, maybe ALGOL. I'm sure I learned ALGOL. Whether I actually programmed in it is another matter and for some classes we were, I believe, using the Burroughs 5000.

Daylight: Did you talk to McCarthy a lot even though he had everyone work independently?

Liskov: No. Once in a while I would see him. It was hard to get an appointment. They tended to be rather brief.

Daylight: Did you nevertheless learn anything about his work on ALGOL?

Liskov: No, and I knew very little about what he was doing on other projects. I was pretty focused on my own stuff and I think I've always kept my vision quite narrow because that's the way to make progress without getting distracted by a lot of other things. I'm not saying it's his fault, it might have also been the way I do things. I was in the lab and Raj Reddy was working on his robot arm which was his PhD thesis. And then there was a fellow named Jim Painter who was working on the theory of computation with McCarthy, which in retrospect would probably have been much more interesting to me than what I did work on because I'm actually a systems person, not an AI person. I took a lot of courses from Dana Scott who was at Stanford at the time. So I learned all that logic stuff, which I've never done anything with. [L: Laughter]

Daylight: Did you learn about Turing machines from Scott?

Liskov: I can't remember. I do recall undecidability and related topics.

6.2   Early Work of Contemporaries

Daylight: I have here this 1956 book *Automata Studies* [272] which is quite theoretical.

Liskov: I don't think I ever took a course in computer science theory. I took a course in compilers. I sat in on a course on numerical analysis because that was required. Of course, I took courses from Dana Scott but they were really more on logic than on computer science. So this book doesn't look at all familiar to me.

Daylight: McCarthy's paper in this book is called 'The Inversion of Functions Defined by Turing Machines' [272, p.157].

Liskov: No, I don't remember that at all.

Daylight: He explains, by means of Turing machines, how to solve intellectual problems. You worked on chess endgames so I thought there might be a link with your work.

Liskov: There wasn't anything formal in my thesis. John McCarthy was working with Dana Scott, probably because John was interested in formal analysis. But I don't know exactly what they were working on.

Daylight: I also brought this 1961 book *Computer Programming and Formal Systems* [27]. This book is a result of some logicians and programmers getting together, in North Holland. McCarthy's contribution is this book is his paper 'A Basis for a Mathematical Theory of Computation' [27, p.33]. He mentions the Advice Taker in this paper.

Liskov: I might have read some papers by John. I remember propositional calculus but I don't remember this paper specifically. The Advice Taker was an AI program. The paper on the Advice Taker was written by Newell and Simon I think. So it probably came out of the group at Carnegie Mellon.

Daylight: In 1970 you married Nate Liskov. You went back to the Mitre Corporation but now on the research staff. I assume that was the time you realized what you really want to do?

Liskov: I had realized that before. I knew in my third or fourth year of graduate school that I was more interested in systems than in AI. It was partly because I felt that AI was too hard. I was very interested in machine learning, but machine learning at that time was all based on the idea that the machines would work like people work. Today, of course, they don't do machine learning like people learn at all. They just use statistics and so forth. I just felt that I wasn't making headway on anything that was interesting. Then I did this thesis which I was able to slug away at and finish. It was interesting in its own little way but I didn't find it extremely compelling. In the meantime, I was much more interested in languages and systems. So I knew that I wanted to switch areas. I just decided not to do it until after I was finished with my PhD. As soon as I got to Mitre I switched and started working in systems.

Daylight: That's where you designed a computer architecture which also led to the Venus operating system. You also became very active in programming methodology, right?

Liskov: Yes, but my work on programming methodology only started in 1970 or so. The first couple of years at Mitre I was working on building the Venus machine on top of the Interdata 3 and then the Venus operating system using the Venus machine. It was only when that project was over that I started working on programming methodology.

Daylight: The 1960s were of course also the years of ALGOL60 and ALGOL68. Did these languages have any direct influence on you?

Liskov: ALGOL68 was definitely an influence. I probably didn't get to know it until after I was at MIT. When I was at Mitre, I was focused on systems work. When I got to MIT I started looking at languages.

Daylight: I have here the proceedings from Garmisch 1968, *Software Engineering* [221]. The words software crisis were introduced there along with Dijkstra's paper 'Complexity controlled by hierarchical ordering of function and variability' [221, p.181].

Liskov: I don't recall that particular paper. Dijkstra wrote a lot of papers and, other than the ones I referenced in my own papers, I couldn't tell you whether I've read other papers of his.

Daylight: The year after Garmisch 1968, a follow-up conference was held. The proceedings were edited by Buxton and Randell [33]. Dijkstra's paper in that proceedings was his 'Structured Programming' [33, p.84] — not to be confused with his 'Notes on Structured Programming' which is in this now famous book called *Structured Programming* [45, p.1–72].

Liskov: That book [45] was one I read very thoroughly. I certainly may have read other works of Dijkstra, but I don't remember.

Daylight: Dijkstra's paper 'Structured Programming' [33, p.84] is about a necklace of pearls. He introduced pearls as a form of analogy.

Liskov: I remember those pearls. If you think about it, it's a strange analogy. Because it isn't really a necklace. Concerning these ideas about top-down design, I'm pretty sure that it was Wirth's paper on stepwise refinement [303] that I found to be the most influential. But they are all talking about the same thing and Dijkstra has a paper here [33, p.84] which is about that too.

Daylight: What about this one, Dijkstra's 'The Structure of the "THE"-Multiprogramming System' [70]?

Liskov: Yes, definitely I read that. That's the paper where Dijkstra introduced the notion of semaphores. I put semaphores into the Venus machine, so I decided that they were very nice and that it would be very good for the hardware to have direct support for synchronization. Actually, when you think about this in retrospect it was an interesting thing to do. Nowadays they have *test* and *set* (or something like that) with basic support from the hardware level but in those days they didn't have that stuff, probably because they weren't thinking much about multiprogramming. I actually met Dijkstra. I believe he came to Mitre and I talked to him sometime in maybe 1969 — I don't remember specifically when it was — and we were talking about the ideas in that paper [70]. It was before I finished working on the Venus hardware.

Daylight: How would you describe Dijkstra? He must have had a Dutch accent I assume.

Liskov: But his English was good. What I recall is that we had a conversation about synchronization primitives.

Daylight: Concerning early data-centric approaches, in your 1975 paper 'Data types and program correctness' [173] you referred to the work of George Mealy [191], Jay Earley [88], and Robert Balzer [12].

Liskov: I vaguely remember Jay Earley doing some work on program languages. I probably read his paper when I was working on abstract data types, so after having joined MIT.

Daylight: Jay Earley advocated a separation between specification and implementation. George Mealy, in turn, advocated user-defined data types. He said:

> [W]hat we really need is fewer data types along with apparatus which will allow the user to define his own. [191, p.532]

Liskov: I did read papers by Mealy but they did not stick in comparison to some of the other ones. But clearly that quote is asking for abstract data types.

Daylight: What about Bob Balzer, did you know him at the time? His manuscript from 1967 is called 'Dataless Programming' [12].

Liskov: That's his PhD thesis. I remember it. I met Bob very early on, I believe it was during the early 1970s. Bob's PhD thesis is one of many papers that I read after 1972. Steve Zilles and I read it. We also read Jay Earley's paper — I remember now. The Mealy paper I had probably read earlier because that was more in the programming methodology domain.

What Bob Balzer proposes in his PhD thesis is a constrained way of viewing data, in terms of a fixed set of operations without any abstraction. So there is no information hiding. He also had syntax tricks so that operations could be written in the syntax in a particular manner. His work was a step along the way but it didn't really get to data abstraction, partly because there was no abstraction and partly because it was too constrained. You have to realize that in preparation for my Turing lecture I went back and reread lots of papers. So I'm not telling you today what I remembered from reading this in 1972. I'm telling you today what I remember because I read it last year.

Daylight: How did Balzer's work fit into the bigger research picture of extensible (higher level) languages? Why were universal languages discussed so heavily at that time?

Liskov: Well, today we know we can write any program in a universal language such as C or Java, but at that time people were worried about whether you could do this. The source of their worry was that whenever you provide a higher level language, you take away the features of the underlying machine, because you replace that machine with a higher level and you're supposed to use the machine only through that higher level. And they were worried that the loss of expressiveness from the lower level to the higher level might be a serious problem. And, it is a problem if you think about writing low-level systems in Java today; you do sometimes dip down into C in order to accomplish a few things very efficiently. But, in general, by now we understand that you can write programs in any universal programming language. The work on extensible languages was intended to try to address this problem with universal languages. As Schuman and Jourrand pointed out in their very interesting paper [271], there were two different approaches being looked at: syntactic and semantic.

What was meant by syntactic was that you could extend the syntax of the programming language. On the surface this is a plausible idea. You say "Well, I have to use factorial a lot, so why can't I take that exclamation point and make it mean the factorial function? That would make it so much easier for me to write my programs." In reality it is an absolutely dreadful idea because we know today that reading programs matters much more than writing them. A program is written once, it's read by its author over and over again, and by the tenth time you read it you forget what you were doing, and then it's read by other people in your group and five years later somebody has to maintain it. So reading programs is what really matters, not writing them. To read a program you have to understand its syntax and so what you'd like is at least a syntax that doesn't change.

The other thing Schuman and Jourrand talked about though was what they referred to as semantic extensions. Bob Balzer's thesis in 1967 was an example of this. Bob assumed that all data types were collections. He said every data type should have four operations. There is an operation to *put* something in the collection, to *remove* something from the collection, to *see* what's in the collection, and to *modify* something in the collection. And then he invented ways of using special syntax for this. So you can see this is a step along the way to abstract data types except, of course, all data types are not collections and it would be very inconvenient to say they all have to have the same set of operations. Not only that, there was no encapsulation. So it was just a kind of a sugaring on the language; it didn't provide you with any way of protecting what you were doing.

Daylight: Balzer said there are typically four steps a programmer takes to code a problem, cited after [12, p.1]:

1. Define the problem.

2. Analyze the processing requirements.

3. Choose a data representation on the basis of these requirements.

4. Code the problem.

He wanted to switch the third and fourth step because:

> [C]hanging the data representations usually involved making extensive changes to the code already written. [12, p.1]

Dataless Programming was the language he proposed to do that.

Liskov: You can see that having a fixed syntax to interact with the data structures would support this idea because then you could freely change the data structures underneath. But there was nothing in his methodology that guaranteed that the code using the data structure didn't use the representation, so it didn't get to data abstraction.

One of the things that struck me when I was thinking about my Turing lecture was how you could see data abstraction all over the place except never quite defined. Mealy is proposing it, Balzer is proposing it. Data abstraction shows up less in the work of Dijkstra and Wirth; they weren't thinking in terms of data abstraction but instead in terms of the programming process.

Daylight: So it would be incorrect to assume that you were aware of this work during the early 1970s?

Liskov: In the early 1970s I was aware of the programming methodology research. I did not read Balzer's thesis at that point because his thesis is about a programming language mechanism. At the time I started working on programming methodology, and before I started working on abstract data types, I was aware of the work of Parnas, Dijkstra, Wirth and some of Mealy's papers.

Daylight: Do you recall Parnas's SODAS which he presented in 1967 at the Fall Joint Computer Conference? SODAS is an abbreviation for: a Structured Oriented Description And Simulation [236, p.449]. In this paper he described what he called a top-down approach to system design. In his words:

> It involves starting at the "top" with a complete specification of the desired behavior of the system, then breaking the system down into smaller and smaller components until the system is specified in terms of the basic building units. [...] The specifications at every level provide evaluation criteria for the next lower level. [236, p.450]

What interests me here is that this way of working top down with different levels seems to have originated in various places. It wasn't just Dijkstra who had the idea.

Liskov: Yes, I believe when it's time for ideas to bubble up that they often come from several places simultaneously. Note also that Dijkstra and Parnas were two very different personalities with Dijkstra representing the European school and Parnas the American school. So there was also something going on there.

THE	Venus
user programs	user programs
buffering for I/O devices	
operator-console device driver	device drivers & schedulers
memory management	virtual memory
	I/O channel
CPU scheduling	CPU scheduling
	instruction interpreter
hardware	hardware

Table 6.1: Comparing between THE and Venus. Source: Silberschatz & Galvin [279, p.72].

6.3 The Venus Operating System

Daylight: I have here a copy of your Venus paper, 'The Design of the Venus Operating System' [172]. You won a best paper price for it in 1972. Do you recall why?

Liskov: I have no idea, I never thought about that question. It might very well have been due to the mixing of programming methodology with operating system design. I was interested in how the notions of programming methodology were playing out in the Venus design. This was in the Spring of 1972, when operating system design was a research topic — I mean it still is but not in the sense it was then when people were trying to understand what an operating system was. The Venus operating system is a little unusual I guess. You can see the influence of THE in it: the idea that you would build things up in layers. And the semaphores, the fact that I put them into the hardware, was very useful in this project.

Daylight: Dijkstra's THE and your Venus system were unique in that they were layered. They were rather similar in their layering too (cf. Table 6.1).

Liskov: This notion of levels of abstraction is something I don't believe in. I believe that things are much more like a graph structure. But at that time there was this notion of hierarchy and each level took over from the previous one. If you look at Figure 2 in the Venus paper [172, p.148], though I may have called these levels, you can see that we are jumping over levels. It's not the strict leveling that some people proposed where at level N you could only make use of level $N - 1$.

Daylight: Do you recall why you introduced this bypassing of levels?

Liskov: If you don't do that, then what you end up with at each level is something that has to provide access to all the functionality of the lower level, which just adds extra complexity to the design. The way I think of it today is that, when you are designing, you have available a set of abstractions. There is no reason why if you use that set of abstractions you should bundle them all up into one super abstraction, that contains all of them. It's better to think of a bunch with which you can work. The fact that some of the abstractions that you're using might be using some of the others doesn't seem to matter.

Daylight: In 1971 in Belfast, Tony Hoare and Ron Perrott organized a conference on operating systems [134]. You didn't attend, nor did Dijkstra. When I study the proceedings I notice three main things. First, they were all talking about Dijkstra's THE system throughout the conference. Second, Hoare was rather skeptical about layers of virtual machines[108]. Third, Hoare, Randell and several others had different views toward what an operating system actually was or was supposed to be. Hoare, for instance, said:

> The basic purpose of a computer operating system is to *share* the hardware which it controls among a number of users, making unpredictable demands upon its resources; and its objectives are to do so efficiently, reliably, and unobtrusively. [134, p.11, original italics]

So sharing was central to Hoare. But then Randell said that sharing was not the main purpose of an operating system:

> I feel that the emphasis on sharing in Hoare's paper is not quite right, sharing is a remedy not a problem. My own characterization of an operating system is that it is something which allows one (or attempts to allow one) to achieve the performance which the hardware should be capable of, and to surpass the reliability which it is capable of. As the system gets bigger and more expensive, sharing is very obviously a way of dealing with the first of these. [134, p. 21]

In short, these researchers didn't yet have a consensus on what an operating system was. Did you experience similar things when you were working at Mitre?

Liskov: I can hardly remember and my view of operating systems is colored by what I know today. At that time multiprogramming was maybe not yet the main thing, which could explain why they were discussing sharing so much. You could view an operating system as supporting a single user and giving access to the power of the machine at a more abstract level. And, in fact, if you think about running an operating system today on your PC, that is what is going on. At that time, I think the mainstream in operating system work was that machines were expensive and you wanted to support many users on them concurrently; obviously they were sharing, and you wanted to find a way that allowed them to share without getting into each other's way and do so efficiently and so on. **Venus** was a multiprogramming system, so it was fundamentally a system that allowed multiple users to be running simultaneously on the same hardware. It was all about sharing. That's why you had these abstractions, these processes or virtual machines and what I think I called segments but they were fundamentally files. These are all ways of abstracting from what the hardware provided to something that is like that thing but abstracting it so that there can be many of them. This is a way to share the underlying resources.

Daylight: When you introduced these virtual machines, did you have the tendency to minimize their number? Was there a cost associated with introducing virtual machines?

Liskov: If I recall correctly, the **Venus** system supported 16 concurrent users. I don't remember the architecture, whether it had some extra processes floating around so that the operating system could do some work in parallel. I don't know whether there is much of a cost of having more virtual machines but switching from one to another is typically expensive. Of course, at the time this paper [172] was written, there wasn't so much understanding of the cost of such a switch.

Daylight: In that 1971 conference in Belfast, the attendees were discussing the implications of having an operating system be built up in levels of abstraction. They were wondering whether that was the right way to design an operating system. Randell mentioned that Dijkstra's **THE** system suffered from thrashing:

> [A]nd Dijkstra's system does suffer from thrashing. So here is a case where the **THE** system's levels of abstraction are not adequate. I'm not trying to preach against levels of abstraction – I like God, Love and Motherhood too. [134, p.191]
> [T]he question of thrashing is a very nice example of a partial inadequacy even in the very nicely argued set of levels which Dijkstra has established. [134, p.204]

Likewise, Hoare and Brinch Hanssen said that abstractions typically broke down for scheduling [134, p.206].

Liskov: Scheduling was a hard problem, several research groups looked at it through the 1970s. I don't think it's abstraction versus scheduling. I think it has more to do with understanding how to implement such functionality correctly. There's been a long sequence of research here. How do you know that this process ought to be preferred over that process, and how do you decide what units to use? Such questions have been studied thoroughly. As I recall, `Venus` had an unsophisticated scheduling system. I don't know that we ever interrupted based on time. I think that once a process couldn't do anything we would switch to another one. Of course, this wouldn't work in a larger environment where resources get tight. And, honestly, I don't think thrashing has anything to do with it. First of all, if you try to run your program and it requires more volatile memory than you have available, it is going to thrash. That has nothing to do with abstractions, it's just a fact, but probably not very well understood at that time. Secondly, you can figure out sophisticated ways to schedule and people did develop those. So you have to think about this discussion in the context of the time. People didn't understand very well how to do these things and lots of it probably doesn't make much sense in terms of what's going on today.

6.4 Design Methodology

Daylight: I'd like to discuss your 1972 design methodology paper 'A design methodology for reliable software systems' [171] in which you said that

> [P]roblems can be solved most effectively *during* the design process. [171, p.191, my italics]

— as opposed to working a posteriori with, for instance, debugging techniques. Dijkstra's work on the `THE` system was also about proving correctness constructively. His levels of abstraction helped him prove the correctness of his system. Did that play any role when you were working with `Venus` and its levels and did you talk to Dijkstra about this matter? You also advocated *"informal* proofs of correctness" [171, p.191, original italics]. Why did you stress the adjective "informal" and what's your take on it today?

Liskov: I never talked to Dijkstra about this. Nevertheless, the community that worked on correct-by-construction programs probably did influence me, even if I didn't believe it was really possible. In my paper on design methodology [171], I made an attempt at organizing the software so that you'd have a better shot at reasoning about its correctness, but I thought the reasoning would be informal. I didn't believe formal reasoning was going to make it, certainly not at that point in time. I'm a great fan of informal reasoning. The problem with formal reasoning is that specifications tend to not be very complete. Also, formal reasoning is difficult, although a lot of progress has been made in the last ten years with theorem provers. They do require formal specifications though and it's hard to get a good formal specification.

Daylight: In your paper on design methodology you discussed levels of abstraction and structured programming. For the levels of abstraction you mentioned two rules:

> Each level of abstraction is composed of a group of related functions. [...] There are two important rules governing levels of abstraction. The first concerns resources (I/O devices, data): each level has resources which it owns exclusively and which other levels are not permitted to access. The second involves the hierarchy: lower levels are not aware of the existence of higher levels [...]. [171, p.193]

For structured programming, you referred to Dijkstra's 'Structured Programming' [33, p.84–88] and Mills's 'Structured programming in large systems' [196]. Here too, you defined two rules:

> The first rule states that structured programs are developed from the top down, in levels. The levels in a structured program are not (usually) levels of abstraction, because they do not obey the rule about ownership of resources. [...]
> The second rule defines which control structures may be used in structured programs. Only the following control structures are permitted: concatenation, selection of the next statement based on the testing of a condition, and iteration. [...] [171, p.193]

I am keen on understanding how you viewed the relationship between levels of abstraction and structured programming, and how you refined your view over the years. If I understand correctly, for the **Venus** system, each level of abstraction corresponds to one module, as shown in Figure 6.1. The figure presents a module-dependency graph: each rectangle depicts a module, each line inside a module depicts a procedure, and an arrow from module A to module B denotes the dependency of A on B in terms of functionality.

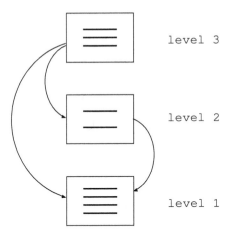

Figure 6.1: Each level contains one module. The arrows depict dependencies between modules.

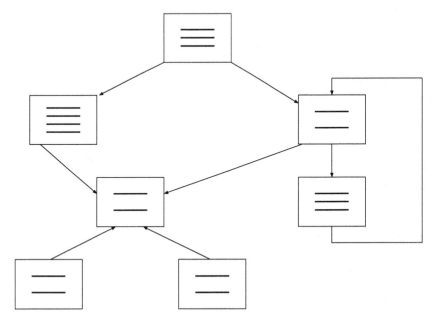

Figure 6.2: A module-dependency graph, similar in spirit to [176, p.307].

Liskov: When I think about this paper [171] today, I consider the notion of what I then called "levels of abstraction" to be the most important. I've also sometimes called them partitions. A partition is really a module. The central idea is that each resource belongs strictly to one partition of the system and nobody else can get access to it. That's what fed in to the later work on data types — that's where abstract data types came from. I also have always advocated a programming methodology that's fundamentally top down, where in the end you have a program graph and there's no rule that says you have the first layer, the second layer, the third layer, etc. Today I would say a little cycle might be OK, because you have to think about what you do with recursion. You can find examples of such module-dependency graphs in my books [175, 176], especially in the second one [176]. The figure on page 307 contains an example. [See Figure 6.2 in this chapter.] You see, there's a cycle, and what I tell my students is that cycles represent recursion. If you have mutual recursion, then this can be problematical.

The rule of no crossing of the boundary is what mattered in this paper [171]. The other thing that I thought was novel was the idea that you could have multiple procedures in each module. So each module had not just one procedure with which you could interact, but a bunch of them. This paper is about design methodology, so it's trying to cover the entire waterfront. It starts with "we should do top-down development and, by the way, well-structured control structures will be adequate", but I don't believe, at this point, that you write programs the way Wirth proposed, where you write abstract programs. I think, instead, you design by inventing abstractions, and what you're doing is saying "well, let me think about how could I implement this" — you're not going to bother writing that code. And you might introduce more than one abstraction at once, because I'm thinking in terms of an abstract machine. Now, that's not all in that paper. What I'm giving you now is the mature version of the methodology that is starting to be sketched in that paper.

Daylight: Were you at that time already skeptical about structured programming? I clearly see these levels of abstraction stand out and I think the paper would be as strong if the part on structured programming were not part of the paper.

Liskov: I think the part that mattered the most was the part about the modules and what they are like. The rest of it is just completing the story. But I was interested in the whole story and I do think of the paper as having two parts. It's just that as I moved forward, I focused on modularity because that seemed to be the most interesting problem to work on. It was probably not until the late 1970s that I went back and started to work on the rest of the problem, like "how do you do design?" and "how do you write specifications?". So it was all there from the beginning but it was a big problem, too big to work on all at once. This paper is trying to lay out the whole problem. When I think about the progression of the work, that's what happened.

Daylight: To summarize a bit: during the early 1970s you advocated layered software with multiple procedures per layer, you had a top-down approach with the possibility of bypassing layers. But, at some point, Parnas scrutinized layered systems and the THE system in particular. He did this by formalizing the "uses hierarchy" [233, 234].

Liskov: Well, the uses hierarchy and my module-dependency diagrams are pretty similar. The uses hierarchy causes this graph on page 307 in [176]. [See Figure 6.2 in this chapter.]

Daylight: Which is very different from a layered software system.

Liskov: Absolutely, so I ended up over here [cf. Figure 6.2]. I think, in a way, if you come out of the operating system world you have a somewhat skewed view of how things work. The operating system completely covers up the machine, and so it is like a complete rewriting. A programming language is like this too. You have the machine language, you have the programming language, you run on top of the programming language, and you never have access to the underlying machine. This is where these ideas came from, that there should be complete hiding. But when you start to build applications, it's not like that any more. So I think some of these ideas were probably influenced by the fact that these people were working on operating systems and programming languages, causing them to think about things in particular ways.

We haven't talked much about Parnas but he was a huge influence on me, perhaps the biggest influence. He was the one, I thought, who was attacking the important question "what are modules?". What I say in my Turing lectures is that programming methodology was actually about two separate topics. One was "how do you do design?". The other one was "what should the system structure be like?".

Daylight: What I take away from the work of Dijkstra, Wirth, and Hoare is that during the mid-1960s electronic technology had advanced so much, compared to the 1950s, that machine efficiency was not the main importance any more. As a result, a software designer was allowed to put structure first. In other words, you were allowed to spend more effort on getting something structured even if that would mean that the end result was less machine efficient than it could have been.

Liskov: I guess my view is a little bit different. I think that what happened is that the Software Crisis became to be perceived as overwhelmingly important. Therefore, it was very important to start using techniques that would have a chance of getting the software to work, and this wasn't necessarily compatible with trying to extract each last little bit of performance out of the machine.

One of the things programmers used to be worried about was whether compilers for higher level languages could produce efficient object code. They sometimes recoded their programs in machine language in order to obtain more efficient implementations. The compilers today do a pretty good job. The place where they can't do such a great job is actually the garbage collector, there are still problems there. And, of course, in those days people didn't have garbage collectors, because they were working in ALGOL60 and its derivatives, and you had to manage storage yourself. Compiler technology has improved, but part of what they were saying then was, "yes, you are going to lose some performance, because you don't have goto statements or you are using this higher level language, but it is much more important to get your program to work". I think that was the fundamental shift in understanding.

Another point is that if you write a program modularly, there's lots of scope for re-implementation. So the methodology I talk about in my book [176] is that you write the program and you don't try to over-optimize. You just try to get a good clean structure and then you do performance debugging and you decide where the bottlenecks are. And then, given that it is a modular structure, you can simply take a module and re-implement it, nobody else is affected. So it is actually a very good way to get an efficient program.

Daylight: From my past experience as a researcher in embedded systems, I would think that breaking the encapsulation between the modules can result in factors of improvement in terms of execution speed or memory footprint. This is a rather drastic way of optimizing with dirty code as a result. I understand the need for modularity, but why not separate the two steps? That is, have a modular approach, followed by a step in which the the modular structure is intentionally broken.

Liskov: First of all, compilers will do this for you today. In-line substitution is an example. They may not get the kinds of things you're talking about, but they can improve performance significantly just by compiling two modules together and doing the optimizations. After all, compilers do a lot of clever optimizations these days. It's also alright if you decide to replace a little group of modules by one module or another group of modules. Mind you, if you do that with the compiler then you are completely protected because you can always go back to the original modular structure, whereas if you do it by hand then you have deviated from the structure of the program and you are likely to have trouble later on. So it's something you want to approach with caution.

6.5   Scrutinizing Layered Systems Further

Daylight: In the late 1990s, Silberschatz and Galvin [279, p.72–73] mentioned that there are at least two problems with layered systems. First of all, how do you actually define and order the layers? Apparently there's no consensus on this. Looking back at Dijkstra's work from 1969, he explicitly mentioned that his ordering in the THE system was not necessarily the best one [221, p.184–185]. Silberschatz and Galvin expressed the same concern some thirty years later. What's your take on it today?

Liskov: Well, I don't believe in layered systems, and probably that's one of the reasons why I don't believe in them. Now, mind you, the same kind of things can happen if you throw out the layers and you just think in terms of the module-dependency diagram I showed you earlier. Obtaining such a module-dependency diagram means that I made a particular design decision somewhere which led me to extend the graph in a particular way. And if I had done it differently, I could have had a very different and maybe better structure. So there is no doubt that as you design, every time you make a decision, you're ruling out a bunch of solutions. You are always constraining as you move through the design process. That's not exactly what Silberschatz and Galvin are talking about because they are trying to superimpose what I think is an artificial structure and then arguing about that artificial structure. But even if you ignore that and look at the real design, still, every time you make a decision, you introduce constraints and you throw out possibilities. This is one of the things that makes design hard.

Daylight: Is there any research going on in formalizing the different design choices that a software engineer can make?

Liskov: Well, typically, people don't do multiple designs. You can't afford to do more than one design. So, what you do is you try to justify your design decisions. In that justification, you might say "I thought about doing it this or that way, and this is the best way because —". But, since I finished working on programming methodology sometime in the 1980s, I have been working in distributed systems and I haven't been paying much attention to the programming methodology community and the software engineering community. So there might be some work going on there, but I don't know what it is.

Daylight: The second remark Silberschatz and Galvin make is that layered systems tend to be less efficient than other types of systems. Perhaps I'm allowed to generalize their findings to modular software, perhaps not. They say that:

> [F]or a user program to execute an I/O operation, it executes a system call which is trapped to the I/O layer, which calls the memory-management layer, through to the CPU scheduling layer, and finally to the hardware. At each layer, the parameters may be modified, data may need to be passed, and so on. Each layer adds overhead to the system call and the net result is a system call that takes longer than one does on a nonlayered system. These limitations have caused a small backlash against layering in recent years. Fewer layers with more functionality are being designed, providing most of the advantages of modularized code while avoiding the difficult problems of layer definition and interaction [279, p.73].

> [As an example] consider the history of Windows NT. The first release had a very layer-oriented organization. However, this version suffered low performance compared to that of Windows 95. Windows NT 4.0 redressed some of these performance issues by moving layers from user space to kernel space and more closely integrating them [279, p.74].

Liskov: Somehow I think we got off into operating system land here. [L: Laughter] So, it's not clear that there is something general being said. But you know that if you enforce modularity there is a cost. It isn't really the cost of the procedure calls, because the compiler can easily get rid of that. The cost arises because I made a design decision and as a result I'm thinking of two things separately rather than together. Nevertheless, I still believe in the methodology that says that you do your performance debugging and then you figure out what to change.

Moreover, I think performance is greatly overrated in the computer science field, because what you need in performance is good-enough performance. You don't need the best performance. It has to be good enough performance for what you are trying to do. The performance requirements become particularly severe as you get lower in the programming stack. So it is very important that the programming languages you use have a good implementation. It is very important that your operating systems have a good implementation. It is much less important that your web services have an outstanding implementation, because by now you are working at the speeds of programs that people can notice and that gives you a lot of flexibility.

6.6   Specifications: Formal versus Informal

Daylight: Concerning formal specifications, my colleague Mark Priestley wrote that:

> Liskov and Zilles also saw a strong connection between the use of abstract data types and issues to do with proving the correctness of programs. [...] They considered various ways in which formal specifications of data abstractions could be given. [246, p.212]

Liskov: Steve Zilles, for his PhD thesis, was working on algebraic specifications for abstract data types. And John Guttag, who is the co-author of my book [175], his PhD thesis was on that too. I never worked on it myself. This tenth chapter 'Writing Formal Specifications' in [175] is coming largely from Guttag's `Larch` language [115].

Daylight: I have the feeling, based on your recent book [176], that you are skeptical about formal specifications.

Liskov: Oh, I was skeptical then too. I thought this work was interesting and I had a PhD student, Valdis Berzins, who worked on an abstract model technique for giving formal specifications, which I believed was more promising than the algebraic technique. I felt that the algebraic technique was so abstract that people would have a lot of trouble thinking in those terms. The problem with any formal technique is that people have a lot of trouble writing formal specifications.

Daylight: In 1975, you and Zilles wrote:

> Formal specifications are superior to informal ones as a communication medium. [177, p.74]

Liskov: [L: Laughter] The trouble is that informal specifications can have a lot of hand waving in them, so it's hard to know what they are saying. But formal specifications can be completely inscrutable. That is, you can look at them and not understand what they are saying at all.

Daylight: Isn't that then one of the major problems today in software?

Liskov: Yes. Even informal specifications are a problem, let alone formal ones. It helps if you have a form for them. So in my book [176], there is a form for informal specifications (e.g., on page 210). The students were taught to write specifications like this and to use examples to illustrate them. Moreover, I had my students implement the abstraction function and the representation invariant. It was extremely useful for them, they saw that these are not just abstract ideas and that they can be used for debugging purposes too.

Daylight: Bertrand Meyer with `Eiffel` works more or less in a similar fashion. I think his work is more formal.

Liskov: He allows you to put in things that are not comments but that are interpreted by the compiler so of course they have to be formal.

Daylight: IFIP working group 2.3 was very much into formal programming methodologies, wasn't it?

Liskov: Yes and for a brief period in time I was member of that working group. Or maybe I was not a member but they were looking at me as a potential member. I don't remember. I didn't personally find those working groups all that useful.

6.7 CLU

Daylight: Your CLU language had data abstraction, iteration abstraction, exception handling, and polymorphic types. I would like to understand how your research group had come up with these ideas during the 1970s. In your 1993 recollections [174] you mentioned `Simula67` and `Smalltalk` in this regard.

Liskov: I was not paying much attention to the approach of the `Smalltalk` group because it was mostly about inheritance. Their early work was very implementation focused and there was no abstraction. It was all about classes and subclasses: making a subclass from a class, adding a few fields and some extra methods, changing the behavior. Preserving the behavior of the superclass was not important to them. Also, I wasn't particularly interested in `Simula67`, because `Simula67` at that time did not have encapsulation. Their primary focus was on simulation and concurrency and so forth. But they certainly had the inheritance mechanism that then was picked up by the object oriented community. The `Smalltalk` group was working on a different problem. I was working on abstraction, they were working on an implementation technique that allowed you to have multiple methods. So you can see the two ideas are related, but the focus was different.

My view of CLU is it had three forms of abstraction: procedural-, data-, and iteration abstraction. Polymorphism is a generalization technique for each form of abstraction. I don't have to define a set of integers,

I can have a set of type T. Likewise, I can have an iterator that is parameterized by a type T. Exceptions is a kind of generalization also. It only refers to procedures and iterators and it is a way of trying to make sure that you define them with the weakest precondition that you can manage, while distinguishing the different kinds of results that can happen. So I viewed exceptions as important because ideally I wanted to have *true* as my precondition, but I wanted to avoid the C solution, which was you just embedded everything in the answer. Of course, the problem with that is that it is very error prone, because people don't even bother to look at the answer. I wanted exceptions in order to bring to the attention of the caller the fact that something unusual had happened. When I started the CLU project iterators were not on my agenda. They came along later when I realized that I needed something to complete the data abstraction story in a way that did not require programmers to make bad abstractions or to write bad programs.

Daylight: What do you mean with bad?

Liskov: I'm thinking now from the perspective of a language designer. I knew that it was going to be important to be able to iterate over objects, because many objects are collections and that's the whole point of collections: you want to do something with all the elements of the collection. In the absence of iterators I had in mind two different solutions. One was to simply empty the collection and then you know you're finished. The problem with that was that sometimes you want to use it again, which would lead to an ugly program. Or, you could complicate the abstraction by, say, turning a set into an indexed set, so that you could then easily iterate over it. But, from a language perspective, I didn't want people to have to make more complicated abstractions than they needed to. So I was worried at the time about how to provide a way for designers to come up with the simplest abstractions that had sufficient expressive power. Because there is this notion for data abstraction of completeness; you have to provide enough operations so that everything the user needs to do can be done easily and efficiently.

Iterators arose from a discussion with the Alphard group at Carnegie Mellon [313]. They were working on generators, not unlike the generators we now have in Java. Though generators solved the problem, we thought they were ugly. It was Russ Atkinson, one of my students, who invented iterators on our plane ride home from Carnegie Mellon, after we had heard about generators. Iterators have less expressive power than generators because there are certain kinds of iterations you can't express with them, like comparing two trees to see whether their elements are equal. We looked at more complex mechanisms but in the end we chose something simple, using the engineering rule that it's better to get 95% of the cases with a simple mechanism rather than have a more complicated mechanism that solves 100% of the problem.

Daylight: So your group followed a very pragmatic approach. Yet, on the other hand, elegance was heavily involved as well.

Liskov: Absolutely, iterators were an elegant solution. We recognized that they didn't have as much power as generators. We thought about more complicated iterators that provided additional power. In the end, we went for the mechanism that was both elegant and sufficiently expressive.

This is the art of design in a nutshell. In my group we always tried to consider all aspects of a decision so that in the end we could make an informed decision. I ran it as a group, we often developed consensus. Sometimes, however, we ended up with two different solutions so that somebody had to make a decision. That was me. And, yes, elegance was very important.

Daylight: What were the opposing forces to elegance? Were there, for instance, deadlines your group had to meet?

Liskov: It was research, so there were no external deadlines. We were, of course, very focused on making progress. Elegance and expressive power were opposing forces. By expressive power we meant making it easy to write the programs that we thought you ought to be writing. So we had some notion of good programs versus bad programs. That was our touchstone. We didn't care to support making it easy to write any program. For example, if you really wanted to program with goto statements, you weren't going to be able to do this easily in CLU — though I'm sure you could have invented structures to accomplish this. So we had a notion of a class of programs we wanted to support even though I probably couldn't tell you what that class was. Then there was performance. Iterators, by the way, had a very efficient implementation. And there was ease of use. These were our design goals and they came into play all the time. We were always writing little programs, trying to evaluate how easy or hard it was to express something and whether this was an important thing to express.

Daylight: Were you aware, from the beginning, of these four criteria? Or did these criteria gradually surface?

Liskov: I think that elegance was so basic that we didn't enumerate it as a design principle, but the others were, I believe, stated up front. Simplicity is another, which is not the same as elegance. Simplicity has to do with people being able to understand what you're talking about. Ease of use is: here's the mechanism, can I easily write programs using it? Expressive power is: can I express everything I need to express? Concerning performance, CLU was a garbage collected language so we knew we weren't going to have the kind of performance you get out of C. But, still, we were very mindful of performance.

Daylight: Each of your students had each of these criteria in mind, right? It's not that one student was working on simplicity and the other on performance?

Liskov: No, definitely not. We were working on language constructs, thinking about example programs and how you would express them in this way versus that way. In the end, we would decide what the solution was and although we didn't talk specifically about these goals, these were the goals that we had in mind.

Daylight: How did you then assign tasks to your students? Each student had to get his PhD, right?

Liskov: I didn't do a good job at that. In retrospect, Russ Atkinson should have gotten his PhD on iterators. One of them should have gotten his PhD on parameterized types. But I didn't think about doing it that way. There were definitely several PhD topics in that project. Instead, we were all working on the language together and I didn't sort it out like that.

Daylight: Maybe that's why it was so successful?

Liskov: Maybe. But I think that even doing it as a group project, I could have broken it up. But I just didn't understand that I could have done that at the time.

Daylight: Were there other groups working in a similar fashion? And what about today, do you still work like this?

Liskov: I have no idea about the other groups. The CLU-group working method continued through the 1990s. I would have weekly group meetings, people would come and we would be talking about the central problems in the group. Today I don't work so much like that any more because my group has become much smaller, but I do continue to work in that vein.

Daylight: With respect to elegance or simplicity, I assume that when a new student joins your group, he has first to get used to what that means, right? I have difficulty imagining everybody assigning the same meaning to such words.

Liskov: I don't train them specifically. Again, my group is probably different today than it was up through the 1990s. It used to be a pretty big group, and the young students would come in and they would work with the older students. The older students probably had all been teaching assistants in my class, so they had all completely consumed this methodology (cf. [175, 176]). Then it would just be learning by osmosis, so that's probably how it worked. Today I work with my students and I'm always saying things like "maybe this is too complicated and let's try think of a simpler way" because elegance and simplicity are very tightly linked. You don't want a solution that is complicated when you can come up with something that is simpler.

Daylight: What about discussing simplicity with other researchers? Dijkstra's notion of simplicity, at some point in his career, corresponded to having a short correctness proof of a program. And there are other notions of simplicity. Did you feel that when you for instance went to that IFIP 2.3 working group?

Liskov: I can't remember. I might have because I certainly felt that they were not interested in the same kind of things I was interested in. Maybe they were more into formal methods than I was. But, since about 1985, I've not been going to conferences except in the systems community. There we don't talk much about these things, but when my group members and I discuss research papers, we often see that the interface of the system isn't nice or the implementation has this little glitch in it that they didn't understand was a glitch. So these things do come through in our discussions.

6.8   ADA **and Academia Today**

Daylight: Is it correct that you were involved with one of the ADA teams?

Liskov: Yes, I was consulting with one of the industrial teams in the Boston area. There were four teams originally, they all had to be industrial. None of them was academic.

Daylight: What was technically your impression about ADA?

Liskov: ADA was too complicated, it was burdened by its specification. There were really two problems. The designers didn't have much flexibility because there were an awful lot of constraints put on what was an acceptable solution. So in some sense the language design was being done by the people in the Department of Defense who probably didn't have that great an idea of what they were doing. The second problem was that the best language designers were not involved in designing the language because of the requirement that it be done by industrial teams.

So you started off with a specification that required too much, and there was very little ability to say "well, we shouldn't do that, we should do this". In fact, I felt that the design that won was much too compliant.

Daylight: Concerning academia today, I would like to quote Wirth:

> [I]n this post-modern academic environment the professor has long ago ceased to be the wise, learned man, penetrating deeper and deeper into his beloved subject in his quiet study. The modern professor is the manager of a large research team of researchers, the keen fund raiser maintaining close relationships with the key funding agencies, and the untiring author of exciting project proposals and astonishing success stories. [310, p.2]

Liskov: I think he's talking about his own institution, ETH. There they run large groups with lots of postdocs and the professor at the top. Not only are they very well funded by ETH, they have to go out and get more money too. He's not talking about computer science in general.

Daylight: How would you describe the situation at MIT?

Liskov: Here most of the groups are relatively small, by their standards very small. My biggest group had nine students. Once in a while I'd have a postdoc, but the model was that I was always working closely with the students directly rather than through an intermediary. Many people here have smaller groups, six students with a postdoc or two, and the group works as a team. The professor is deeply involved and the amount of money being brought in is enough to support that team. So it isn't more and more and more.

Daylight: So research funding is not so problematical?

Liskov: It is harder to get funding than it used to be. We used to get most of our funding from DARPA, which became problematical during the 1990s; but maybe we're recovering now.

Daylight: To put it bluntly, isn't it easier to get funding at MIT than at other universities in the USA?

Liskov: Perhaps. But people here are spending more time writing proposals than they used to. Things are a little better now than they were three or four years ago, when things were really bad. NSF was funding only, say, 10% of the proposals that came in, and DARPA was focused almost entirely on industrial work. So there was a real problem then.

Daylight: Wirth also says it is technically "depressing" today. He mentions C, C++, C#, and Java as being poor languages. Academics are forced to use these languages and technically make good a posteriori.

Liskov: Yes, but things have not changed. In fact, if anything, it is a little easier now to get a research language out and used, because you can put software out as open source on the Internet. Pascal, more than any other academic language, had a really good run. But, by and large, it is the languages that were supported by industrial places that were the ones that are really widely used up until recently. Today there are languages coming out — they may not be very good languages — like Python, PHP, and Ruby. They don't come from the mainstream and they may also not come from academics.

Daylight: Barbara Liskov, thank you very much for this discussion.

Liskov: You're welcome.

7. Peter Naur and Turing's 1936 Paper

For the cause of the history of programming languages, I have conducted an extensive discussion with Peter Naur, the 2005 Turing Award winner. Naur was a renowned astronomer before he became a successful programming language designer and antagonist of formal methods. My discussion with him was spread over three afternoons. The fragments about `ALGOL60` and Turing are presented in this chapter. For the complete discussion, and especially for Naur's critical remarks about Dijkstra, I refer to my booklet *Pluralism in Software Engineering: Turing Award Winner Peter Naur Explains* [55].

Meeting Peter Naur

My discussion with Naur took place on 5 April, 14 May, and 17 May 2011 at his home in Gentofte, Denmark. Its digital recordings were transcribed by me and subsequently edited by Naur, De Grave, and myself.

Short Biography of Peter Naur

Peter Naur was born in 1928 in Frederiksberg, Denmark. He graduated from Copenhagen University in astronomy in 1949 and was a research student at King's College, Cambridge in 1950–51 where he programmed the `EDSAC` in order to solve an astronomical problem. After a year's stay in the USA and a brief return to Cambridge, Naur spent the rest of the 1950s in Copenhagen. In 1957 he received his PhD in astronomy and in 1959 he joined the staff of Regnecentralen, specializing in high-level programming languages. He became heavily involved in the design and implementation of `ALGOL60` and organized the `ALGOL` Bulletin. From 1969 until his retirement in 1999 he was professor at the Copenhagen University Institute of Datalogy. Since the mid-1990s until this day, Naur actively studies and writes about psychology and in particular about how human life is like at the neural level of the nervous system. He has received several awards, including the Computer Pioneer Award of the IEEE Computer Society in 1986 and the ACM Turing Award in 2005.

7.1   Early Years

Daylight: Peter Naur, you were born in Frederiksberg, Denmark in 1928.

Naur: Yes, Frederiksberg is a part of Copenhagen really. It's not very far from here.

Daylight: Did you have siblings?

Naur: I had one sister and one brother, five years and two years older than me.

Daylight: As a child, did you enjoy playing football?

Naur: No, not really. I liked to play Meccano until I got caught in astronomy. Those were two very different hobbies. The switch in interest happened when I changed schools. I must have been 11 or 12 years old. The geography teacher had suggested that we should watch the stars and the Big Dipper in particular. I did this and made several drawings because I thought it was an excellent exercise. It turned out that I was the only one in the class who had done a sensible job. This fired my interest in astronomy. For years thereafter, I was just very keen on understanding astronomy.

After a few years, I got interested in the computation of orbits of newly discovered comets and planets. It was an activity that was well supported by the observatory of Copenhagen. I got very much help from the people there. One of their staff members, Jens P. Møller, helped and supported me with my computations. I got access to their hand-driven calculating machines. In a few years, I understood all of this and did useful work in astronomy, which was published. I also got a lot of support from my parents. That was how it all started.

Daylight: During the second world war you learned English from the school books written by the Danish linguist Otto Jespersen. Were you at that time already intrigued by Jespersen's research on linguistics?

Naur: No, no. By that time I had become very interested in modern physics, including the works of Einstein and Bohr. I read about such things in the semi-popular literature: James Jeans's books on astronomy and Eddington's books, etc.

Daylight: Was your interest in physics related to the fact that you wanted to specialize in astronomy, or were you reading these books because you wanted to obtain a general understanding?

Naur: It's hard to say. But I was definitely keen on astronomy. Of course, all this physics had a lot to do with astronomy. This was the time when it was discovered how the energy of the sun comes out by atomic processes. That is atomic theory. So things were completely wielded together. In later years I worked on the interior of stars. When I got to America I computed models of the sun. It was published at that time, in 1952/53.

Daylight: Did you during your school years also become acquainted with the works of some philosophers, such as Hume, Locke, Kant? I am asking this because you mentioned to me in private correspondence that you had read Harald Hoffding's *Den nyere filosofis historie*, 1894.

Naur: You see, I always wanted to understand everything. I liked nothing better than the public library. I would browse through the books and ask myself what is psychology about.

Daylight: So it wasn't just astronomy?

Naur: No not at all. But I got much further in astronomy because I was specializing in that.

Daylight: Wasn't that difficult for you? On the one hand, doing that as a child must have been fun, you had lots of time to dig into these books. On the other hand, you were probably surrounded by children who had other interests. Did you sense any difficulty?

Naur: Not a difficulty really. But I felt quite clearly that I was to some extent exceptional in my striving to understand science. The school work I found very easy, including the languages such as English and German. I started reading astronomy in German. The texts on computations of orbits was in German. So I knew more German before I started reading English.

Daylight: You were not discouraged in any way to work on scientific problems in your teens?

Naur: No, no. I felt perfectly happy.

7.2 Cambridge: 1950–51

Daylight: You went to King's College in Cambridge between October 1950 and June 1951.

Naur: That was after I had finished my degree in Copenhagen.

Daylight: Could you elaborate a bit on the kind of work you did in Cambridge, compared to your work in Copenhagen? You worked on astronomy in both places, didn't you?

Naur: By 1950 it was already well known that Cambridge had the EDSAC computer. I had this double bill. I was working on astronomy and also on automatic computing. They had developed a technique for photometry with electronic means. That never got off the ground because the weather was so bad in Cambridge. Therefore, at a certain stage, I switched completely to programming and computation. I was also well prepared for this kind of work thanks to the computational work that I had done at the observatory in Copenhagen. I knew the techniques by hand, how to do these calculations such as integrating differential equations of motions of a small planet. I had been doing this for hundreds of hours in Copenhagen. So I was quite ready to prepare these computations for the EDSAC.

Daylight: Did you keep a diary? Did you note down how you were progressing in your research on astronomy?

Naur: Well, I do have a skeleton of a diary. I can't remember when I started this. But I have been doing this for years. It has one page for every year. [Naur shows his notebook.] Here I started a computation on this comet and here I had a discussion about a specific topic, etc.

Daylight: At a later age, when you were working on your PhD, did you extensively write down your ideas on paper in a form of a diary?

Naur: No, not like that. I do remember during my trip to the USA which was in 1952–53, when traveling around and visiting computing centers, that I started to write down my findings — I made a report on computers in the USA as I had perceived them. That report [202] is in Danish and was my way of formulating my experience. The most important part of it was the lesson from Cambridge, how they had organized their programming, the initial orders of Wheeler. His work on transforming the external form into the internal form was a very flexible and simple approach really. I immediately rearranged it so that it would suit our DASK machine that was being built in Copenhagen and which I believe was finished around 1957.

The DASK machine was inspired by the design and electronics of the Stockholm machine, called the BESK, which was an excellent electronic device: high speed, very good design. But the programming style in Stockholm was very primitive and inconvenient. So I had the chance to contribute a much better system for the machine language of the DASK. This work led straight on to our later research on compilers for ALGOL.

Daylight: You mentioned Wheeler, but there were also Hartree, Wilkes, and Gill at Cambridge. How would you describe these people? Did some of them impress you? Did you know some better than others?

Naur: It was simply that I had gotten the chance to work on the EDSAC in Cambridge, it is not that I got to know any of those people personally. I got a table and the book *Report on the Preparation of Programs for the EDSAC and the Use of the Library of Subroutines* [254] and that was about it. That book contains a library of subroutines for the EDSAC and was also published in America a few years later. It was the source of insight which I could immediately use to start programming for my particular astronomical problem.

Daylight: That was your only source? During the 1940s you had already worked on manual computations. You already knew how to do the numerical mathematics.

Naur: I was completely familiar with the technique of computation: developing numbers step by step according to a particular algorithm. That was completely by hand. It was just a matter of putting it on the EDSAC machine. My background as an astronomer was essential in this, as I've described in [210].

Daylight: Did some of these people at Cambridge speak to you about Alan Turing? Did you meet Turing?

Naur: I never met Turing. I have a sort of a feeling that there was some antagonism between the Cambridge group and Turing's group at the National Physical Laboratory. How that was, I've never been able to understand. I have a feeling that they were not able to get on particularly well. I'm not sure whether Wilkes got on well with Turing or understood him too well.

Daylight: It's not that they stressed Turing's 1936 paper [291] to you while you were at Cambridge?

Naur: No, no. The relation between Turing's work and the EDSAC I did not realize at that time at all. I'm not sure there was any relation because I think what Wilkes took over was the American work from Von Neumann, Mauchly, and others. I'm sure Wilkes attended their course in Philadelphia on the `UNIVAC`. That's not directly derived from Turing, I'm quite sure about that. The American style was also in large part due to Atanasoff. It's explained in Randell's excellent account on *The Origins of Digital Computers: Selected Papers* [249]. Atanasoff invented so many things. His computer was automatic, binary, electronic, but it didn't do programming. [Pause] Turing's universal machine is of course a programmed computer. How exactly Von Neumann got into that, I don't know.

Daylight: Did you have a roommate at Cambridge? Did you have a lot of contact with other students?

Naur: I had an excellent relation with Peter Remnant, a Canadian research student of philosophy who later became professor of philosophy at Vancouver. I lived in an hostel, across the street from King's College. There were 20 or 30 students there and one kitchen. That's where I got into contact with Peter Remnant and also one physicist, Oliver Penrose, who is now professor in Edinburgh.

Daylight: Is that the famous Penrose?

Naur: It's the brother of Roger Penrose. Oliver is a physicist and we were very friendly. I've seen him many times after my year in Cambridge. Nowadays I often have correspondence with him and discuss problems which we think are interesting.

Daylight: About Peter Remnant, you mentioned to me in private correspondence that you talked to him regularly about a variety of subjects, including the work of Ryle, Wittgenstein, Russell, Peirce, and Quine. Can you elaborate on this?

Naur: We had our society of two for the discussion of meaningless questions. That was Remnant's idea, inspired by Kant who wrote somewhere that the man who asks a meaningless question and the other man tries to answer it, that is like one man milking a he-goat and the other man holding a sieve to catch the milk. Remnant was a real philosopher; he was five years older than me.

Daylight: Did you read Wittgenstein in Cambridge?

Naur: At that time I was not much aware of Wittgenstein, not really.

Daylight: Ryle?

Naur: He was one that Peter Remnant would have mentioned as a very prominent modern-day English philosopher. I didn't read Ryle's book *The Concept of Mind* until much later. That of course is an interesting book because so many people find it so very hard to understand or to grasp. Ryle criticized Descartes's idea of a soul in the body, or what he called the ghost in the machine. I realized decades later that he was 60 years late in that because William James [150] had already made that very clear in 1890. Ryle was not into James's work at all. He was strangely ambivalent about the subject of his book; it is not clear whether it was psychology or behavioralism. In this way, I found his book to be very unclear really.

Daylight: Remnant and you probably talked about Bertrand Russell's work.

Naur: We talked about it. I remember that was just when Russell had published *History of Western Philosophy.* I recall Remnant quoting his teacher, professor C.D. Broad if I'm not mistaken, by referring to Russell's new book as "that absurd book".

Daylight: Remnant was also the one who mentioned William James's book *The Principles of Psychology* [150] to you.

Naur: I would say that was the most striking advice he gave me. I didn't act on it at all at that time. But that was the source and it took some twenty years before I really got down to it. But he understood James's work perfectly.

Daylight: In your recollections you wrote that Easter 1951 was an important moment for you [210]. The EDSAC was closed down so you were not able to run your program on the machine.

Naur: That's right. I had just revised my astronomical program so it was ready to be run on the machine. But since that was not possible, all I could do was sit down and look at my program carefully, trying to find the mistakes by hand. The result is that the day after the break holiday it all worked beautifully.

Daylight: I do wonder, what were the other people in Cambridge doing during Easter? They weren't able to work on the machine either. Didn't they check their programs similarly to the way you did?

Naur: I don't know what they were doing. I didn't have close contact with them. We could come and go at the laboratory, just like that.

Daylight: You have written that

> No one [in Cambridge] had any idea of how to analyse what went wrong in his program. [210, p.417]

Naur: The people at Cambridge had a particular prime-number test, a complicated program that was used to test the machine. It tested whether the machine was in a happy state or not. Those words you just quoted are Wilkes's which he sent to me around 1980, after I had sent him a draft version of my recollections [210]. No one knew how to analyze a program. Nowadays, I would cut it down section-wise, but nobody tried to do that.

Daylight: So you were looking at the program text?

Naur: No no, it was just a tape with a machine. A tape with a handful of other tapes, auxiliary tapes for the machine. If you wanted to check whether the store was in a good state, you'd put in a particular tape and you could adjust the pulse frequency somewhere in the panel. They were all paper tapes.

Daylight: When the EDSAC was shut down, you were looking at your paper tape. You didn't have the luxury at that moment to go to the machine and run your paper tape. Did your English colleagues have more of a tendency to go to the machine and operate it?

Naur: I couldn't tell for sure. But, of course, the group there was very much oriented to helping people find their mistakes. They had a whole family of auxiliary programs overlooking what happened, these programs could modify what happened. For example, instead of just executing the code, they would have an auxiliary program run at the same time which would take the instructions one by one. Besides executing these instructions, useful information would be printed out for each of these instructions as well. In this way you could then check whether your expectations with regard to execution were met. Another technique was to survey one particular storage cell. Every time something happened to that cell, you would be told what. These were the techniques that were developed there. I found Cambridge to be an excellent school of how to eliminate programming mistakes. All the business about library subroutines was just the same; that you should use as much as possible things that had already been checked out.

Daylight: In Cambridge you were programming the EDSAC in order to solve an astronomical problem. It is clear from what we have been discussing that you had a strong urge to understand science and, in particular, to further the state of the art in astronomy. But were you also carefully planning your career at that time? Were you pursuing an academic career?

Naur: I already had a degree finished from Copenhagen. The next natural step would have been a doctorate. I only realized much later that I could have used my EDSAC program as the central topic of my PhD thesis. Instead, it was just published in a paper. I accomplished my actual doctorate thesis five years later. Though it was also based on my work with the EDSAC, it had a lot more results with regard to astronomical observations and positions.

7.3 From Astronomy to ALGOL

Daylight: Did you, during the early 1950s, delve more into the work of Einstein?

Naur: Not really. I continued with astronomy after leaving Cambridge. I taught astronomy in Copenhagen for a while and then worked at the observatory in Copenhagen. Later, I moved into the new observatory which was being built in the middle of Sjaelland in Denmark, where I continued working on things which I had observed during my stay in the USA (1952–53).

Daylight: What did you do during your stay in the USA?

Naur: Besides looking into American computers, I continued my work on astronomy. For instance, I made observations from the McDonald observatory in Texas. That was in cooperation with Bengt Strömgren. He was a very outstanding Danish astronomer and I owe him much gratitude. He became director of the Yerkes observatory in Wisconsin. I spent a month with him at the top of the mountains in Texas and observed the magnitudes and colors of a certain selection of stars. He had a particular program for which this was useful. I also computed models of the interior of the sun: how the temperature and pressure increases when you go into the sun, and how the state is such that there will be an energy production from nuclear processes. That was all in the USA. Pure astronomy with lots of calculations.

I also spent a summer in the Watson Lab in Manhattan, New York. The computing machines there were more primitive than the EDSAC. They were IBM punch-card machines: the 602A electromechanical calculator and the 604 electronic calculator. That was for working on the structure of stars, integrating differential equations.

Daylight: The reason I mentioned Einstein again is because you wrote in your letter to me that you had a copy of Einstein's *The meaning of relativity*, dated 17 June 1950. You also wrote an obituary of Einstein [203] and you had a copy of his *Out of my later years* from around that time.

Naur: Yes, I wrote his obituary which shows that I was very well aware of his activities.

Daylight: You also wrote that you had become acquainted with the following authors by the mentioned dates:

- Whitehead's *Adventures of Ideas*, by 31 January 1951.

- Gallie's *Peirce and Pragmatism*, by 1952.

- Britton's *John Stuart Mill*, by 25 January 1957.

- Russell's *Mysticism and Logic,* by 25 January 1957.

Naur: That were Pelican books which I happened to pick up. I would usually read it and get an impression of what was happening there.

Daylight: Did you discuss these books with any of your colleagues in astronomy?

Naur: It was Peter Remnant, no one in Danish astronomy.

Daylight: In 1957 you had Russell's *Mysticism and Logic.* Do you recall whether you also bought this book, or did you borrow it?

Naur: Well, I have a copy here. [Naur also shows the four aforementioned Pelican books.] They were easy accessible you see, they were cheap too. Definitely, Peter Remnant mentioned Peirce to me, the inventor of pragmatism. My book is dated 1952 you see.

Daylight: In your 1995 book *Knowing and the Mystique of Logic and Rules*, you have countered Russell's claim that "there are such things as meanings that have one-to-one relationships with words" [219, p.52]. Were you during the late 1950s already delving deep into Russell's writings?

Naur: No. Definitely not.

[Naur gets some more books from his shelves and shows them.]

Much later, I picked up these books as well on psychology:

- *Criticism and the Growth of Knowledge*, edited by Lakatos and Musgrave, Cambridge University Press.

- Chomsky's *Language and Mind.*

- Quine's *Word & Object.*

- Quine's *From a Logical Point of View.*

- Quine's *Quiddities: an Intermittently Philosophical Dictionary.*

- Ayer's *The Problem of Knowledge.*

- Miller's *Psychology: the Science of Mental Life.*

- Wittgenstein's *Philosophische Untersuchungen.*

- Russell's *The Analysis of Mind.*

- Kuhn's *The Structure of Scientific Revolution*, second edition.

My interest in Quine definitely came from Peter Remnant, but I didn't study it thoroughly until around 1984. I believe Ayer was a student of Russell.

Daylight: I don't think many people in your field read Wittgenstein.

Naur: I'm sure that Dijkstra admired Wittgenstein.

Russell's *The Analysis of Mind* I got in 1991. In my 1995 book [219] I tried to find out how people wrote about mental life before 1950, that is before computers. I quote Russell at length in my Antiphilosophical Dictionary on perception [220]. Russell is so specific that I easily show how absurd his approach really is.

Kuhn's book I bought in 1983.

Daylight: In the late 1950s you started working at Regnecentralen in Copenhagen. So you had switched from astronomy to computing. That's quite a drastic switch, from the respectful field of astronomy to programming a machine. This looks like an abrupt change in your career.

Naur: In a way yes, in a way no. For me it was a great opportunity. It was the best thing that happened in my whole career. The new observatory in Sjaelland was in a completely absurd state. It was built to satisfy the ambitions of Bengt Strömgren, the Danish professor who was in charge but who was sitting in the USA for ten years! The people here didn't know what to do about it. It was an extremely frustrating situation. I did some work trying to put the meridian circle in working order, but that was impossible because it was understaffed to an extreme degree. As an astronomer it was extremely frustrating.

At the same time I was a consultant to the DASK project. It was in that capacity that I had the opportunity to propose the language of the machine, which was immediately adopted. So I had excellent contacts with them. I had advised them also in techniques to find programming mistakes, along the same lines of what I had done in Cambridge. My experience from Cambridge thus became extremely useful to this group. When I switched to Regnecentralen on the 1st of February 1959, it was very well prepared in advance. I was very happy to get out of astronomy and into an excellent group in Regnecentralen, headed by Niels Ivar Bech. He was the most fantastic leader of this sort of activities that I have ever encountered. That was how I got the opportunity to work on ALGOL.

Daylight: You just explained why your expertise from Cambridge was helpful at Regnecentralen. What was the background of your colleagues at Regnecentralen?

Naur: All the best staff were engineers. Regnecentralen was very much directed towards commercial applications of computing. They had to make a living. Some of my first tasks at Regnecentralen were engineering tasks.

One project was the calculation of radiation fields from antennas. It was related to the American space activity. You have a cylindrical rocket and you want to have an antenna so that you can communicate with it. The idea was to cut an helix around the rocket. The question was how that radiated. There was an expert at the technical university who was able to develop a theory of how the field would be in terms of formulae, infinite series of complex numbers. They wanted to tabulate it, so that was one of my tasks. It was with Bessel functions and all these sorts of things. I didn't understand the theory really, but I could take the formulae and write efficient programs for them.

I also had an application which was with a physicist at the Niels Bohr Institute. He had a very strange integral which he wanted me to evaluate. I did that for him and it was quite successful.

So these were applications that people would pay for. They were all problems in numerical analysis and thus very similar to the kind of things I had done in astronomy. For example, solving the equations of motion of a planet is a numerical analysis problem. I also taught numerical analysis at the technical university of Copenhagen for several years: integration, matrices, eigenvalue problems, etc.

Daylight: I don't have the impression that you felt you lacked some kind of expertise with regard to programming. It all went pretty well as I understand it. [N: Yes] Pretty soon, after joining Regnecentralen, you met several people on the international scene. You met Bauer, Samelson, Van Wijngaarden, Zonneveld, Dijkstra and others. Many of them were numerical analysts too.

Naur: They were very much so. Rutishauser in Zurich was very famous in numerical analysis. I'm sure Bauer and Samelson were primarily numerical analysts as well.

Daylight: How would you describe the first meeting you had with these people? You all had a similar technical background, so do you think you were perceived as their equal?

Naur: No. Not only was I quite a bit younger than most of them, I also clearly felt this central-European professor attitude — professor this, professor that. It is a style that I never much enjoyed and it is very different from the Anglo-Saxon relation. In this regard, I got very well along with Van Wijngaarden from Amsterdam. He was very strong in setting the informal style of discourse for the ALGOL meetings. I wrote a little article on Van Wijngaarden's contributions to ALGOL60 in [211].

Daylight: In 1959 you met Bauer, Samelson, Rutishauser, Van Wijngaarden, and others. Van Wijngaarden made an impression on you in that he set the tone, stressing that everyone was to be treated equally, regardless of whether he was a professor or not. But what about the subject matter itself, did someone make an impression on you technically? Did you feel that you and your colleagues at Regnecentralen were lagging behind technically compared with some of the other European and American players?

Naur: The ALCOR group (with Bauer, Samelson, Rutishauser) was to me a sort of central-European power play. They said that explicitly. They definitely wanted to be the most influential on the international scene. In the first phase, with our DASK machine, we at Regnecentralen tried to use the ALCOR techniques. That was a useful exercise because it showed ALCOR's limitations. Quite soon, we decided that we could do better on our own.

Daylight: Afterwards you started to collaborate with the Amsterdam group. [N: Yes, much more.] The Amsterdamers were much more in favor of dynamic memory management. [N: Yes] They had recursion, they didn't follow the static approach. Was this technically appealing to you? Did Wilkes's ideas from Cambridge have an influence on your work on compilers?

Naur: No, not Wilkes from Cambridge. [Pause] The whole thing about dynamic storage allocation — we were forced into that due to the severe storage limitations of our computer. Of course, Dijkstra developed the stack storage of variables. Then we also developed dynamic storage of the program, which Dijkstra and his colleagues did not consider.

Daylight: Can you elaborate on that? What do you mean with dynamic storage of the program?

Naur: Well, this was our `GIER` compiler for `ALGOL60`. It could handle the dynamic allocation of programs.

Daylight: Ah, are you referring to what was later called paging?

Naur: Paging yes. That was invented in Manchester. Jensen picked up the idea from there. We were forced into that because our computer had only 1K working store and the drum. So we developed this paging mechanism, both at run time and at translation time. We made a multi-pass compiler, which was very original. Most people would be proud if they had a one-pass compiler. We said: "Why should you? We have ten passes."

Daylight: So the Amsterdamers didn't go so far?

Naur: Not on the program, because they had a much bigger store.

The other thing is the checking of the program. We did a much better job at that compared to the Amsterdam group. I think Dijkstra admitted that quite clearly somewhere.

Daylight: Yes. He was impressed by the `GIER` compiler.

We are discussing the early 1960s. You must have corresponded a lot with Van Wijngaarden and Dijkstra.

Naur: Not a lot. Not a lot. I paid visits to them and they came here at a certain stage. That must have been the spring of 1960; they spent a few days with us. We learned a lot about their techniques: Dijkstra's stack solution of variables and blocks and so on.

Daylight: That's March 1960.

Naur: Yes, that could be. I also went to Amsterdam at a certain stage and stayed with Dijkstra for a week or so. Well, he came in the summer with his whole family and stayed with my family up in our little summer cottage. So we had quite a lot of private interchange.

Daylight: Did you talk about Wittgenstein then?

Naur: No, I don't think so.

Daylight: I have here your words, which are about the `ALGOL` compiler for the `DASK`:

> [In March 1960, t]he Dutch group impressed us greatly by their
> very general approach. However, although they were prepared to
> put their solution of the problem of recursive procedures at our
> disposal we decided to stick to the more modest approach which
> we had already developed to some extent. The reasons for this
> reluctance were practical. [205][217, p.118–119]

For technical reasons, you chose to initially stick to Bauer and
Samelson's compiler approach.

Naur: That's right.

Daylight: I also brought this paper about the `ALGOL60` compiler for
the `DASK`, entitled 'A Storage Allocation Scheme for `ALGOL60`'. Jensen,
Mondrup and you allowed the `ALGOL` programmer to explicitly express
information transfers between the core store and the drum [151].

Naur: I've forgotten all of this. [N: Laughter] I don't think I ever ran a
single `ALGOL` program on the `DASK`. I believe I was in America when the
`DASK ALGOL` was finished and when I came back we immediately started
on the `GIER` project. I had prepared the `GIER` project in the second half
of 1961 in North Carolina where I was research-associate lecturer in the
department of mathematics. This was with John Carr III.

Daylight: How was Carr like? He was an older man?

Naur: No, not that much. He was a little bit... I'm not quite sure I
really understood him. On the one hand, he had invited me. But at
a certain stage I had the impression he reacted against me — it was
hard to say. When I came back to Copenhagen, we at Regnecentralen
immediately started working on the `GIER` project, which ran until August,
1962. While doing that, I also went to a summer school in Chapel Hill in
1962 where I explained our methods for the `GIER`.

Daylight: Were you inspired by Carr when you were preparing the `GIER`
project?

Naur: No, not at all. But I did get inspired somewhat by some of
the other American projects. For example, using the inverse Polish
notation as an intermediate form of instructions during compilation. We
used this systematically in what I called pseudo evaluation. We had an
article describing this technique: 'Checking of Operand Types in Algol
Compilers' [206]. During compilation, you do a sort of evaluation. That
is, you form your operands in the stack in the way you would do at
execution time, but the operands are not values, they are descriptions
of the operands. They allow you to express very simply the instructions

you have to produce. It could be used both in type checking (pass 6 in our compiler) and in addressing of variables (pass 7).

Daylight: You were thus much more heavily involved in the GIER compiler, compared with the DASK.

Naur: Oh absolutely. The DASK was an attempt to use the ALCOR method. Jensen and Mondrup were mainly involved in this. The big problem was storage allocation; they had this 1K and magnetic tapes. It was a three-pass compiler and the second pass was too big for anything. It was very clumsy. The programming was very difficult because they always had to squeeze for space.

Daylight: Maybe your colleagues wanted to stick to the ALCOR agreement, instead of following Dijkstra's dynamic approach, because "the ALCOR train" had already departed and was heading somewhere.

Naur: The Dijkstra approach was concerned with the stack at run time. While the ALCOR group was much concerned with the translation process and their use of the "cellar" principle. Of course, we took over the details of their "cellar" operations during translation. We had one man, Willy Heise, he had spend some time there and later worked for Siemens. He was in Regnecentralen when I arrived. He had already been to the meeting about ALCOR in November 1958, before I had really joined Regnecentralen. We felt that it was a great help to have their logic for the translation process, and so it was used, but I wasn't concerned with it really.

Before we move on to the mid-1960s, I would like to stress the influence that my numerical analysis methods as an astronomer had on my later work in computing. I started as an astronomer doing computational work. At a certain stage in the 1960s, I had started teaching numerical analysis to engineers at the technical university. My teaching was based on the book *Modern Computing Methods* [198] which is about numerical analysis methods. Since part of my work was making up exercises for my students, I ended up writing the booklet *Twelve Exercises in Algorithmic Analysis*. This booklet contains numerical methods which the mathematicians called numerical analysis and which I called algorithmic analysis. I liked this field very much, I liked to play with it. When we had gotten the ALGOL60 compiler running, I had great fun in using it for experimenting with algorithms published in the Communications of the ACM. I tried them out and this is all reported in the Communications of the ACM. In a sense that was a sort of ultimate continuation of my work in this area. That was why we made a good programming language and compiler, it was a useful tool for our work with problems in this particular field.

7.4   Syntax and Semantics

Daylight: In your 1985 paper 'Intuition in software development' [214], you wrote about syntax and semantics as follows:

> In much recent discussion of text and language there is a strong tendency to take for granted that in dealing with texts one has to distinguish between things called syntax and semantics, and a corresponding unquestioned belief that the reading of a text must involve separate syntactic and semantic analyses. [214, p.66]

Last month you mentioned to me that the Swiss linguist Ferdinand de Saussure may have been the one who, unfortunately, introduced this in the beginning of the 20th century. [N: Yes] Nevertheless, you also wrote in your paper that this distinction between syntax and semantics is useful in compiler work, in programming languages. Could you elaborate?

Naur: A "programming language" is an inappropriate term. There is no similarity to the way we normally talk about language. That has been disgusting me all along, right from the beginning in the 1950s when I got into all of this. All these logicians from America, such as Saul Gorn, would immediately come with their formal languages. He had a Baker's Dozen of such languages [110] and that was all based on the idea of syntax and semantics.

Daylight: Did you meet Saul Gorn? Was he a logician?

Naur: I met him several times. He must have been a kind of logician, I suppose so. He was certainly influential in computing at that time. He wrote his paper on the Baker's Dozen in the Communications of the ACM. I was uneasy about his usage of the term language. Why should ALGOL60 be called a language? I was always uneasy about that.

Daylight: Yet, you say that in compiler work it is useful to distinguish between syntax and semantics. Why is that?

Naur: I suppose it is, yes. [Pause] In our early ALGOL60 compiler we had a number of passes, nine altogether. One may say that the first three were concerned with all that was syntax, because they were described in terms of the syntax notation. Some people used this formal description as a basis of a scanner; to analyze an incoming program. I was never fond of it and viewed it as a rather clumsy approach. At the syntax stage you use letters to identify things, but what they identify is at this stage immaterial. You are only concerned with the delimiters, the symbols in between them, and finding the structure.

Then comes the later processing where you take up which objects are identified by each of these names. That, you may say, is semantics.

Daylight: When you say semantics, do you also mean how the program is supposed to execute? The computational model? For example, the runtime system?

Naur: It's part of the semantics. The interpretation of the structure in terms of the order of execution, you have to repeat certain things and you have to skip certain things under certain conditions. That's part of semantics, surely.

Daylight: I would associate syntax with BNF notation, as presented in the ALGOL60 report [10].

Naur: That report indeed distinguishes between syntax and semantics. [Naur takes the ALGOL60 report from his shelves.] I was sure people would like this distinction. That's why I made it explicit throughout the report. Up here you are only concerned with how symbols are put together (the syntax), down here I explain how they are executed (the semantics). Usually I start with the assignment statement, syntax, in terms of BNF notation, then some examples, and then semantics, which explains how things are done.

Daylight: When you just talked about the passes of your ALGOL60 compiler, is the syntax-semantics distinction the same as in the ALGOL60 report?

Naur: Not really. [Pause] Well, in a sense one may say so.

Daylight: What is your reaction to those people who, in later years, also wanted to formalize the semantics of ALGOL60 and other programming languages? That's what Cliff Jones, for instance, wanted to accomplish with the Vienna Definition Language.

Naur: I am sure, and Van Wijngaarden very much. Well, that was a demonstration to me, of how you get into terrible trouble. In the case of Van Wijngaarden, the result was ALGOL68, a monstrum of complication. I am sure it is valid, it works because these people were extremely clever, but I don't think it is helpful. It is like Cliff Jones's paper on formalization where he formally specifies a permutation by taking up a lot of space. Putting that next to Donald Knuth's very simple explanation, expressed in ordinary language, shows what I mean. (See Daylight [55, p.64].)

Daylight: You stressed that syntax and semantics only serve a posteriori. In your words:

> [T]he essential point about such concepts as syntax and semantics
> is that they are not issues in terms of which a language may first
> be presented to a person. Rather, they may, at best, serve to
> bring out aspects of a language to someone who already has the
> language, intuitively. [214, p.67]

Naur: Yes, rules are descriptive. It is a form of description of something already known. And describing, of course, is a useful thing. All sciences are about describing.

Daylight: This brings me to your rejection of Turing's Test, which you elaborated on in your 1986 paper 'Thinking and Turing's Test' [215]. You wrote that if intelligent behavior could be accounted for in terms of rules of behavior, then this would lead to an infinite regress of rules, which is absurd [215, p.179].

Naur: If intelligent behavior depended on using certain rules, then there would have to be rules about how to apply the rules, etc., ad infinitum. I have also used this kind of argument against Russell which we have already discussed. (See Daylight [55, p.57].)

7.5 Understanding Turing's Universal Machine

Daylight: In the early 1990s you tested whether a description found useful to one programmer was equally useful to another programmer, by having your students study Turing's 1936 paper [291]. You wrote your findings down in:

- Understanding Turing's Universal Machine — Personal Style in Program Description [218].

I am curious why you chose Turing's paper for this project.

Naur: Turing presented a program in his paper which is totally different from what we have today. Of course, he didn't have anything better, he invented it all on the spot by his genius. Just understanding that is a challenge to any present-day person, a challenge which was a good way of having people think about program understanding. I've known the existence of Turing's 1936 paper for decades. I had glanced at it several times throughout my career and saw this strange symbolism with ancient German notation, altogether completely different from what we have nowadays. At a certain stage, I decided that I had to read and understand it, and I could only do so by adding to it a formal description.

I had to invent a supplementary description of his program, which is not in his work, so that I could formally describe the states of his machine in certain terms. This description is also explained in my 1995 book *Knowing and the Mystique of Logic and Rules* [219, p.198]. It's a snapshot representation of Turing's machine, inspired by my paper on snapshots from the 1960s [207]. As a result, I could make formal demonstrations of the correctness of his program. Then I challenged my students by asking them to develop a description that they would find helpful in understanding Turing's program. Furthermore, while doing that, they were asked to indicate the mistakes that are present in Turing's program. I found that this was a useful course activity with the students. It gave the challenge to test out whether formal descriptions appealed.

The course activity had two phases. In the first phase, every student had to study Turing's program and formulate an additional description that would help other people understand Turing's program. Every student would then submit a report, and then I would mix into that my own report which they were not aware of. All reports were anonymous. In the second phase, everyone had to look at all the other reports and note down whether they found them to be clear and helpful. In this way, I forced them to look at my very formal description, which was somewhat unique compared to the other reports. I was curious how people would react to it. I found that the reaction to my description was very much person dependent. Some students considered it simply hopeless. Others thought it was a great aid. That shows something about the personal aspects of understanding.

As you can read from the introduction of my paper, my purpose to do this project was two-fold:

> The primary purpose of the present study is to present some empirical evidence related to the programmers' understanding and their use of descriptions in computer programming. Key issues are the importance of individual style differences and of formalized descriptions in programming. A secondary purpose is to demonstrate a technique for empirical investigation of issues of programming. [219, p.189]

Empirical evidence was what I wanted. The conclusion is that some people like formal descriptions and others don't. It's a very personal matter. There's no middle way so to speak.

Daylight: You're saying that each individual has his or her own preferred style of program development. But is it possible that there are, say, at most ten different styles?

Naur: No, my style, for instance, was developed solely for Turing's program and served no other purpose. For another program, I would very likely develop another style.

Daylight: It is Turing's original 1936 paper that you gave to your students. [N: That's right.] That paper also interested you a lot, you wanted to finally get down to understanding it.

Naur: Yes, and it should also interest the students because it is a fundamental paper of the whole field and it is unknown. Nobody knows about Turing's paper. I've talked about this in working conferences in the United States. This is the most famous paper in computing, and I asked how many people in the audience had ever read it. Nobody. [N&D: Laughter] That's what it is like.

Daylight: I think you may be one of the few who has actually read his paper.

Naur: Probably. And of those who were aware of his 1936 paper, very few understood the difference between a Turing Machine and the Universal Machine. Many people have mixed up the two, thinking that a Universal Machine must be a Turing Machine. Any computer you see in this room is controlled by a program and thus is a Universal Machine. In this way you can simulate any other machine's program by programming.

Daylight: Was it difficult to organize such a project at the university?

Naur: No difficulty at all.

Daylight: In your paper you wrote:

> On this background, one relevant question is whether there is a clear correlation between the formal properties of the description forms used by a programmer and the understanding achieved by the programmer. [218, p.351]

Naur: The understanding achieved was partly measured in terms of the number of errors found by the students. Some of the students, themselves, introduced and used their own formal notation. Others used examples, which can be quite effective too. That's what Polya would say: start with concrete examples and then get the knack of it. Some did step-by-step execution of the program which is reasonable if you are completely unfamiliar with Turing's program. They would then get stuck rather quickly, because there is an error in Turing's paper which entails that you will get stuck rather quickly if you follow a step-by-step approach. One of the students did get stuck and could not continue reading Turing's paper. [N&D: Laughter]

Daylight: These errors that Turing made, can't they all be easily resolved?

Naur: Some of them, not all of them. There were some subtle errors. I listed all errors in my paper and I discussed the corrections [218, p.353]. The list also shows who corrected which errors, again showing the individuality of such understanding.

Daylight: Many thanks Peter Naur for this discussion.

Naur: You are most welcome.

8. Deromanticizing Turing's Role in History

This book is primarily about Turing's influence on programming and his influence on Dijkstra's thinking in particular. As a result, several other major historical actors, like Aiken, Atanasoff, Babbage, Eckert, Goldstine, Hopper, Mauchly, Stibitz, and Zuse have only been mentioned briefly or not at all.

It should at least not go unmentioned that the American computer builder Howard Aiken was already building computing machines during the early 1940s at Harvard. Similar to the German engineer Konrad Zuse, Aiken did not depend on Turing's 1936 paper to further his early research in computer building [245, p.123]. In the mid-1940s, Grace Hopper joined Aiken's group and would soon thereafter become a leading researcher in automatic coding, later called automatic programming. In her field there were only a few people during the 1950s, like Gorn and Carr, who became sufficiently acquainted with mathematical logic in order to connect metamathematics and Turing's 1936 notion of universal machine with their own profession of instructing a real computing machine.

Taking the above observations into consideration, I now turn to the mid-1940s when Turing himself was connecting his theoretical 1936 paper to real computing machinery. In 1947, for example, Turing said the following:

> Let us now return to the analogy of the theoretical computing machines [...] It can be shown that a single special machine of that type can be made to do the work of all. It could in fact be made to work as a model of any other machine. **The special machine may be called the universal machine.**

This passage, cited from the introduction of Davis's bestseller[109], illustrates Turing's clear vision in 1947. As elaborated on in Chapter 2, it would take some more years before others, like the switching theorist

Moore and Davis himself, would see the connection between Turing's 1936 paper and real computing machinery. In fact, seeing this connection in the early 1950s led Davis to start writing his book *Computability & Unsolvability* [47], an undertaking which took several years. The book was published in 1958 and was very novel exactly because it brought Turing machines to the fore and in connection with real computing machinery. One of its reviewers even derided that very connection, as Davis has recollected in a recent interview (see Chapter 2).

During the 1950s many, if not most, computer practitioners were not in a position to connect Turing's work with real computing machines. It is in this intellectual climate that Aiken, a leading researcher of his time, made the following statement in a 1955 lecture:

> If it should turn out that the basic logics of a machine designed for the numerical solution of differential equations coincide with the logics of a machine intended to make bills for a department store, I would regard this as the most amazing coincidence I have ever encountered. [50, p.xi][53, p.xiii]

This passage, too, comes from the introduction of Davis's bestseller[110]. During the past decades, Davis contributed greatly to increasing the public awareness of Alan Turing. This is for the good but, unfortunately, it comes with little appreciation of other researchers, like Zuse and Aiken. Consider, for instance, the following reference by Davis to the above words of Aiken:

> Aiken made this *remarkable* assertion in *1956 [1955]* when computers that could readily be programmed to do both of these things were already commercially available. If Aiken had grasped the significance of Alan Turing's paper, published two decades earlier, he would never have made such a *preposterous* statement. [50, p.140, my italics][53, p.124, my italics]

According to Davis, the computer pioneer Aiken was clearly lagging behind on the current events of his time. Conformance with Mahoney's histories of computing [182], by contrast, leads to a more positive characterization of Aiken. Speaking as a leading figure in computing, Aiken did not depend on Turing's 1936 theory of computation to further his research. Moreover, as mentioned before, Davis himself did not initially see the connection between Turing's 1936 paper and real-world computing machines either. In 1955, when Aiken made his "preposterous" statement, Davis was still writing his book to get the message across!

According to Jack Copeland, Davis has taken Aiken's quote out of context and has misunderstood Aiken's point. Copeland defends the case that

Aiken's quote had nothing to do with Turing's theoretical concept of universality [44, p.36]. My interpretation of Copeland's critique is that Aiken was not "lagging behind" as Davis proclaims.

I disagree with Copeland's claim that Aiken's quote had nothing to do with Turing's theoretical concept of universality. As opposed to using one machine for data processing applications and another for scientific computations, Aiken, in his 1955 lecture, was coming to grips with the possibility that a single machine could be used for both application domains. In retrospect then, Aiken *was* discussing some important practical implications of Turing's theoretical notion of 'universal machine' but without being intimately aware of Turing's role in this matter. My disagreement with Davis is that it was very normal *not* to see this connection between Turing's 1936 paper and practice during the 1950s.

In this regard I also present Gerrit Blaauw's 2011 recollections. Blaauw was a colleague of Aiken during the late 1940s and early 1950s, a colleague of Dijkstra in Amsterdam during the early to mid 1950s, and an employer of IBM in New York from the mid 1950s to the mid 1960s. Blaauw was involved with the IBM STRETCH computer and became a leading architect of the IBM System 360. The "general purpose" character of these two computers stood in sharp contrast to the many special-purpose stored-program machines that IBM had been building during the 1950s and early 1960s [30][54]. Instead of building a special machine for data processing and another one for scientific computing, Blaauw and his close colleagues (including Turing Award winner Fred Brooks) started, during the late 1950s, to see the all-purpose character of their stored-program computers. This realization was reflected in the names of their computers: the word "stretch" alluded to stretching over different application domains, and "360" referred to 360 degrees; that is, to a machine that could handle all application domains. Just like the majority of IBM employees, Blaauw was an engineer, not a theoretician who was aware of earlier developments in logic. Blaauw recalls the engineering work that led to the System 360 in the following manner:

> We had a really new idea, namely that you have a modest machine that can execute exactly the same instructions as the big machine; the only difference is that the big machine runs faster and has more memories. So that was a key insight, that a bigger machine need not be designed differently. [Translated from a Dutch oral interview [54].]

Blaauw was only one of many who, during the course of history, became aware of the all-purpose character of contemporary computers without relying on theoretical research into logic.

8.1 Turing's Influence on Programming was Felt Gradually

Instead of plunging into the history of the computing machine, I have pondered Turing's influence on programming and his indirect influence on Dijkstra's thinking in particular. Doing so has, I believe, brought Turing's true legacy to the fore. Logicians and programmers recast Turing's 1936 notion of universal machine. Gradually, during the 1950s, recast notions helped some leading switching theorists, hardware engineers, and researchers in automatic programming to see the bigger picture of what they were accomplishing. In later years, Church's and Turing's undecidability results, in the form of Davis's 1958 Halting Problem or in a form equivalent to it, influenced some experts in the emerging field of high-level programming. Dijkstra was definitely one of them.

Turing's 1936 paper, and computability theory in general, only impacted programming in some quarters and only gradually. For example, the design and implementation of the ALGOL60 programming language took place too soon for Turing's 1936 paper on computability to make a noticeable impact. It was during the 1960s and later that people like Strachey, Böhm, Jacopini, Dijkstra, and Hoare did become sufficiently acquainted with some of the practical implications of computability theory in order for them to write about it[111]. McCarthy was a bit earlier in this respect in that he had already written about Turing machines by 1956 and had learned some practical implications of Turing's work in later years in connection with his LISP language. Similar remarks hold for McCarthy's early but limited reception of Church's λ-calculus.

The notable exception, not mentioned so far, is Henry Gordon Rice who by 1960 was not only well versed in computability theory by education but had also become an experienced computer programmer. In a 1960 letter to the editor of the Communications of the ACM, he explained *both* the theoretical implications of recursion in programming with regard to computability and its practical implications with regard to machine efficiency. Moreover, he also conveyed Van Wijngaarden and Dijkstra's linguistic incentive to include the recursive procedure in ALGOL60, well aware of the fact that these Amsterdamers did not necessarily intend to use it in their ALGOL60 programs.

To express my appreciation for Rice's insight in 1960, I first fast forward to the 1962 Rome symposium (discussed in Chapter 3) where Dijkstra,

Duncan, and a few others were advocating recursive procedures in `ALGOL`-like languages. Duncan, in accordance with Dijkstra's views, compared a restricted version of `ALGOL60` with the actual `ALGOL60` language in the following way:

> [T]here may be a significant class of problems for which, because of the restricted language, the source program may need to be more cumbersome and complicated than it would have been had the full powers of Algol 60 been available. [230, p.368]

An example of Duncan's 'restricted language' is a language in which procedures cannot call other procedures. As we have seen, such a restriction was most notably supported by the West-Germans Bauer and Samelson much in line with programming tradition.

Dijkstra, on the other hand, allowed the programmer to use procedure calls in full generality. In response to Duncan's comment, Dijkstra went even a step further by stating that

> [...] you are not only hindered by restrictions that prohibit you to do things, it is even so that you gain by possibilities *that are not actually used in the program* at all. [230, p.368, my italics]

These words capture Dijkstra's insistence on generality. By allowing all kinds of procedure activations, including those that are not used in practice like the recursive procedure activation, one obtains a very general language. The gain, mentioned by Dijkstra, lies in the reduced amount of effort needed to understand and implement the generalized language in comparison with a language that is defined in terms of many case distinctions.

Dijkstra wanted procedure calls of any kind to be expressible, so that the language would be simple and, hence, easy to implement. Allowing some kinds of procedure calls and prohibiting others, was in violation of his and Van Wijngaarden's linguistic ideals. It seems that Dijkstra's prime, if not only, concern was to pursue simplicity by means of general principles. Finding a way to implement recursive procedures was merely a byproduct of his urge to generalize.

I now elaborate on Rice's two-page letter [255] which was published in September 1960, one month after Dijkstra and Zonneveld stunned the computing world by completing their `ALGOL60` implementation, an implementation which could handle recursive procedures. In his letter, Rice used the term recursion in a mathematical context. It is important to recall that recursion can be implemented on a computer in several ways, for example by means of the modern *while–do* construct, the goto statement, or the recursive procedure. ALGOL60 did not have the modern *while–do* construct but it did have an equally powerful *for* construct as well as the goto statement and the recursive procedure.

ALGOL60's widely used *for* construct and goto statement made the recursive procedure superfluous in terms of computability, a fact which only became common knowledge among ALGOL researchers during the late 1960s. Rice, however, seems to have already been aware of this in 1960.

Rice started his letter by describing the controversy surrounding ALGOL60's recursive procedure.

> There appears to be a certain amount of programmer interest, currently, in recursively-defined functions and in self-calling subroutines to evaluate these functions. The ability of some new programming systems to handle such situations has been claimed. Programmers without these powerful tools, however, wonder about other ways of handling the same functions. In the interest of practical, economical computing, and with the help of some basic facts from the theory of recursive [i.e. computable] functions, the following suggestions are made. [255]

These words from Rice show, again, that several computer practitioners were, during the 1960s, debating the practical merit of ALGOL60's recursive procedure. When recast into the terminology of computability theory, these practitioners wanted to know whether it was a superfluous language construct in terms of computability.

Rice suggested to the readership of the Communications of the ACM not to use recursion if it could be avoided. To Rice, machine efficiency was more important than a beautiful mathematical argument expressed in terms of recursion. In his words:

> When to recur? Never if you can avoid it. Recursive definitions provide a neat way for mathematicians to define functions, and are very convenient for proving things about functions by mathematical induction. However, they are a poor form in which to specify functions for computation. [255]

To clarify why recursion required an enormous amount of machine time, Rice made the following analogy. Computing a function from a recursive definition is like looking up its value in a serial memory, while computing a function from a closed form or analytical expression is like looking up its value in a random access memory and, hence, far more efficient [255].

Based on his theoretical knowledge, Rice noted that some form of recursion was, however, needed in the programming language at hand in order to be able to compute any computable function.

> Unfortunately, however, *recursion cannot always be avoided*. It can be proved that certain functions cannot be defined in terms of certain sets of primitive functions except by recursion or something equivalent to it. [255, my italics]

Following the literature of the 1930s–1960s, much of the discussion in this book is about one simple method to compare programming languages, namely that of definability of functions on the natural numbers. In this setting, and as mentioned before, the distinction between the recursive procedure and the goto statement (or the modern *while–do* construct) vanishes. The reason is that one can use numeric tricks to encode essentially all storage management as manipulations of natural numbers.

Rice, however, also made the following observation in 1960. He noted that although in practice only primitive recursive functions are computed[112] it is not always easy, and sometimes very difficult, to recognize that the function at hand is indeed a primitive recursive one. Rice thus realized that some form of recursion in a program can come in handy, even though the function to be computed is primitive recursive. Today we can refine Rice's observation by elaborating on two language constructs that can be used to implement recursion: the iterative and potentially unbounded *while–do* construct and the recursive procedure. The former is a far less powerful technique than the latter in terms of what many people today call *expressive power*, a metric that has yet to be precisely characterized among programming language researchers. In Liskov's words from Chapter 6: "By expressive power we [mean] making it easy to write the programs that we [think] you ought to be writing." The reader is thus warned not to slip into the "Turing tarpit" of thinking that because all common programming languages are Turing equivalent they are therefore indistinguishable from one another.[113]

Definability of functions on the natural numbers is one way to compare programming languages. Expressive power is a second (albeit informal) way to compare programming languages. As we have seen, Van Wijngaarden and Dijkstra used a third calibration technique based on their sense of mathematical aesthetics. Rice ended his 1960 letter by implicitly referring to the linguists Van Wijngaarden and Dijkstra and thereby demonstrating his understanding of their incentive to introduce recursive procedures in ALGOL60.

> There are circumstances, other than the computing of functions

> from recursive definitions, in which the problem arises of a
> subroutine operating simultaneously on more than one level.
> Usually the question is one of producing extremely general and
> unrestricted program components, which may be interconnected
> with complete *freedom*. The preceding remarks of course do not
> apply here. [255, my italics]

Rice understood the linguists' appeal for generality in the interest of implementation simplicity, regardless of whether the recursive procedure was to be used in an ALGOL60 program or not.

Unlike Rice, most computer practitioners did not during the early 1960s see that ALGOL60's recursive procedure is superfluous in terms of computability. In fact, if the West-Germans Bauer and Samelson had grasped the contents of Rice's 1960 letter and applied Kleene's Normal Form theorem from a programming perspective, as explained in Chapter 2, then they would have had a strong theoretical argument not to implement recursive procedures for the ALGOL60 language.

The debate about the recursive procedure continued through all of the 1960s. In 1963, the computer practitioner James A. Ayer wrote a letter entitled 'Recursive Programming in FORTRAN II'. Ayer explained how he was able to implement recursive activations in FORTRAN II by "deceiving the FORTRAN compiler into allowing a subprogram to call itself". He also wrote that

> It is hoped that the technique described [in my letter] will draw the
> poison from the FORTRANers' wounds by allowing them to recurse
> to their complete satisfaction [5].

Ayer's letter is only one of many that illustrates the widening gap between the ALGOL60 academics and the FORTRAN practitioners or, more generally but at the expense of over-simplification, between the soon-to-be computer scientists and the real-world computer practitioners. Dijkstra's later case against the goto statement widened the gap even further.

The controversy surrounding the recursive procedure was in large part due to the machine inefficiency of early ALGOL60 implementations. Recursive procedures required an enormous amount of machine time, not to mention dynamic storage, in comparison with the many iterative FORTRAN programs. Rice's follow-up letter from 1965 addressed this issue in greater detail by discussing a specific example:

> [T]here may not exist a case [in ALGOL60] that will run recursively
> in an economically feasible amount of machine time, and yet that
> takes long enough in FORTRAN to be able to time it. [256]

In 1969, the debate about the recursive procedure remained unsettled to many, as Sammet's book illustrates (see Chapters 2 and 4). With hindsight, this is not surprising. Böhm and Jacopini's 1966 paper was only a few years old and was, and still is, by no means easy to understand. Furthermore, theoretically inclined men like Hoare had yet to make the connection between computability theory and programming explicit in their own writings.

Did Dijkstra Read Turing's 1936 Paper?

The influence of computability theory on imperative programming was only felt gradually from the second half of the 1960s and onwards. Dijkstra's impact on programming, on the other hand, was felt directly in 1960. Van Wijngaarden and Dijkstra's generalizing style had paved the way for implementation simplicity of ALGOL-like languages. In August 1960, Dijkstra and Zonneveld completed their ALGOL60 implementation, months and even years ahead of their European colleagues[114]. Dijkstra's 1962 keynote address in Munich illustrates how far apart his ideas on generalization stood from contemporary programming practice.

It seems fair to conclude that Dijkstra's reception of Turing's 1936 paper was indirect but, nevertheless, very relevant for his own work. In later years he confirmed that he did not read the mathematical logic literature in detail, nor with any great interest[115]. My educated guess is that Dijkstra never eagerly studied Turing's 1936 paper either, even though he very likely had come across it during the 1950s and most probably by the early 1960s[116]. However, it took several more years before he started to apply the unsolvability of the Halting Problem. Minsky's 1967 book *Computation: Finite and Infinite Machines* [197] made all the difference to him. Not only did Dijkstra write about Turing by citing Minsky's book in his 1971 lecture notes, he most likely had already studied Minsky's book in 1967 before finishing EWD 117. In Section 2.3.1 we saw that Dijkstra's EWD 117 referred to the "well known" fact that "there exists no algorithm to decide whether a given program ends or not" [80, p.10].

Just like McCarthy's limited reception of Church's λ-calculus and Hoare's limited reception of Kleene's *Metamathematics*, Dijkstra, too, was eager to advance his field of programming as opposed to becoming a mathematical logician or an historian of science. He did not have any strong incentive to read Turing's 1936 paper in detail.

8.2   Important Points

To conclude, I reiterate over some important points that I have either mentioned briefly or discussed in detail in this book. First, I urge the reader to doubt the claim that Turing played a crucial role in the advent of the first universal computers. Defending such a strong statement about Turing's priority requires elaboration on the earlier work of Zuse, Aiken, and others. Both Zuse and Aiken had already built "universal" computers by 1941 and 1944, respectively. They did not use the adjective "universal" to describe their machines because they did not depend on Turing's 1936 notion of universal machine to further their research.

Second, to examine logic's role in the history of computing, it is fruitful to investigate where and how papers from logic were cited and why those papers were discussed at conferences. In Chapter 2 I have tried to do just that with regard to Turing's 1936 paper and primarily for the field of automatic programming. Similar investigations have yet to be conducted for artificial intelligence and complexity theory. My thesis is that Turing's influence was felt more in programming and after his death than in computer building during the 1940s. From this historical perspective, it is no surprise that the first Turing Award went to Alan J. Perlis for his contributions in the area of advanced programming techniques and compiler construction (i.e. automatic programming).

Third, Turing's 1936 paper and the mathematical logic literature at large were only received gradually and only in some quarters of computing. This raises the question whether Turing Award winners, themselves, ever read Turing's work. Turing's 1936 paper influenced the 1972 Turing Award winner Dijkstra indirectly but significantly. The 1973 Turing Award winner Bachman, by contrast, did not even know who Turing was prior to 1973. While Dijkstra conducted research in an academic environment, Bachman worked in the database industry.

Fourth, the crucial developments concerning `ALGOL60` during the 1950s and early 1960s took place too soon for Turing's work to make a noticeable impact. In particular, Dijkstra's incentive to include the recursive procedure in `ALGOL60` had nothing to do with recursive function theory (i.e. computability theory). In fact, if some of Dijkstra's proponents, like Bauer and Samelson, had grasped the theoretical superfluousness of the recursive procedure in terms of computability, then they would have had a strong argument not to admit the recursive procedure in the `ALGOL60` language. In later years, Dijkstra was one of the first to do that albeit with regard to the superfluousness of the goto construct and by an appeal to Böhm and Jacopini's theoretical 1966 paper.

Fifth, as Turing acknowledged himself in his 1936 paper, Church scooped him in resolving the Entscheidungsproblem. Also, contrary to what many believe, it was not Turing who defined the Halting Problem. It was Church who did so in 1936 without using those specific words. During the 1950s, Davis introduced the words "Halting Problem" and defined them in terms of the recast notion of a "Turing machine", not in terms of Turing's original automatic machines. In short, by seeking a hero like Turing we are often, albeit unintentionally, disrespecting his true accomplishments and at the expense of others.

Errata

Errata are available at *www.dijkstrascry.com/dawn*

Acknowledgments

My gratitude goes first and foremost to Robert Harper who discussed every chapter of this book with me and who provided me with extra motivation to write this book in the first place. Many endnotes are in large part due to him. I also thank John Reynolds for commenting in no less than 9 pages on the Advance Reading Copy of this book and thereby contributing to several technical improvements.

I furthermore thank the following people for providing me with valuable feedback: Gerard Alberts, Tony Dale, David Nofre, Jos Peeters, Raphael Poss, Wilfried Sieg, Robert Soare, Paul Vitànyi, and several anonymous reviewers.

I thank the Dijkstra family for handing over a large part of Edsger W. Dijkstra's documents, including the two pictures shown on the front cover. I am indebted to Tracy Wilkinson and King's College for permitting me to use the two pictures of Turing on the front cover.

Last but not least, I thank the editor, Kurt De Grave. His painstaking efforts in repeatedly scrutinizing the form and content of this text along with his care for the cover design have led to what I believe is a high-quality book.

Endnotes

[1]See [51]. The paperback version of the book is entitled *Engines of Logic: Mathematicians and the origins of the Computer* [50]. The second edition of the book [53] was published in 2012. There is essentially no difference between the first and the second edition except for some technical editing.

[2]Davis claims that Turing played a central role in the advent of the "first universal computers" and, in particular, in influencing Von Neumann's work with the `EDVAC` [50, p.186–187][53, p.166].

[3]As Davis states himself in [50, p.xii][53, p.xiv]. Some engineers *are* treated toward the end of the book.

[4]See Chapters 5 and 6 in Mark Priestley's book *A Science of Operations* [245]. Zuse's 1941 machine was called the Z3 and Aiken's 1944 machine was called the Mark I. See page 46 in Zuse's biography for his *later* reception of the propositional calculus [316].

In the first edition of his book, Davis does not mention Zuse who started building computing machines even before Turing began writing his 1936 paper [249, p.155]. A similar concern has also been raised by Blank in his book review of Davis's bestseller [21]. In the second edition of his book, Davis has only added two stand-alone sentences about Zuse. See [53, p.158].

Davis's writings nevertheless suggest that he was aware of Zuse's achievements. In his 1988 paper 'Mathematical Logic and the Origin of Modern Computers' [49] and also in his later 2000 bestseller, Davis referred to Brian Randell's popular 1973 book *The Origins of Digital Computers: Selected Papers* [249] which contains a chapter about Zuse's early engineering work.

Furthermore, recent work by Bruderer shows that Zuse and Turing even met in 1947 [29, p.4]. Such a meeting may, or may not, be of extreme significance in the history of the first universal computer*s*.

Moreover, as I will explain later, Zuse may also have been very influential in the history of programming. According to Zuse's biography [316, p.34,53,135], he was initially not aware of Babbage nor of Turing. Other sources that back up this claim are presented later in Chapter 2.

I will discuss Davis's brief account of Aiken's work in the last chapter of this book.

[5]Extensive support for this conclusion can be found in Priestley [246, p.89][245, p.125].

In addition, the following words from January 1945 by Von Neumann contradict Davis's central thesis.

> The ENIAC was an absolutely pioneer venture, the **first** complete automatic, **all-purpose** digital electronic computer. [223, my emphasis]

The ENIAC was a program-wired machine and a precursor to the EDVAC. Neither Turing nor Von Neumann participated in the ENIAC project. The leading engineers of the ENIAC, Mauchly and Eckert, had thus already built an all-purpose computer according to Von Neumann himself! Hence, the ENIAC is yet another example, besides the machines of Zuse and Aiken, that can be used to discredit Martin Davis's bestseller.

The above quote is also presented on page 73 in George Dyson's just published book *Turing's Cathedral* [87]. My review of Dyson's book is available on my website (*www.dijkstrascry.com/dawn*).

[6]In the sequel, I will avoid using the word "science" as in "computer science" and "theoretical computer science", because it has been contested by historical actors. See, for example, Oettinger [228] and Naur [216]. Instead I will use the word computing to encompass several fields, including programming languages (and, more generally, software engineering), artificial intelligence, and complexity theory.

[7]Moreover, on page 231 in his 1936 paper, Turing explicitly referred to Church's papers [40, 41] and acknowledged that Church had already reached similar conclusions with regard to computability and the Decision Problem.

According to Turing's biographer, Andrew Hodges [136], Turing was not aware of any of Church's work while he wrote (most of) his 1936 paper, even though he submitted his paper for publication right after having received Church's 1936 published paper 'A Note on the Entscheidungsproblem' [40]. Hodges has backed up this claim by presenting the personal correspondence of Turing, his colleagues, and his family. Turing may thus have been scooped to a significant extent, but that does not mean we should credit him for the result without abandoning the whole idea of academic credit in the first place.

Later research conducted by Gandy [103] and by Sieg [277, 278] does not alter Church's priority over Turing. Sieg claims that *both* Church's proof and Turing's proof of the unsolvability of the Decision Problem require further justification. His general point, in modern day terminology, is that whatever model of computation is used to prove the undecidability result at hand, the primitive steps must be self-evidently "computable" in some prior sense to the sense being defined. In subsequent work, Sieg has tried to remedy the problem by articulating axioms for the abstract notions of "Turing Computor" and "Gandy Machine" and proving appropriate representation theorems. I am not in a position to judge whether Sieg has been successful in this respect.

[8]Church showed that it is undecidable whether a λ-term normalizes or not [41].

[9]The Halting Problem is defined in Martin Davis's 1958 book *Computability and Unsolvability* [47]. According to Copeland [43, p.40, footnote 61], Davis may have already formulated the Halting Problem in 1952.

[10]See, for example, Chapters 2 and 7, and also Petzold [240].

[11]ACM is an abbreviation for Association for Computing Machinery.

[12]In particular, the influence of Church's λ-calculus on programming lies outside the scope of this book but should definitely be taken up in future research.

In this book I shall moreover not discuss Church's thesis nor Turing's thesis but instead refer to Wilfried Sieg's 'On Computability' [278], Robert Soare's 'Computability and Recursion' [282], and their extensive bibliographies.

[13]See also Priestley [245, p.136–137, 139] for scrutiny of Davis's account of Turing's role in influencing Von Neumann's work with the EDVAC.

[14]In retrospect one can say that the stored-program computer embodies the universal Turing machine in the way the modern computer does. But this does not mean that the stored-program computer emerged simply as a byproduct of theoretical research into logic, as, according to Mark Priestley, Martin Davis wants his readership to believe [53, Chapter 8]. It was primarily due to *engineering* arguments that the EDVAC became the first stored-program computer [245, p.138–139].

It should then also be stressed again that, in retrospect, the earlier machines of Zuse (1941) and Aiken (1944) were all-purpose computers too, even though they were not stored-program computers. A similar remark holds for the ENIAC of Mauchly and Eckert (1945/46).

Turing's universal machine can serve as a model for the aforementioned non-stored-program machines too, irrespective of whether historical actors actually did so during the 1940s and 1950s. Recall from Endnote 5 that at least one person, John Von Neumann by January 1945, *did* see the connection between Turing's universal machine and the already-existing ENIAC, i.e. a program-wired and all-purpose machine.

[15]The adjectives "universal" and "all-purpose" are used as synonyms in this book. The first adjective refers to Turing's theoretical 1936 notion of universal machine. The second adjective mainly comes in handy for the many engineers and programmers who, during the course of history, also became aware of the universal character of their computers but *without* relying on theoretical research into logic.

[16]See, for example, the accounts of Knuth [158, 163], Valdez [294], Zuse [316], Barton [13], Waychoff [297], and Galler & Rosin [101].

[17]See Knuth [162, p.24–25], de Beer [19, p.9], Slater [280, p.41–50], Randell [249, p.155–157], and Priestley [245, p.121].

[18]Cited after Valdez [294, p.35]. See also Bruderer [29, p.4] for an indication of Zuse's indirect yet influential role and Rutishauser's role in the development of ALGOL60.

[19]The word "compiler" used in this ALGOL60 context refers to *both* the actual compiler and the corresponding runtime system. This is in conformance with the way actors like Dijkstra used the term "compiler". In this book, context will disambiguate the intended meaning of the word "compiler".

[20]Again, an executed ALGOL60 program exhibits dynamic behaviour in terms of memory requirements compared with the a priori fixed storage of the machine.

[21]Virtual memory was already implemented in the Atlas system at the University of Manchester between 1959 and 1961 [294, p.82].

[22]Only in the early 1970s did Dijkstra become an ardent supporter of Hoare's logical approach to programming language semantics. See Dijkstra's recollections [79, p.346].

[23]The axioms have to be sufficiently powerful in that they can support encoding of syntax as numbers in the theory. Otherwise the incompleteness theorem does not apply.

[24]To be more precise: the axioms have to be computably enumerable. One could formulate a theory in which the axioms are all true statements of arithmetic, and then of course one does not have any incompleteness. But, on the other hand, one cannot tell whether a given proposition is an axiom or not. So the requirement for enumerable axioms is the requirement that it can be computable whether or not something actually is an axiom.

[25]See Gödel [105]. Gödel called his primitive recursive functions "recursive functions". Only after Kleene's 1936 paper [153] were they renamed to "primitive recursive functions" [156, p.371].

Gödel and Rosser also showed that such a system cannot demonstrate its own consistency [52, p.230–231].

Gödel definitely proved that there are undecidable sentences in any system that adheres to the previously described constraints. But to claim that he proved that there are *true* but undecidable sentences in any such system implicitly relies on the assumption that arithmetic is interpreted in the standard model, an assumption that I only make explicit here because there is no disagreement about it.

[26]Gödel numbering is similar to Descartes's numbering of the x- and y- axis in the Cartesian plane in that it shows similarity between two apparently different structures. In the case of Descartes, geometric statements correspond to algebraic statements. In the case of Gödel, syntactical metamathematical statements correspond to arithmetic statements (cf. DeLong [58]).

[27]Moreover, Ackermann's result had already been discussed heavily before 1928 [278, p.551].

[28]Kleene actually used ϵ to denote his least number operator but would two years later change it to the now-familiar μ operator [153, 154]. See also Sieg [278, p.557].

[29]Besides Turing, also Post conducted research along these lines [246, p.36]. And, it was Church who, in 1937, had reformulated Turing's machines as modelling arbitrary machines instead of human calculators [137, p.8–9].

[30]According to Hodges and Priestley [137, p.4,6][246, p.76].

[31]Cf. Priestley [246, p.79, 84]. I stress, however, that Turing and Von Neumann became aware of this connection (between theory and practice) by observing *already-existing* all-purpose computing machines. I refer to my review of Dyson's book *Turing's Cathedral* on my website (*www.dijkstrascry.com/dawn*) for further details.

[32]Priestley mentions Wilkes, Prinz, and Oettinger as people who, during the early 1950s, had clearly grasped the practical implications of Turing's theoretical notion of universal machine [246, p.86–87]. Other examples are presented later.

[33]Kleene's monumental *Introduction to Metamathematics* [155] was published in 1952. It covers several topics of mathematical logic, including the concepts of "recursively defined functions" and "Turing machines". In Chapter XIII, Kleene showed that both concepts are equivalent, thereby reformulating what he, Church, Turing, and others had accomplished during the 1930s.

[34]Functions whose domains and ranges are restricted to the integers.

[35]See Calude [34, p.66]. Martin Davis thinks the anonymous reviewer was the logician J. Barkley Rosser as he conveyed to me in a private discussion in Ghent, Belgium on 8 November 2011.

[36]Cf. Davis [47, p.70]. The essential ideas underlying the proof were not novel, due to the prior work of Church and Turing [40, 41, 291].

[37]See Hasenjaeger [119, p.182], Zuse [316, p.34,53,135], Blank [21], Rojas [259], and Randell [249, Chapter IV].

[38]Hasenjaeger was also aided by the work of Moore and by Shannon's seminal paper 'A universal Turing machine with two internal states' [273].

[39]In this regard, see also the register machines proposed by Shepherdson and Sturgis in 1963 [276]. Their paper can be viewed as furthering Wang's research agenda, namely closing the gap between the theoretical and practical aspects of computation.

[40]The first occurrence of the words "programming language" in a technical paper seems to be in 'Empirical Explorations of the Logic

Theory Machine: A Case Study in Heuristic' [225], by Newell, Shaw, and Simon in 1957. An earlier occurrence can be found in a 1956 newsletter [97]. Source: Nofre et al. [227] which covers the metaphor "programming language" in greater detail.

[41] All papers were collected in a book, edited by Richard Goodman [106]. That book is dedicated to Alan Mathison Turing and Appendix One contains Turing's 1936 paper [291] and his follow-up correction [292].

[42] Cited from [286]. Strachey's description is, however, not entirely satisfactory. Under the realistic assumption that Strachey associated a 'program' with a Turing machine or something equivalent, a program can go on forever by *either* running in a 'closed loop' (forever), *or* by using an unbounded amount of memory space. A more accurate wording of the unsolvability of the Halting Problem is presented in Section 2.3.2 by citing Minsky [197, p.153].

[43] Combined Programming Language

[44] To be precise, Strachey had proved a modified version of the unsolvability of the Halting Problem as stated in Davis's 1958 book [47]. He had proved a version related to CPL programs instead of Turing machines.

[45] Since U is a primitive function and T a primitive recursive predicate, Kleene's Normal Form theorem states that exactly one *while–do* construct suffices in theory.

[46] I have received comments from people who claim that Dijkstra had already understood Turing's work during the 1950s. I do not contradict this claim in this chapter, but I do not have any evidence to support it either.

[47] See Dijkstra [68, p.55]. Dijkstra did not *refer* to Turing's 1936 paper, however.

[48] ALGOL researchers are researchers who were studying ALGOL-like languages, their formal semantics, and the like; these researchers were not necessarily advocates of ALGOL60 or ALGOL68 per se.

[49] As Dijkstra stated in [79, p.346]. See also: DuWorks & Smoliar [86], Moore [199], and Rubin [261].

[50] Cf. Dijkstra [79, p.346], Santini [267, p.128], and Valdez [294, p.205].

[51] Cited from Knuth [161, p.262].

[52]Cf. Dijkstra's own words based on an interview in [294, p.211].

[53]We have already seen that what is "well known" to one group of researchers may be unknown to another.

[54]Dijkstra has explicitly acknowledged this [73]. Similar observations have been made by David Harel [118, p.383] in 1980, concerning theoretical results that were published during the late 1960s and 1970s.

[55]The critical reader will note that I am relying on the Church-Turing thesis. Furthermore, ALGOL60 does not contain a modern *while–do* construct [10], but its *for* command is just as powerful. The modern command *while B do C* can be translated to the following ALGOL60 code: *for dummy:=0 while B do C* where *dummy* is a fresh variable.

[56]Minsky's proof of the unsolvability of the Halting Problem was conducted at the low level of Turing machines, not at the higher level of ALGOL60 programs (see Section 8.2, page 148 in [197]). Minsky did show in his book the computational equivalence between Turing machines and various other systems, including "Universal Program Machines with Two Registers" on page 255, but he did not prove the unsolvability of the Halting Problem directly in any of those computationally equivalent systems.

[57]Contrary to the computer practitioner, the computability theorist (e.g. Kleene, Post) was primarily interested in algorithms that do not halt on every input.

[58]Dijkstra did not use the words "Halting Problem" [72, p.15].

[59]The use of the word "linguistic" in connection with Dijkstra may seem strange today but it is in accord with the terminology he and others used during the 1960s. Dijkstra used it [65, p.241] and so did Perlis in his recollections [238]. See also my blog: *www.dijkstrascry.com/node/25*.

[60]See Bauer & Samelson [17, p.121–122] and Naur [212, p.100–101].

[61]An example Rutishauser gave was calculating the factorial of a positive number n. It is more economical, both in space and time, to calculate it by iteration by means of a *for* loop than by recursive procedure activations.

[62]He published his recursive pseudo-ALGOL60 program in [111]; that is, before the publication of Hoare's QuickSort. Also Irons [147] should be mentioned in this regard.

[63]For example, the ALCOR compilers described in [265], the Danish DASK ALGOL compiler [151, p.441], and SMALGOL61 [6, p.502].

[64]The word "implementation" refers to both the compiler and the corresponding runtime system. The previous quote shows that during the 1960s the word "compiler" often referred to both the actual compiler and the runtime system.

[65]See [244]. The critical reader will note that the obtained definition is still unsatisfactory. The number π, for instance, adheres to the definition but cannot be stored on a finite machine.

[66]Rutishauser was also the inventor of the now-famous QD algorithm, which he explained in a 74-page booklet *Der Quotienten-Differenzen-Algorithmus* [269, p.3].

[67]See the comments of the American Perlis in [238] or Chapter 3 in De Beer [19].

[68]Gesellschaft für Angewandte Mathematik und Mechanik (Association of Applied Mathematics and Mechanics).

[69]Cf. Naur [212, p.112]. Today we know that it is almost impossible to write recursive grammar rules preventing the use of recursion. This was, however, not obvious to many ALGOL60 actors at the time.

[70]Van Wijngaarden and Dijkstra also made other contributions to the design of ALGOL60. See for example the proposal about complex numbers in Algol Bulletin section 7.35.

[71]Further support for this claim, involving also Van Wijngaarden and Dijkstra, can be found by reading Bauer's remarks in [212, Appendix 5] and, in particular, Bauer's words: "the Amsterdam plot on introducing recursivity" [212, p.130].

[72]Cited from a panel discussion which was held at the 1962 Rome symposium [230, p.368]. Incidentally, it is interesting to note that Strachey used the verb 'simplifying' to denote the opposite action of what Dijkstra associated with that verb.

[73]The question remains whether the analogy made by Dijkstra (and others) is warranted. Noting a similarity between the mathematician and a programmer does not exclude the possibility that there are one or more differences which make the analogy ineffective. Arguments of this kind have been presented repeatedly during the later course of history. For example by De Millo et al. [195], Fetzer [91], Dobson &

Randell [83], Naur [55], Van der Poel [242, p.6,17], Robinson et al. [258], and Zemanek [315].

[74]See Chapter 2 in LaForest [164].

[75]Dijkstra emphasized that one universal stack was sufficient to implement ALGOL60 [66, p.344].

[76]Contrary to what is suggested in [145, p.5] and [140, p.96].

[77]Cf. McCarthy [187, p.192–193]. Also, in John Reynolds's words in correspondence with me:

> Although one could write recursive programs in IPL-V, one had to explicitly code the stack manipulations that implement the recursion, using lists to represent the stack. In contrast, in LISP, a function recurred simply by calling itself. Moreover, LISP provided garbage collection, which avoided most storage leaks and permitted a more flexible use of aliasing.

[78]See Carpenter & Doran [37] and Davis [50, p.188, 237].

[79]Rutishauser, himself, mentioned in his 1963 paper [263, p.50] that he had implemented recursive subroutines for the ERMETH in the "pre-ALGOL days".

[80]Today we could view Dijkstra's work as a precursor to the Java virtual machine.

[81]See, for example, Samelson & Bauer [265, p.210] and Naur et al. [151, 205]. Also, the account of Randell and Russell [251, p.3] indicates that Dijkstra's machine-independent object language was unconventional at that time. However, once again, I stress that *no* claim is made in this chapter that Dijkstra was the *first* person to introduce a machine-independent object language. Other people had come up with similar ideas independently — see, for example, the remarks of Galler and Gallie in [232, p.528] and McCarthy's work on LISP in particular [284].

[82]See Naur [205, p.118, 120–124][208, p.94]. Also Samelson described the Amsterdam and ALCOR approaches as two different "schools of thought" [264, p.490].

[83]See Dijkstra [64, p.538]. Dijkstra and others used the word "translator" as a synonym for "compiler". In this context, the word "translator" is used in the strict sense of the word; that is, it excludes the runtime system of an ALGOL60 implementation.

[84]Cf. Randell [248, p.2]. See also Samelson's 1978 recollections in which he contrasts between "liberalists" such as Naur and "restrictionists" such as himself, and states that: "[U]nification burdens the normal case [in terms of machine efficiency] with the problems arising from the exceptional case" [212, p.132–133]. But, as Naur correctly points out [212, p.136], this partitioning of the ALGOL60 community into two opposing groups only took place in the years following the publication of the ALGOL60 report. See, in particular, the opposing views expressed at the Rome 1962 conference.

[85]See Randell & Russell [252, p.34]. Also Rutishauser, in 1962, had expressed the desire for such an approach [232, p.527].

[86]In this respect, see also Knuth's later comments on Dijkstra's "strong sense of aesthetics" and that Dijkstra "didn't want to compromise his notions of beauty" [90, p.41].

[87]It is perhaps safer to ascertain that the gap has widened between the 1960s and 1990s and to avoid making claims about the recent past.

[88]Note that this does *not* imply, however, that their research contributions have always led to industrial applications. Furthermore, Hoare has discussed his involvement with industry with me (Sections 4.2.2–4.2.3). He has also provided his own views concerning the contradistinction between practice and theory (Section 4.2.6), views which can be contrasted with those of Naur [55].

[89]It is for this very reason why one should also remain skeptical when reading an historical essay or an oral history such as those presented in this book!

[90]Some of the best research is conducted across disciplinary borders, according to both Hoare [131] and Naur [216].

[91]The word "interviews" is used on the front cover of this book for marketing reasons.

[92]An anonymous referee correctly pointed out to me that it would have been more correct to say that Turing's paper is on mathematical logic. Furthermore, the problem Turing was solving was one that concerns the foundations of mathematics. Finally, stating that Turing's paper does not contain a link to computing machines is, to say the least, ambiguous, since it is all about computing machines, be it, symbolic ones (and Turing explicitly used the word "computing machine" in his paper — see [240, p.72]).

[93]IFIP WG2.2, *Working Conference on Formal Language Description Languages*, Vienna, 15–18 September, 1964 [283].

[94]As discussed in Chapter 3, the famous sentence states that:

> Any other occurrence of the procedure identifier within the procedure body denotes activation of the procedure. [10, p.311]

[95]Efficiency here refers to execution speed. The fact that I mentioned it here is perhaps misleading given Hoare's previous statement that speed was less of a concern for him than space.

[96] The 'West-Germans' here solely refer to Bauer and Samelson. Their compiler *did* have a runtime stack for handling dynamic arrays, but it was deliberately restricted in *not* handling recursive procedure calls [265, p.214].

[97]Correction: the cellar principle and the compilation of arithmetic expressions were due to Bauer and Samelson [16, 18]. Dijkstra's 1960 paper was on implementing recursion by means of the stack [60].

[98]The precise remark made by Hoare in Vienna 1964 was:

> There seem to be two intensely practical problems which have not excited very much interest so far at this conference. First, we must give a great deal of thought to deciding which things we want to leave imprecisely defined. Second, in any formal or informal description of a language, we must have a *mechanism* for failing to define things. [283, p.143, original italics]

[99]In retrospect, I was mainly thinking about [32].

[100]Which Böhm presented at the 1964 Vienna conference.

[101]See e.g. Naur's papers 'Formalization in program development' and 'Intuition in software development' [213, 214].

[102]See Naur's paper 'Understanding Turing's Universal Machine—Personal Style in Program Description' [218]. See also Chapter 7.

[103]See 'An Axiomatic Definition of the Programming Language Pascal' [135].

[104]The following comment by John Reynolds (in correspondence with me) is relevant:

> [T]he question of whether an ALGOL compiler permitted recursion was not all-or-nothing. The ALGOL compiler for the Burroughs 5000 computers permitted recursion, but limited the use of global variables. In a recursive procedure, one could only use local variables, or globals that were declared at the beginning of the program. This avoided the need for a mechanism such as Dijkstra's display.

[105]The year 1965 is probably incorrect. Dijkstra wrote his EWD249 'Notes on Structured Programming' in 1969 [78].

[106] Reference made to 'An Axiomatic Definition of the Programming Language Pascal' [135].

[107]Cited after 'Thoughtful Programming and Forth' [98] and 'The Evolution of Forth' [253].

[108]See [134, p.23, 219, 388] in particular.

[109]See [50, p.xi, Davis's emphasis][53, p.xiii, Davis's emphasis]. Turing's 1947 quote implicitly refers to his 1936 paper [291], in which 'the universal machine' was defined.

[110]The quotation is not entirely correct. Aiken's exact words are:

> [I]f it should ever turn out that the basic logics of a machine designed for the numerical solution of differential equations coincide with the basic logics of a machine intended to make bills for a department store, I would regard this as the most amazing coincidence that I have ever encountered. [1, p.33]

[111]A similar remark can also be made about Church's λ-calculus, a topic which lies outside the scope of this book.

Furthermore, Robert Floyd in his 1962 article 'On ambiguity in phrase structure languages' [95] demonstrated that no algorithm can accept an arbitrary context-free grammar and decide whether it is ambiguous. I thank John Reynolds for bringing Floyd's work to my attention.

[112]With the one exception being Ackermann's function, as he clarified in his follow-up letter 'Recursion and Iteration' [256].

[113]I thank Robert Harper for bringing this to my attention.

[114]A similar strong claim holds for Dijkstra and Zonneveld's American colleagues with the possible exception of one or two research groups. See also my discussion about the work of Irons and Feurzeig in Section 3.3.2.

[115]As far as I know, Dijkstra never cited Turing's 1936 paper. Concerning his limited reception of the work of Gödel and Kleene, see Dijkstra [73]. Another source is an unpublished 1994 interview between Dale and Dijkstra which MacKenzie was so kind to send to me in private correspondence.

[116]Recall from Chapter 2 that Turing's work was well received by 1959 in the field of automatic programming. Turing's 1936 paper was even included in Appendix One of Richard Goodman's 1960 book: *Annual Review in Automatic Programming I* [106].

Bibliography

[1] H.H. Aiken. "The Future of Automatic Computing Machinery". In: *Elektronische Rechenmaschinen und Informationsverarbeitung*. Ed. by A. Walther and W. Hoffmann. 1957.

[2] G. Alberts and H.T. de Beer. "De AERA. Gedroomde machines en de praktijk van het rekenwerk aan het Mathematisch Centrum te Amsterdam". In: *Studium* 2 (2008), pp. 101–127.

[3] K.R. Apt. "Edsger Wybe Dijkstra (1930–2002): A Portrait of a Genius". In: *Formal Aspects of Computing* 14 (2002), pp. 92–98.

[4] B.W. Arden, B.A. Galler, and R.M. Graham. "The Internal Organization of the MAD Translator". In: *Communications of the ACM* 4.1 (1961), pp. 28–31.

[5] J.A. Ayers. "Recursive Programming in FORTRAN II". In: *Communications of the ACM* 6.11 (Nov. 1963).

[6] G.A. Bachelor et al. "SMALGOL-61". In: *Communications of the ACM* 4.11 (1961), pp. 499–502.

[7] J.W. Backus. "The syntax and semantics of the proposed international algebraic language of the Zürich ACM-GAMM Conference". In: *IFIP Congress*. UNESCO, Paris. 1959, pp. 120–125.

[8] J.W. Backus. "Programming in America in the 1950s — Some Personal Impressions". In: *A History of Computing in the Twentieth Century*. Ed. by N. Metropolis, J. Howlett, and G-C. Rota. Orlando: Academic Press, 1980.

[9] J.W. Backus and H. Herrick. "IBM 701 Speedcoding and Other Automatic-Programming Systems". In: *Symposium on Automatic Programming for Digital Computers, Washington, D.C., 13-14 May*. Navy Advisory Math. Panel, Office of Naval Research. 1954, pp. 106–113.

[10] J.W. Backus et al. "Report on the algorithmic language ALGOL 60". In: *Communications of the ACM* 3.5 (1960). Editor: P. Naur, pp. 299–314.

[11] F.T. Baker and H.D. Mills. "Chief programmer teams". In: *Datamation* 19.12 (Dec. 1973), pp. 58–61.

[12] R.M. Balzer. *Dataless Programming*. Tech. rep. Memorandum RM-5290-ARPA. The RAND Corporation, July 1967.

[13] R.S. Barton. "Functional design of computers". In: *Communications of the ACM* 4.9 (1961).

[14] F.L. Bauer. "From the Stack Principle to ALGOL". In: *Software pioneers: contributions to software engineering*. Ed. by M. Broy and E. Denert. Berlin: Springer, 2002.

[15] F.L. Bauer. "My years with Rutishauser". In: *LATSIS Symposium, ETH Zurich*. 2002.

[16] F.L. Bauer and K. Samelson. "Sequentielle Formelübersetzung". In: *Elektronische Rechenanlagen* 1 (1959). Published in English as [18]., pp. 176–182.

[17] F.L. Bauer and K. Samelson. "The problem of a common language, especially for scientific numeral work (motives, restrictions, aims and results of the Zurich Conference on ALGOL)". In: *IFIP Congress*. UNESCO, Paris. 1959.

[18] F.L. Bauer and K. Samelson. "Sequential formula translation". In: *Communications of the ACM* 3 (1960), pp. 76–83.

[19] H.T. de Beer. *The History of the ALGOL Effort*. Masters thesis, Eindhoven University of Technology, http://heerdebeer.org/ALGOL. 2006.

[20] B.A. Benander, N. Gorla, and A.C. Benander. "An Empirical Study of the Use of the GOTO Statement". In: *Journal of System Software* 11 (1990), pp. 217–223.

[21] B.E. Blank. "The Universal Computer: The Road from Leibniz to Turing". In: *Notices of the AMS* 48.5 (May 2001), pp. 498–501.

[22] C. Böhm. "The CUCH as a formal descriptive language". In: *IFIP Working Conference*. Baden, Sept. 1964.

[23] C. Böhm and G. Jacopini. "Flow diagrams, Turing machines, and languages with only two formation rules". In: *Communications of the ACM* 9.5 (May 1966), pp. 366–371.

[24] L. Böszörményi, J. Gutknecht, and G. Pomberger, eds. *The School of Niklaus Wirth: the Art of Simplicity*. dpunkt.verlag, 2000.

[25] L. Böszörményi and S. Podlipnig. *People Behind Informatics*. With contributions from M. Broy, T. Dahl, and M. Nygaard. Institute of Information Technology, University of Klagenfurt, 2003.

[26] J.P. Bowen. "An Interview with C.A.R. Hoare". In: *Communications of the ACM* 52.3 (Mar. 2009). L. Shustek (ed), pp. 38–41.

[27] P. Braffort and D. Hirschberg, eds. *Computer Programming and Formal Systems — Special Issue 1963 in Studies in Logic and the Foundations of Mathematics*. North-Holland Publishing Company Amsterdam, 1963.

[28] J. Brown and J.W. Carr III. "Automatic Programming and its Development on the MIDAC". In: *Symposium on Automatic Programming for Digital Computers*. Office of Naval Research, Department of the Navy. Washington D.C., May 1954, pp. 84–97.

[29] Herbert Bruderer. "Verhalf eine unscheinbare Fussnote der ETH Zürich zu Weltruhm?" In: *IT Business* (May 2011), pp. 2–4.

[30] W. Buchholz, ed. *Planning a Computer System: Project STRETCH*. McGraw Hill, 1962.

[31] A.W. Burks and I.M. Copi. "The logical design of an idealized general-purpose computer". In: *J. Franklin Inst.* 261 (1956), pp. 299–314, 421–436.

[32] R.M. Burstall and J. Darlington. "A transformation system for developing recursive programs". In: *Journal of the ACM* 24 (1977), pp. 44–67.

[33] J.N. Buxton and B. Randell, eds. *Software engineering techniques*. Report on a Conference Sponsored by the NATO Science Committee Rome Italy, 1969. Apr. 1970.

[34] C.S. Calude, ed. *People and Ideas in Theoretical Computer Science*. Springer, 1999.

[35] M. Campbell-Kelly. *From Airline Reservations to Sonic the Hedgehog: A History of the Software Industry*. Boston: MIT Press, 2003.

[36] M. Campbell-Kelly and W. Aspray. *Computer: A History of the Information Machine*. Basic Books, 1996.

[37] B.E. Carpenter and R.W. Doran. "The Other Turing Machine". In: *The Computer Journal* 20 (1977), pp. 269–279.

[38] J.W. Carr III. "Lecture given at the Purdue University, Computer Symposium, November 15, 1957". In: *Computers and Automation* 7 (1958), pp. 21–22, 25–26.

[39] P.E. Ceruzzi. *A History of Modern Computing*. Boston: MIT Press, 2003.

[40] A. Church. "A Note on the Entscheidungsproblem". In: *Journal of Symbolic Logic* 1 (1936).

[41] A. Church. "An Unsolvable Problem of Elementary Number Theory". In: *American Journal of Mathematics* 58.2 (Apr. 1936), pp. 345–363.

[42] R.L. Clark. "A linguistic contribution to GOTO-less programming". In: *Datamation* 19.12 (Dec. 1973), pp. 62–63.

[43] B.J. Copeland. *The Essential Turing*. Oxford University Press, 2004.

[44] B.J. Copeland. "Unfair to Aiken". In: *IEEE Annals of the History of Computing* (2004), pp. 33–36.

[45] O.-J. Dahl, E.W. Dijkstra, and C.A.R. Hoare. *Structured Programming*. London - New York - San Francisco: Academic Press, 1972.

[46] J. Darlington and R.M. Burstall. "A system which automatically improves programs". In: *3rd International Conference on Artificial Intelligence*. Stanford University. California, 1973, pp. 479–485.

[47] M. Davis. *Computability and Unsolvability*. McGraw-Hill, 1958.

[48] M. Davis. "Why Gödel didn't have Church's Thesis". In: *Information and Control* 54 (1982), pp. 3–24.

[49] M. Davis. "Mathematical Logic and the Origin of Modern Computers". In: *The Universal Turing Machine - A Half-Century Survey*. Ed. by R. Herken. Originally in: Studies in the History of Mathematics. Mathematical Association of America, 1987, pages 137-165. Oxford University Press, 1988.

[50] M. Davis. *Engines of Logic: Mathematicians and the origins of the Computer*. 1st ed. New York NY: W.W. Norton & Company, 2000.

[51] M. Davis. *The Universal Computer: The Road from Leibniz to Turing*. 1st ed. Norton, 2000.

[52] M. Davis, ed. *The Undecidable: Basic Papers on Undecidable Propositions, Unsolvable Problems and Computable Functions*. Dover Publications, Inc., 2004.

[53] M. Davis. *The Universal Computer: The Road from Leibniz to Turing*. 2nd ed. CRC Press, 2012.

[54] E.G. Daylight. *Interview with Blaauw on 29 November 2011, conducted by Gerard Alberts and Edgar Daylight*. Tech. rep. 2011.

[55] E.G. Daylight. *Pluralism in Software Engineering: Turing Award Winner Peter Naur Explains*. Ed. by E.G. Daylight, K. De Grave, and P. Naur. www.lonelyscholar.com. Lonely Scholar, Oct. 2011.

[56] E.G. Daylight and S. Nanz, eds. *The Future of Software Engineering: Panel discussions, 22–23 November 2010, ETH Zurich*. Conversations. www.lonelyscholar.com. Lonely Scholar, Oct. 2011.

[57] J.W.R. Dedekind. *Was sind und was sollen die Zahlen?* 6th ed. Braunschweig, 1930.

[58] H. DeLong. *A Profile of Mathematical Logic*. Dover Books, 1971.

[59] E.W. Dijkstra. *Communication with an Automatic Computer*. Academisch Proefschrift. Universiteit van Amsterdam, Oct. 1959.

[60] E.W. Dijkstra. "Recursive Programming". In: *Numerische Mathematik* 2 (1960), pp. 312–318.

[61] E.W. Dijkstra. *On the Design of Machine Independent Programming Languages*. Tech. rep. MR 34. Mathematisch Centrum, Amsterdam, 1961.

[62] E.W. Dijkstra. *EWD 28: Substitution Processes (Preliminary Publication). I.e., a preliminary draft of [65]*. Tech. rep. 1962.

[63] E.W. Dijkstra. "Operating Experience with ALGOL60". In: *The Computer Journal* 5.2 (1962), pp. 125–127.

[64] E.W. Dijkstra. "Some Meditations on Advanced Programming". In: *IFIP Congress*. Munich, 1962, pp. 535–538.

[65] E.W. Dijkstra. "Unifying Concepts of Serial Program Execution, Rome, 26-31 March". In: *Proceedings of the Symposium Symbolic Languages in Data Processing*. New York and London: Gordon and Breach Science Publishers, 1962, pp. 236–251.

[66] E.W. Dijkstra. "Making a Translator for ALGOL60". In: *Annual Review in Automatic Programming 3*. Ed. by R. Goodman. New York: Pergamon Press, 1963.

[67] E.W. Dijkstra. "On the Design of Machine Independent Programming Languages". In: *Annual Review in Automatic Programming 3*. Ed. by R. Goodman. New York: Pergamon Press, 1963.

[68] E.W. Dijkstra. "Over de beperkte omvang van ons rekentuig". In: *NRMG '59/'64* (Apr. 1964). Uitgave ter gelegenheid van het eerste lustrum van het Nederlands Rekenmachine Genootschap (NRMG), Voordrachten gehouden op 3 April, 1964, 2e Boerhaavestraat 49, Amsterdam, pp. 55–71.

[69] E.W. Dijkstra. "Go To Statement Considered Harmful". In: *Letters to the Editor, Communications of the ACM* 11 (1968), pp. 147–148.

[70] E.W. Dijkstra. "The structure of the 'THE'-multiprogramming system". In: *Communications of the ACM* 5 (1968), pp. 341–346.

[71] E.W. Dijkstra. "Structured Programming". In: *Software Engineering Techniques*. Ed. by J.N. Buxton and B. Randell. Apr. 1970, pp. 84–88.

[72] E.W. Dijkstra. *EWD 316: A Short Introduction to the Art of Programming*. Tech. rep. Aug. 1971.

[73] E.W. Dijkstra. *EWD 463: Some questions*. Tech. rep. Nov. 1974.

[74] E.W. Dijkstra. *EWD 450: Correctness concerns and, among other things, why they are resented*. Tech. rep. Invited paper, to be presented at the 1975 International Conference on Reliable Software, 21-23 April 1975, Los Angeles, California, USA. 1975.

[75] E.W. Dijkstra. *EWD 514: On a language proposal for the Department of Defence*. Tech. rep. Sept. 1975.

[76] E.W. Dijkstra. *EWD 658: On language constraints enforceable by translators, an open letter to Lt. Col. William A. Whitaker*. Tech. rep. Mar. 1978.

[77] E.W. Dijkstra. "A Programmer's Early Memories". In: *A History of Computing in the Twentieth Century*. Ed. by N. Metropolis, J. Howlett, and G-C. Rota. New York: Academic Press, 1980.

[78] E.W. Dijkstra. *EWD 1308: What led to "Notes On Structured Programming"*. Tech. rep. Nuenen, June 2001.

[79] E.W. Dijkstra. "EWD 1308: What led to Notes on Structured Programming". In: *Software pioneers: contributions to software engineering*. Ed. by M. Broy and E. Denert. Springer, 2002, pp. 341–346.

[80] E.W. Dijkstra. *EWD 117: Programming Considered as a Human Activity*. Tech. rep. written between 1964 and 1967.

[81] E.W. Dijkstra. *EWD 682: The Nature of Computer Science (first draft)*. Tech. rep. written between 1976 and 1979.

[82] "Discussion: The Burroughs B-5000 in Retrospect". In: *Annals of the History of Computing* 9.1 (1987), pp. 37–92.

[83] J. Dobson and B. Randell. "Program Verification: Public Image And Private Reality". In: *Communications of the ACM* 32.4 (Apr. 1989), pp. 420–422.

[84] J.R. Donaldson. "Structured programming". In: *Datamation* 19.12 (Dec. 1973), pp. 52–54.

[85] S. Drobi. "A Conversation with Sir. Tony Hoare". Conducted on June 25, 2009, Recorded at QCon, www.infoq.com/interviews/tony-hoare-qcon-interview.

[86] R.J. DuWorks and S.W. Smoliar. "The Arrogant Programmer: Dijkstra and Wegner Considered Harmful". In: *SIGCSE Bulletin* 4.4 (Dec. 1972), pp. 19–21.

[87] George Dyson. *Turing's Cathedral: The Origins of the Digital Universe*. Penguin Books, 2012.

[88] J. Earley. "Toward an Understanding of Data Structures". In: *Communications of the ACM* 14.10 (1971), pp. 617–627.

[89] *Faster Than Thought: A Symposium on Digital Computing Machines*. 1953.

[90] E. Feigenbaum. *Oral History of Donald Knuth*. Tech. rep. CHM Reference number: X3926.2007. Mountain View, California, Computer History Museum, 2007.

[91] J.H. Fetzer. "Program Verification: The Very Idea". In: *Communications of the ACM* 31.9 (1988), pp. 1048–1063.

[92] D.A. Fisher. "DoD's Common Programming Language Effort". In: *IEEE Computer* (Mar. 1978), pp. 24–33.

[93] M. Fitting. *Incompleteness in the Land of Sets*. College Publications, 2007.

[94] R.W. Floyd. "An Algorithm for Coding Efficient Arithmetic Operations". In: *Communications of the ACM* 4.1 (1961), pp. 42–51.

[95] R.W. Floyd. "On Ambiguity in Phrase Structure Languages". In: *Communications of the ACM* 5.10 (1962), pp. 525, 534.

[96] R.W. Floyd. "Assigning Meanings to Programs". In: *Proceedings of Symposia in Applied Mathematics*. Vol. 19. American Mathematical Society. 1967.

[97] *Formation of USE — A Cooperative Organization of 1103A Users*. Central Exchange 1103.8 (Feb. 1956). pages 264-265.

[98] J. Fox. *Thoughtful Programming and Forth*. www.ultratechnology.com/forth.htm.

[99] P.L. Frana. "Oral history interview with Charles Antony Richard Hoare". OH 357, Conducted on 17 July 2002 in Cambridge, England. Copyright: Charles Babbage Institute, University of Minnesota, Minneapolis.

[100] A. Galler. *Remarks on Compiler Construction*. p.525 in Panel on Techniques for Processor Construction, Information Processing 1962 –Proceedings of IFIP Congress 1962, Munich, 27 August – 1 September, pp. 524-531. North-Holland. 1962.

[101] B.A. Galler and R.F. Rosin. *The Burroughs B 5000 Conference*. Tech. rep. OH 98. Charles Babbage Institute, 1986.

[102] T. Gallie. *Techniques for Processor Construction*. pp. 526-527 in Panel on Techniques for Processor Construction, Information Processing 1962 –Proceedings of IFIP Congress 1962, Munich, 27 August – 1 September, pp. 524-531. North-Holland. 1962.

[103] R. Gandy. "The confluence of ideas in 1936". In: *The Universal Turing Machine: A Half-Century Survey*. Oxford University Press, 1988.

[104] J.V. Garwick. "The definition of programming languages by their compiler". In: *IFIP Working Conference*. Baden, Sept. 1964.

[105] K. Gödel. "Uber formal mentscheidbare satze der Principia Mathematica und verwandter systeme. I". In: *Monatsch. Math. Phys.* 38 (1931), pp. 173–178.

[106] R. Goodman, ed. *Annual Review in Automatic Programming I: Papers read at the Working Conference on Automatic Programming of Digital Computers held at Brighton, 1–3 April 1959.* Pergamon Press, 1960.

[107] R. Goodman, ed. *Annual Review in Automatic Programming 4.* Pergamon Press, 1964.

[108] S. Gorn. "Planning Universal Semi-Automatic Coding". In: *Symposium on Automatic Programming for Digital Computers.* Office of Naval Research, Department of the Navy. Washington D.C., May 1954, pp. 74–83.

[109] S. Gorn. "Standardized Programming Methods and Universal Coding". In: *Journal of the ACM* (July 1957). Received in December 1956.

[110] S. Gorn. "Specification Languages for Mechanical Languages and Their Processors — A Baker's Dozen". In: *Communications of the ACM* 4 (Dec. 1961), pp. 532–541.

[111] A.A. Grau. "Recursive processes and ALGOL translation". In: *Communications of the ACM* 4.1 (Jan. 1961), p. 10.

[112] D. Gries, ed. *Programming Methodology.* Springer-Verlag, 1978.

[113] D. Gries, M. Paul, and H.R. Wiehle. "Some Techniques Used in the ALCOR ILLINOIS 7090". In: *Communications of the ACM* 10.12 (1965), pp. 804–808.

[114] J.V. Guttag. "The Electron and The Bit - EECS at MIT: 1902-2002". In: 2003. Chap. VII: Pioneering Women in EECS, pp. 225–239.

[115] J.V. Guttag and J.J. Horning. "An Introduction to the Larch Shared Language". In: *IFIP Congress.* 1983, pp. 809–814.

[116] T. Haigh. "An interview with Charles W. Bachman OH XXX". Conducted on 25-26 September, 2004, Tucson, Arizona. Interview conducted for the Special Interest Group on the Management of Data (SIGMOD) of the Association for Computing Machinery (ACM). Transcript and original tapes donated to the Charles Babbage Institute, Center for the History of Information Processing, University of Minnesota, Minneapolis, Copyright 2004.

[117] P. Brinch Hansen, ed. *The Origin of Concurrent Programming: From Semaphores to Remote Procedure Calls.* New York: Springer-Verlag, 2002.

[118] D. Harel. "On Folk Theorems". In: *Communications of the ACM* 23.7 (1980), pp. 379–388.

[119] G. Hasenjaeger. "On the Early History of Register Machines." In: *Computation Theory and Logic'87*. 1987, pp. 181–188.

[120] J. van Heijenoort, ed. *From Frege to Gödel, A Sourcebook in Mathematical Logic, 1879-1931*. Harvard University Press, 1967.

[121] S. Henriksson. "A brief history of the stack". In: *SHOT, Pittsburgh, October. SIGCIS*. 2009.

[122] T.A. Henzinger and J. Sifakis. "The Discipline of Embedded Systems Design". In: *IEEE Computer* (2007), pp. 32–40.

[123] D. Hilbert and W. Ackermann. *Grundzuge der Theoretischen Logik*. Springer, 1928.

[124] C.A.R. Hoare. "Algorithm 64: Quicksort". In: *Communications of the ACM* 4.7 (1961), p. 321.

[125] C.A.R. Hoare. "An Axiomatic Basis for Computer Programming". In: *Communications of the ACM* 12.10 (1969), pp. 576–580.

[126] C.A.R. Hoare. *Hints for programming language design*. Tech. rep. STAN-CS-74-408. Stanford, California: Stanford University, Jan. 1974.

[127] C.A.R. Hoare. "Recursive Data Structures". In: *International Journal Computer and Information Sciences* 4.2 (June 1975), pp. 105–132.

[128] C.A.R. Hoare. "The Emperor's Old Clothes". In: *Communications of the ACM* 24.2 (1981), pp. 75–83.

[129] C.A.R. Hoare. "Programming: sorcery or science?" In: *IEEE Software* 1 (Apr. 1984), pp. 5–16.

[130] C.A.R. Hoare. "Mathematics of programming". In: *BYTE* (Aug. 1986), pp. 115–149.

[131] C.A.R. Hoare. "How Did Software Get So Reliable Without Proof?" In: *FME '96: Industrial Benefit and Advances in Formal Methods, Third International Symposium of Formal Methods Europe*. Lecture Notes in Computer Science 1051. Co-Sponsored by IFIP WG 14.3, Oxford. Springer, Mar. 1996, pp. 1–17.

[132] C.A.R. Hoare. "Retrospective: An Axiomatic Basis for Computer Programming". In: *Communications of the ACM* (Oct. 2009).

[133] C.A.R. Hoare and D.C.S. Allison. "Incomputability". In: *ACM Computing Surveys* 4.3 (1972), pp. 169–178.

[134] C.A.R. Hoare and R.H. Perrott, eds. *Operating Systems Techniques*. A.P.I.C. Studies in Data Processing No. 9. Seminar held at Queen's University, Belfast, 1971. London and New York: Academic Press, 1972.

[135] C.A.R. Hoare and N. Wirth. "An Axiomatic Definition of the Programming Language Pascal". In: *Acta Informatica* 2 (1973), pp. 335–355.

[136] A. Hodges. *ALAN TURING: The Enigma.* Burnett Books, 1983.

[137] A. Hodges. "Alan Turing: the logical and physical basis of computing". In: *British Computer Society* (2007). http://www.bcs.org/ewics.

[138] M.E. Hopkins. "A case for the GOTO". In: *Proc. ACM Annual Conference.* Boston, 1972, pp. 787–790.

[139] G.M. Hopper. "Keynote Address of the Opening Session and the corresponding transcript of question and answer session". In: *History of Programming Languages.* Ed. by R.L. Wexelblat. New York: Academic Press, 1981, pp. 7–22.

[140] G. van den Hove. *Edsger Wybe Dijkstra: First Years in the Computing Science (1951-1968).* Masters thesis, University of Namur. 2009.

[141] H.D. Huskey. "NELIAC—A Dialect of ALGOL". In: *Communications of the ACM* 3.11 (1961), pp. 463–468.

[142] H.D. Huskey. "Machine Independence in Compiling". In: *Symbolic languages in data processing: Proc. of the Symp. organized and edited by the Int. Computation Center, Rome, 26-31.* Ed. by Gordon and Breach. New York, 1962, pp. 219–228.

[143] H.D. Huskey, R. Love, and N. Wirth. "A Syntactic Description of BC NELIAC". In: *Communications of the ACM* 6.7 (July 1963).

[144] H.D. Huskey and W.H. Wattenburg. "A Basic Compiler for Arithmetic Expressions". In: *Communications of the ACM* 4.1 (1961), pp. 3–9.

[145] *In Memoriam: Edsger W. Dijkstra (1930–2002).* Available from: http://userweb.cs.utexas.edu/users/EWD/MemRes(A4).pdf.

[146] "Interview with Martin Davis". In: *Notices of the AMS* 55.5 (May 2008), pp. 560–571.

[147] E.T. Irons. "A syntax directed compiler for ALGOL 60". In: *Communications of the ACM* 4.1 (1961), pp. 51–55.

[148] E.T. Irons and W. Feurzeig. "Comments on the Implementation of Recursive Procedures and Blocks in ALGOL60". In: *ALGOL Bulletin Supplement* 13.2 (1960), pp. 1–15.

[149] *Jaarverslag 1953.* Tech. rep. 2e Boerhaavestraat 49, Amsterdam: Mathematisch Centrum, 1953.

[150] W. James. *The Principles of Psychology, Vol. I-II.* Reprinted in Dover, 1950. Henry Holt, 1890.

[151] J. Jensen, P. Mondrup, and P. Naur. "A Storage Allocation Scheme for ALGOL 60". In: *Communications of the ACM* (1961), pp. 441–445.

[152] W.M. Keese and H.D. Huskey. "An Algorithm for the Translation of Algol Statements". In: *Information Processing 1962 –Proceedings of IFIP Congress 1962*. Ed. by C.M. Popplewell. 1962, pp. 498–502.

[153] S.C. Kleene. "General recursive functions of natural numbers". In: *Math. Ann.* 112 (1936), pp. 727–742.

[154] S.C. Kleene. "On notation for ordinal numbers". In: *Journal of Symbolic Logic* 3 (1938), pp. 150–155.

[155] S.C. Kleene. *Introduction to Metamathematics*. Van Nostrand, 1952.

[156] S.C. Kleene. "Origins of Recursive Function Theory". In: *IEEE Annals of the History of Computing* 3 (1981), pp. 371–382.

[157] R. Kline. *Cybernetics, Automata Studes, and the Dartmouth Conference on Artificial Intelligence*. Tech. rep. Draft version of a paper accepted for publication in the IEEE Annals of the History of Computing; doi: 10.1109/MAHC.2010.44. Cornell University, 2010.

[158] D.E. Knuth. "A History of Writing Compilers". In: *Computers and Automation* 11.12 (1962). Reprinted in [162]., pp. 8–18.

[159] D.E. Knuth. "Backus Normal Form vs. Backus Naur Form." In: *Letters to the Editor, Communications of the ACM* 7.12 (1964), pp. 735–736.

[160] D.E. Knuth. "The Dangers of Computer-Science Theory". In: *Logic, methodology and philosophy of science.* 1971, pp. 189–195.

[161] D.E. Knuth. "Structured Programming with go to Statements". In: *Computing Surveys* 6.4 (Dec. 1974).

[162] D.E. Knuth. *Selected Papers on Computer Languages*. Center for the Study of Languages and Information: Leland Stanford Junior University, 2003.

[163] D.E. Knuth. "The Early Development of Programming Languages". In: *Selected Papers on Computer Languages*. Center for the Study of Languages and Information, Leland Stanford Junior University, 2003.

[164] C.E. LaForest. *Second-Generation Stack Computer Architecture*. Thesis for Bachelor of Independent Studies, University of Waterloo, Canada. 2007.

[165] P. Landin. "The mechanical evaluation of expressions". In: *The Computer Journal* 6.4 (Jan. 1964).

[166] P. Landin. "A correspondence between ALGOL 60 and Church's Lambda-Notation". In: *Communications of the ACM* 8.2-3 (1965), pp. 89–101, 158–165.

[167] P.J. Landin. "The Next 700 Programming Languages". In: *Communications of the ACM* 9 (Mar. 1966), pp. 157–166.

[168] B.M. Leavenworth. "Programming with(out) the GOTO". In: *Proc. ACM Annual Conference*. Boston, Aug. 1972, pp. 782–786.

[169] J.A.N. Lee. *Computer pioneers*. IEEE Computer Society Press, 1995.

[170] J.A.N. Lee. ""Those Who Forget the Lessons of History Are Doomed To Repeat It" or, Why I Study the History of Computing". In: *IEEE Annals of the History of Computing* 18.2 (1996), pp. 54–62.

[171] B.H. Liskov. "A design methodology for reliable software systems". In: *Fall Joint Computer Conference*. 1972, pp. 191–199.

[172] B.H. Liskov. "The Design of the Venus Operating System". In: *Communications of the ACM* 15.3 (1972), pp. 144–149.

[173] B.H. Liskov. "Data types and program correctness". In: *National Computer Conference*. 1975, pp. 285–286.

[174] B.H. Liskov. "A History of CLU". In: *History of Programming Languages*. Ed. by T.J. Bergin and R.G. Gibson. Addison-Wesley, 1996, pp. 471–497.

[175] B.H. Liskov and J.V. Guttag. *Abstraction and Specification in Program Development*. MIT Press, 1986.

[176] B.H. Liskov and J.V. Guttag. *Program Development in Java: Abstraction, Specification, and Object-Oriented Design*. Addison-Wesley, 2001.

[177] B.H. Liskov and S. Zilles. "Specification Techniques for Data Abstractions". In: *IEEE Transactions on Software Engineering* (1975), pp. 72–87.

[178] J. Low et al. "Read this and change the way you feel about software engineering". In: *Information and Software Technology* 38 (1996), pp. 77–87.

[179] M.S. Mahoney. "The Roots of Software Engineering — An expanded version of a lecture presented at CWI on February 1990". In: *CWI Quarterly*. 1990.

[180] M.S. Mahoney. "What Makes History?" In: *History of Programming Languages*. Ed. by T.J. Bergin Jr. and R.B. Gibson Jr. New York: ACM Press, 1996.

[181] M.S. Mahoney. "The histories of computing(s)". In: *Interdisciplinary Science Reviews* 30.2 (2005), pp. 119–135.

[182] M.S. Mahoney. *Histories of Computing*. Ed. by T. Haigh. Harvard University Press, 2011.

[183] J. McCarthy. "The Inversion of Functions Defined by Turing Machines". In: *Automata Studies*. Ed. by C. Shannon and J. McCarthy. Princeton University Press, 1956.

[184] J. McCarthy. "On Conditional Expressions and Recursive Functions". In: *Letters to the Editor, Communications of the ACM* 2.8 (1959), pp. 2–3.

[185] J. McCarthy. "Recursive Functions of Symbolic Expressions and Their Computation by Machine, Part I". In: *Communications of the ACM* 3.4 (1960), pp. 184–195.

[186] J. McCarthy. "Towards a Mathematical Science of Computation". In: *Information Processing 1962 –Proceedings of IFIP Congress 1962*. Ed. by C.M. Popplewell. 1962, pp. 21–28.

[187] J. McCarthy. "History of Programming Languages". In: ed. by R.L. Wexelblat. New York: Academic Press, 1981. Chap. 'History of LISP' and the transcripts of: presentation, discussant's remark, question and answer session, pp. 173–195.

[188] D.D. McCracken. "Revolution in programming". In: *Datamation* 19.12 (Dec. 1973), pp. 50–52.

[189] C.L. McGowan. "The most-recent-error: its causes and correction". In: *Proc. ACM Conf. on Proving assertions about programs, SIGPLAN Notices* 7.1 (1972), pp. 191–202.

[190] R.M. McKeag, R. Wilson, and D.H.R. Huxtable, eds. *Studies in Operating Systems*. APIC Studies in Data Processing 13. Academic Press, 1976.

[191] G.H. Mealy. "Another look at data". In: *Fall Joint Computer Conference*. 1967, pp. 525–534.

[192] N. Metropolis, J. Howlett, and G-C. Rota. *A History of Computing in the Twentieth Century*. New York: Academic Press, 1980.

[193] A.R. Meyer and D.M. Ritchie. "The complexity of loop programs". In: *Proceedings A.C.M. National Meeting*. 1967.

[194] E.F. Miller Jr. and G.E. Lindamood. "Structured programming: top-down approach". In: *Datamation* 19.12 (Dec. 1973), pp. 55–57.

[195] R.A. De Millo, R.J. Lipton, and A.J. Perlis. "Social Processes and Proofs of Theorems and Programs". In: *Communications of the ACM* 22.5 (1972), pp. 271–280.

[196] H.D. Mills. "Structured programming in large systems". In: *Debugging Techniques in Large Systems*. Ed. by R. Rustin. Englewood Cliffs, New Jersey: Prentice-Hall, 1971, pp. 41–55.

[197]   M. Minsky. *Computation: Finite and Infinite Machines*. Prentice-Hall, Inc, 1967.

[198]   *Modern Computing Methods*. 2nd ed. Notes on Applied Science, No. 16. National Physical Laboratory, 1961.

[199]   D. Moore. ""GOTO Considered Harmful" Considered Harmful". In: *Notes in the Communications of the ACM* 30.5 (1987), pp. 351–352.

[200]   E.F. Moore. "A simplified universal Turing machine". In: *Proc. ACM* (Sept. 1952).

[201]   S. Nanz, ed. *The Futurue of Software Engineering*. Springer, 2011.

[202]   P. Naur. "Beretning om programstyrede elektronregnemaskiner i England, U.S.A. og Sverige (Report on programmed electronic computers in England, the U.S.A. and Sweden)". May 1954.

[203]   P. Naur. "Albert Einstein (obituary)". In: *Nordisk astronomisk tidsskrift* 2 (1955), pp. 36–40.

[204]   P. Naur. "Goto statements and good ALGOL style". In: *BIT* 3.3 (1963), pp. 204–208.

[205]   P. Naur. "The design of the Gier Algol Compiler". In: *BIT Nordisk Tidskrift for Informationsbehandling* 3 (1963). Reprinted in [107, p. 49-85] and [217, Sec. 3.1]. Russian translation: Sovremennoye Programmirovanie, Sovjetskoye Radio, Moskva 1996, p. 161-207., pp. 124–140, 145–166.

[206]   P. Naur. "Checking of Operand Types in Algol Compilers". In: *BIT Nordisk Tidskrift for Informationsbehandling* 5 (1965). Originally presented in NordSAM 64 Stockholm, August 1964. Reprinted in [217, Sec. 3.2]., pp. 151–163.

[207]   P. Naur. "Proof of Algorithms by General Snapshots". In: *BIT Nordisk Tidskrift for Informationsbehandling* 6 (1966). Reprinted in [217, Sec. 5.2]., pp. 310–316.

[208]   P. Naur. "Successes and failures of the Algol effort". In: *Algol Bulletin* 28 (July 1968). Reprinted in [217, Sec. 2.2]., pp. 58–62.

[209]   P. Naur. "Programming Languages, Natural Languages, and Mathematics". In: *Communications of the ACM* 18.12 (Dec. 1975). Reprinted in [217, Sec. 1.3]., pp. 676–683.

[210]   P. Naur. "Impressions of the early days of programming". In: *BIT Nordisk Tidskrift for Informationsbehandling* 20 (1980), pp. 414–425.

[211]   P. Naur. "Aad van Wijngaarden's contribution to ALGOL 60". In: *Algorithmic Languages*. Ed. by de Bakker and van Vliet. Reprinted in [217, Sec. 2.3]. North-Holland, 1981, pp. 293–304.

[212] P. Naur. "The European side of the last phase of the development of ALGOL 60". In: *History of Programming Languages*. Ed. by R.L. Wexelblat. New York: Academic Press, 1981.

[213] P. Naur. "Formalization in program development". In: *BIT Nordisk Tidskrift for Informationsbehandling* 22 (1982). Reprinted in [217, Sec. 7.1]., pp. 437–453.

[214] P. Naur. "Intuition in software development". In: *Formal Methods and Software Development, Vol. 2: Colloquium on Software Engineering*. Ed. by H. Ehrig et al. Lecture Notes in Computer Science 186. ISBN 3-540-15199-0. Reprinted in [217, Sec. 7.2]. Berlin: Springer-Verlag, 1985, pp. 60–79.

[215] P. Naur. "Thinking and Turing's Test". In: *BIT Nordisk Tidskrift for Informationsbehandling* 26 (1986). Reprinted in [217, Sec. 8.2]., pp. 175–187.

[216] P. Naur. "Computing and the so-called foundations of the so-called sciences". In: *Informatics Curricula for the 1990s*. Invited lecture. Reprinted in [217, Sec. 1.5]. IFIP Wokring Group 3.2 Workshop. Providence, Rhode Island, Apr. 1990.

[217] P. Naur. *Computing: A Human Activity*. New York: ACM Press/Addison-Wesley, 1992.

[218] P. Naur. "Understanding Turing's Universal Machine—Personal Style in Program Description". In: *The Computer Journal* 36.4 (1993), pp. 351–372.

[219] P. Naur. *Knowing and the Mystique of Logic and Rules*. ISBN 0-7923-3680-1. Kluwer Academic Publishers, 1995, xii + 365 pages.

[220] P. Naur. *Antiphilosophical Dictionary: Thinking - Speech - Science/Scholarship*. ISBN 87-987221-1-5. naur.com publishing, 2001.

[221] P. Naur and B. Randell, eds. *Software Engineering*. Reprinted in [222]. Report on a Conference sponsored by NATO Science Committee, held in 1968. Jan. 1969.

[222] P. Naur, B. Randell, and J.N. Buxton, eds. *Software Engineering: Concepts and Techniques*. New York: Petrocelli/Carter, 1976.

[223] J. von Neumann. *Memo on Mechanical Computing Devices, to Col. L. E. Simon, Ballistic Research Laboratory, January 30, 1945, VNLC*. Tech. rep.

[224] A. Newell and J.C. Shaw. "Programming the logic theory machine". In: *Proc. Western Joint Computer Conf.* 1957, pp. 230–240.

[225] A. Newell, J.C. Shaw, and H.A. Simon. "Empirical Explorations of the Logic Theory Machine: A Case Study in Heuristic". In: *Proc. Western Joint Computer Conf.* 1957, pp. 218–230.

[226] D. Nofre. "Unraveling Algol: US, Europe, and the Creation of a Programming Language". In: *IEEE Annals of the History of Computing* 32.2 (2010), pp. 58–68.

[227] D. Nofre, M. Priestley, and G. Alberts. "When technology becomes language: New perspectives on the emergence of programming languages, 1950-1960". In: *Presented at SHOT 2011 and in preparation for publication* (2011).

[228] A.G. Oettinger. "The Hardware-Software Complementarity". In: *Communications of the ACM* 10.10 (1967), pp. 604–606.

[229] K. Van Oudheusden. *The Advent of Recursion and Logic in Computer Science.* Masters thesis, University of Amsterdam. 2009.

[230] *Panel Discussion: 'Efficient Processor Construction'.* Proceedings of the International Symposium of Symbolic Languages in Data Processing. C.M. Popplewell (ed). Mar. 1962.

[231] *Panel Discussion: 'Languages for Aiding Compiler Writing'.* Proceedings of the International Symposium of Symbolic Languages in Data Processing. C.M. Popplewell (ed). Mar. 1962.

[232] *Panel on Techniques for Processor Construction.* Proceedings of IFIP Congress 1962, Rome, March, pp. 524-531. 1962.

[233] D.L. Parnas. "On the Criteria to be Used in Decomposing Systems into Modules". In: *Communications of the ACM* 15.12 (Dec. 1972), pp. 1053–1058.

[234] D.L. Parnas. "On a "Buzzword": Hierarchical Structure". In: *IFIP Congress 74.* North-Holland, 1974, pp. 336–339.

[235] D.L. Parnas. "Education for Computing Professionals". In: *IEEE Computer* 23.1 (1990), pp. 17–22.

[236] D.L. Parnas and J.A. Darringer. "SODAS and a methodology for system design". In: *Fall Joint Computer Conference.* 1967, pp. 449–474.

[237] G. Peano. "Sul concetto di numero". In: *Rivista di Matematica* 1 (1891), pp. 87–102, 256–267.

[238] A.J. Perlis. "The American side of the last phase of the development of ALGOL". In: *History of Programming Languages.* Ed. by R. Wexelblat. New York: Academic Press, 1981.

[239] A.J. Perlis and K. Samelson. "Preliminary Report: International Algebraic Language". In: *Communications of the ACM* 1.12 (1958).

[240] C. Petzold. *The Annotated Turing: A Guided Tour through Alan Turing's Historic Paper on Computability and the Turing Machine.* Wiley Publishing, Inc., 2008.

[241] W. van der Poel. "A Simple Electronic Digital Computer". In: *Appl. sci. Res.* 2 (1952), pp. 367–399.

[242] W.L. van der Poel. *Een leven met computers.* TU Delft. Oct. 1988.

[243] E. Post. "Recursive unsolvability of a problem of Thue". In: *Journal of Symbolic Logic* 12 (1947), pp. 1–11.

[244] *Preliminary Report – Specifications for the IBM Mathematical FORmula TRANslating System.* Tech. rep. New York: IBM, Programming Research Group, 1954.

[245] M. Priestley. *A Science of Operations: Machines, Logic and the Invention of Programming.* Ed. by M. Campbell-Kelly. Springer, 2011.

[246] P.M. Priestley. *Logic and the Development of Programming Languages, 1930-1975.* PhD thesis. University College London, May 2008.

[247] W.V.O. Quine. *Mathematical Logic.* Harvard University Press, 1955.

[248] B. Randell. "Whetstone ALGOL Revisited, or Confessions of a Compiler Writer". In: *APIC Bulletin Issue* 21, Automatic Programming Information Centre, College of Technology, Brighton. (May 1964).

[249] B. Randell, ed. *The Origins of Digital Computers: Selected Papers.* Springer-Verlag, 1973.

[250] B. Randell. *Reminiscences of Whetstone ALGOL.* Technical Report Series CS-TR-1190. Newcastle University, 2010.

[251] B. Randell and L.J. Russell. *Discussions on ALGOL Translation, at Mathematisch Centrum, W/AT 841, Atomic Power Division, English Electric Co., –a record of discussions with Dr. E. W. Dijkstra, at Mathematisch Centrum, Amsterdam, during 4-8 Dec., 1961. http://www.cs.ncl.ac.uk/publications/trnn/papers/34.pdf.* Tech. rep. 1962.

[252] B. Randell and L.J. Russell. *Implementation: The Translation and Use of Programs on a Computer.* London: Academic Press, 1964.

[253] E.D. Rather, D.R. Colburn, and C.H. Moore. "The Evolution of Forth". In: *ACM SIGPLAN Notices* 28.3 (Mar. 1993).

[254] *Report on the preparation of programmes for the EDSAC and the use of the library of subroutines.* Tech. rep. University Mathematical Laboratory Cambridge, Sept. 1950.

[255] H.G. Rice. In: *Communications of the ACM* 3.9 (Sept. 1960).

[256] H.G. Rice. "Recursion and Iteration". In: *Communications of the ACM* 8.2 (Feb. 1965), pp. 114–115.

[257] J.R. Rice. "The Go To Statement Reconsidered". In: *Letters to the Editor, Communications of the ACM* 11.8 (Aug. 1968), p. 538.

[258] H. Robinson et al. "Postmodern Software Development". In: *The Computer Journal* 41.6 (1998), pp. 363–375.

[259] R. Rojas. "How to Make Zuse's Z3 a Universal Computer". In: *IEEE Annals of the History of Computing* 20.3 (1998), pp. 51–54.

[260] S. Rosen, ed. *Programming Systems and Languages.* New York: McGraw Hill, 1967.

[261] F. Rubin. ""GOTO Considered Harmful" considered harmful". In: *Notes in the Communications of the ACM* 30.3 (1987), pp. 195–196.

[262] B. Russell. *The Principles of Mathematics.* Originally published in 1903. New York: W.W. Norton & Company, Inc.,

[263] H. Rutishauser. "The Use of Recursive Procedures". In: *Annual Review in Automatic Programming 3.* Ed. by R. Goodman. New York: Pergamon Press, 1963.

[264] K. Samelson. "Programming Languages and their Processing". In: *Information Processing 1962 — Proceedings of IFIP Congress 1962, Munich, 27 August – 1 September.* North-Holland, 1962, pp. 487–492.

[265] K. Samelson and F. Bauer. "The ALCOR project". In: *Symbolic languages in data processing.* Ed. by Gordon and Breach. International Computation Center, Rome. New York, 1962, pp. 207–218.

[266] J.E. Sammet. *Programming Languages: History and Fundamentals.* Prentice-Hall, 1969.

[267] S. Santini. "We Are Sorry to Inform You ..." In: *Computer* (Dec. 2005), pp. 126–128.

[268] K. Sattley and P.Z. Ingerman. "The Allocation of Storage for Arrays in ALGOL60". In: *Communications of the ACM* 4.1 (1961), pp. 60–65.

[269] *School of Mathematics and Statistics University of St. Andrews, Scotland. JOC/EFR Copyright.* http://www-history.mcs.st-andrews.ac.uk/Biographies/Rutishauser.html. 2008.

[270] P. Schulthess. "Lean Systems in an Intrinsically Complex World". In: *The School of Niklaus Wirth: The Art of Simplicity.* dpunkt.verlag, 2000, pp. 87–93.

[271] S. Schuman and P. Jourrand. "Definition Mechanism in Extensible Programming Languages". In: *AFIPS.* 1967.

[272] C. Shannon and J. McCarthy, eds. *Automata Studies.* Annals of Mathematics Studies 34. Princeton University Press, 1956.

[273] C.E. Shannon. "A universal Turing machine with two internal states." In: *Automata Studies*. Ed. by C.E. Shannon and J. McCarthy. Princeton University Press, 1956, pp. 157–166.

[274] D. Shasha and C. Lazere. *Out of their minds: The Lives and Discoveries of 15 Great Computer Scientists*. Copernicus, Springer-Verlag, 1995.

[275] D. Shell. "A high-speed sorting procedure". In: *Communications of the ACM* 2 (1959), pp. 30–32.

[276] J.C. Shepherdson and H.E. Sturgis. "Computability of Recursive Functions". In: *Journal of the ACM* 10 (1963), pp. 217–255.

[277] W. Sieg. "Mechanical procedures and mathematical experience". In: *Mathematics and Mind*. Ed. by A. George. Oxford University Press, 1994, pp. 71–117.

[278] W. Sieg. "On Computability". In: *Handbook of the Philosophy of Science. Philosophy of Mathematics*. Ed. by A. Irvine et al. Elsevier BV, 2008.

[279] A. Silberschatz and P.B. Galvin. *Operating System Concepts*. 5th ed. Addison-Wesley, 1998.

[280] R. Slater. *Portraits in Silicon*. Boston: MIT Press, 1989.

[281] P. Smith. *An Introduction to Gödel's Theorems*. Cambridge University Press, 2007.

[282] R.I. Soare. "Computability and recursion". In: *Bulletin of Symbolic Logic* 2 (1996), pp. 284–321.

[283] T.B. Steel, ed. *IFIP Working Conference on Formal Language Description Languages*. Amsterdam: North-Holland, 1966.

[284] H. Stoyan. "Early LISP History (1956-1959)". In: *LISP and Functional Programming*. 1984, pp. 299–310.

[285] H. Stoyan. "The Influence of the Designer on the Design – J. McCarthy and LISP". In: *Artificial Intelligence and Mathematical Theory of Computation: Papers in Honor of John McCarthy*. Ed. by V. Lifschitz. Academic Press Professional, Inc, 1991.

[286] C. Strachey. "An impossible program". In: *Letter to the Editor of the Computer Journal* (1965), p. 313.

[287] C. Strachey and M.V. Wilkes. "Some proposals for improving the efficiency of ALGOL 60". In: *Communications of the ACM* 4.11 (1961). Also in: University Mathematical Laboratory Technical Memorandum, No. 61/5, pp. 488–491.

[288] *Symposium on Automatic Programming for Digital Computers*. Office of Naval Research, Department of the Navy. Washington D.C., May 1954.

[289] D. Tamari. *Machines de Turing et problemes de mot*. Tech. rep. 2e Boerhaavestraat 49, Amsterdam, DR 10: Stichting Mathematisch Centrum, Mar. 1953.

[290] B.A. Trakhtenbrot. "Comparing the Church and Turing Approaches: Two Prophetical Messages". In: *The Universal Turing Machine A Half-Century Survey*. Ed. by R. Herken. 2nd ed. Springer-Verlag, 1994 and 1995, pp. 557–582.

[291] A.M. Turing. "On Computable Numbers, with an Application to the Entscheidungsproblem". In: *Proceedings of the London Mathematical Society, 2nd series* 42 (1936), pp. 230–265.

[292] A.M. Turing. "On Computable Numbers, with an Application to the Entscheidungsproblem. A Correction". In: *Proceedings of the London Mathematical Society, 2nd series* 43 (1937).

[293] A.M. Turing. "Computing machinery and intelligence". In: *Mind* 59 (1950), pp. 433–460.

[294] M.E.P. Valdez. *A Gift from Pandora's Box: The Software Crisis*. PhD University of Edinburgh, 1988.

[295] H. Waldburger. *Gebrauchsanleitung für die ERMETH*. Tech. rep. Institut für Angewandte Mathematik der ETH, Zürich, 1960.

[296] H. Wang. "A variant of Turing's theory of computing machines". In: *Journal of the ACM* 4.1 (Jan. 1957). Presented in 1954., pp. 63–92.

[297] R. Waychoff. *Stories About the B5000 and People Who Were There*. Tech. rep. 1979.

[298] P. Wegner. "Programming Languages – The First 25 Years". In: *IEEE Transactions on Computers* 25.12 (1976), pp. 1207–1225.

[299] L.H. Weiner. "The Roots of Structured Programming". In: *ACM SIGCSE Bulletin* 10.1 (Feb. 1978). The papers of the SIGCSE/CSA technical symposium on computer science education.

[300] W.A. Whitaker. "History of Programming Languages". In: ed. by T.J. Bergin and R.G. Gibson. Addison-Wesley Publishing Company, 1996. Chap. ADA—THE PROJECT: The DoD High Order Language Working Group, pp. 173–232.

[301] A. van Wijngaarden. "Generalized ALGOL". In: *Annual Review Automatic Programming*. Ed. by R. Goodman. Vol. 3. Pergamon Press, 1963, pp. 17–26.

[302] A. van Wijngaarden. "Recursive definition of syntax and semantics". In: *IFIP Working Conference*. Baden, Sept. 1964.

[303] N. Wirth. "Program Development by Stepwise Refinement". In: *Communications of the ACM* 14 (Apr. 1971), pp. 221–227.

[304] N. Wirth. "On the Composition of Well-Structured Programs". In: *Computing Surveys* 6.4 (Dec. 1974), pp. 247–259.

[305] N. Wirth. "Type Extensions". In: *ACM TOPLAS* 10.2 (1988), pp. 204–214.

[306] N. Wirth. "A Plea for Lean Software". In: *Computer* (Feb. 1995).

[307] N. Wirth. "Recollections about the development of Pascal". In: *History of Programming Languages*. Ed. by Bergin and Gibson. Addison-Wesley, 1996, pp. 97–111.

[308] N. Wirth. "Transcript of Question and Answer Session". In: *History of Programming Languages*. Ed. by Bergin and Gibson. Addison-Wesley, 1996, pp. 117–120.

[309] N. Wirth. "Embedded Systems and Real-Time Programming". In: *EMSOFT 2001*. Ed. by Henzinger and Kirsch. LNCS 2211. Berlin Heidelberg: Springer-Verlag, 2001, pp. 486–492.

[310] N. Wirth. "Computing Science Education: The Road not Taken". 2002.

[311] N. Wirth. "A Brief History of Software Engineering". In: *IEEE Annals of the History of Computing* (2008), pp. 32–39.

[312] N. Wirth and H. Weber. "EULER: A Generalization of ALGOL, and its Formal Definition: Part I". In: *Communications of the ACM* 9.1 (Jan. 1966).

[313] W. Wulf, R. London, and M. Shaw. "An introduction to the construction and verification of Alphard programs". In: *IEEE Transactions on Software Engineering* 2.4 (1976), pp. 253–265.

[314] W.A. Wulf. "A case against the GOTO". In: *Proc. ACM Annual Conference*. Boston, Aug. 1972, pp. 791–797.

[315] H. Zemanek. "Abstract Architecture". In: *Abstract software specifications*. Ed. by D. Bjorner. Vol. 86. Lecture Notes in Computer Science. Berlin - Heidelberg - New York: Springer, 1980, pp. 1–42.

[316] K. Zuse. *The Computer — My Life*. Springer-Verlag, 1993.

Index

Pluralism in Software Engineering: Turing Award Winner Peter Naur Explains

Edgar G. Daylight

What mathematical rigor has (not) to offer to software engineers

Peter Naur wrote his first research paper at the age of 16. Soon an internationally acclaimed astronomer, Naur's expertise in numerical analysis gave him access to computers from 1950. He helped design and implement the influential ALGOL programming language. During the 1960s, Naur was in sync with the research agendas of McCarthy, Dijkstra, and others. By 1970, however, he had distanced himself from them. Instead of joining Dijkstra's structured programming movement, he made abundantly clear why he disapproved of it. Underlying Naur's criticism is his plea for pluralism: a computer professional should not dogmatically advocate a method and require others to use it in their own work. Instead, he should respect the multitude of personal styles in solving problems.

"What an absolutely cool guy!"
— Dennis Shasha, New York University

"Fascinating... the interview is a very worthwhile contribution to documenting the history of the field, and will be of strong interest both to computer scientists and to professional historians."
— Robert Harper, Carnegie Mellon University

What philosophy has to do with software engineering

Though Peter Naur definitely does not want to be called a philosopher, he acknowledges having been influenced by Popper, Quine, Russell, and others. Naur's writings of the 1970s and 1980s show how he borrowed concepts from philosophy to further his understanding of software engineering. In later years, he mainly scrutinized the work in philosophy and mathematical logic & rules in particular. By penetrating deeply into the 1890 research of William James, Naur gradually developed his own theory of how mental life is like at the neural level of the nervous system. This development, in turn, helps explain why he always opposed the Turing Test and Artificial Intelligence, why he had strong misgivings about the Formal Methods movement and Dijkstra's research in particular.

Table of Contents

LONELY SCHOLAR™
SCIENTIFIC BOOKS

Paperback, 127 + iii pages
Published October 2011
ISBN 9789491386008
www.lonelyscholar.com

www.ingramcontent.com/pod-product-compliance
Lightning Source LLC
LaVergne TN
LVHW022307060326
832902LV00020B/3313